Praise for
THE POWER OF PULL

"In a ferociously dynamic world, what happens if we can't plan but can only adapt? We must move, say the authors, from push to pull. At the center of the pull strategy is an individual (not a corporation) who has access to knowledge flows, takes advantage of porous boundaries and serendipitous interactions, and occupies new creative spaces to achieve a novel order of performance. I know. It's a complex model with several moving parts. But it makes for an exhilarating read as the authors sublimely reinvent the world of enterprise."

—*Harvard Business Review*

"[T]his year's must-read book on innovation. . . . The book is a smart analysis of why executives need to broaden their thinking about innovation—and take action, now." —*Bloomberg Businessweek*

"Provocative. . . . [T]he beauty of *The Power of Pull* is that the authors bring such seemingly disparate ideas into one simple, overarching imperative: Stop pushing; start pulling."—*MIT Sloan Management Review*

"Hagel, Brown, and Davison have given us a provocative and insightful look at the power of today's knowledge flow. If you want to meet the challenges of working and living in the 21st century, this book should be your guide."—Eric Schmidt, Chairman and CEO of Google

"*The Power of Pull* will do for our 21st-century information-age institutional leadership what Peter Drucker's *The Concept of the Corporation* did for industrial-era management. This book begins to create a body of learnable principles that will revolutionize our ability to access and work with knowledge flows."

—Newt Gingrich, former Speaker
of the US House of Representatives

"Connecting many important threads through beautiful metaphors and wonderful narratives, the authors provide both a mind-expanding view of how the world is changing and a solid framework and context to approach the future for anyone interested in surviving and enjoying it."
—Joichi Ito, CEO of Creative Commons and Internet venture investor

"In times of unprecedented change, we as individuals and institutions can have extraordinary leverage and influence if we marshal the passion, knowledge and resources necessary to achieve great things. *The Power of Pull* empowers and guides us to make the most of today's enormous possibilities." —John Naisbitt, author of *Megatrends*

"Stop whatever you are doing and read this amazing book. The authors totally nail it. Digging beneath the surface of stuff that distracts us on a daily basis, they unpack the deep forces that really truly matter and provide a guidebook each of us can use to unleash passion, transform how and why we work, and restore destiny and dignity to our lives."
—Richard Florida, author of
The Rise of the Creative Class and *The Great Reset*

"We live in a global village, where borders are blurred, where all humanity could and should be responsible for the well-being of others. *The Power of Pull* proposes fresh insights that coalesce into a powerful way forward in this new world. This erudite manual for change is a testament to the creativity and insight of its authors."
—Mark E. Tucker, Former Group Chief Executive of
Prudential plc, Member of the Court of the Bank of England

"As social media and enterprise cloud computing continue to exert their democratizing influences, *The Power of Pull* will become a key principle for success. The individuals who learn how to use these tools most effectively are the ones who will pull their institutions into new heights of rapid innovation, improved performance, and significant achievement." —Marc Benioff, CEO of Salesforce.com

"This brilliant and exciting book shows how to pursue your passions by harnessing the power of networks. Success no longer comes from possessing knowledge; instead, you have to participate with others in creating a flow of knowledge. The power of 'pull'—the ability to draw out people and resources for each endeavor—can transform both individuals and institutions."
—Walter Isaacson, President and CEO,
the Aspen Institute, and author of *Steve Jobs*

"This is a seminal work that explores the personal and professional implications of a powerful convergence of technologies, ranging from in memory databases for speed, massive parallel processing in the cloud, access via telephone for anything, anytime, everywhere. We are just beginning to understand what this means for us. The authors help us to understand where and how pull will change our lives and our work given the new digital infrastructures re-shaping our landscape. It offers us a roadmap that we neglect at our peril."
—Hasso Plattner, Founder and Chairman of SAP Supervisory Board

"*The Power of Pull* is a powerful new meme for navigating and networking in the 21st century."

—John Doerr, Partner at
Kleiner Perkins Caufield & Byers venture capital

"*The Power of Pull* provide[s] great insight into the quickly changing world of information. On the surface, [it is a] book about technology and business, but on a deeper level, reveal[s] much more about the future of communication, culture, and people."—*800-CEO-READ*

"A good book with strong views on the future nature of enterprises and their relationship to individuals. . . . [O]ne of the most comprehensively thought-out books on the subject of social media and the future of the enterprise to have come out. It goes way beyond the buzz-word or branding driven works that concentrate more on staking out territory than investigating the future of companies, individuals and technology."

—Mark P. McDonald, GVP and Head of Research
at Gartner Executive Programs

"*The Power of Pull* explains the seeming inexplicable."
—The Cook Report on Internet Protocol

"*Pull* isn't just a chronicle of the past, or a set of predictions about the future: it's a pioneering, authoritative guide to getting hands-on with 21st century economics, igniting new institutions, creating stuff of greater worth, and, just maybe, rebooting prosperity. . . . [D]on't just read *Pull* because it tells you what to do next. Read it because it paints a nuanced, compelling picture of *why* to do next—because it will help you see, and more importantly, feel, the contours of a new paradigm for 21st century prosperity."

—Umair Haque, Director of Havas Media Labs
and author of *Betterness: Economics for Humans* and
The New Capitalist Manifesto: Building a Disruptively Better Business

"The book brings a tight, logical, structure to this transformed world. . . . *The Power of Pull* is a compelling primer to navigate a new landscape at work, at home, and at play. Its message resonates beyond the business world." —PR Newswire

"Business and social issues collections alike will relish this."
—*The Bookwatch*

"A very important body of work. . . . *The Power of Pull* succinctly argues that in this emerging 21st century economy, scalable mass collaboration brings together the people-centered expertise and innovative ideas needed to address the very complex challenges, as well as the ample opportunities all around us. This is hugely different from the last century model of mass production. The book convinces us that it is clear that our existing institutions, firmly rooted in the world of push, will require significant redesign in order to effectively harness the potential of pull." —blogcritics.org

THE POWER OF PULL

THE POWER OF PULL

How Small Moves, Smartly Made,
Can Set Big Things in Motion

John Hagel III

John Seely Brown

Lang Davison

BASIC BOOKS
A Member of the Perseus Books Group
New York

Designed by Jeff Williams

The Library of Congress has catalogued the hardcover as follows:
    Hagel, John.
    The power of pull : how small moves, smartly made, can set big things in motion/
John Hagel III, John Seely Brown, and Lang Davison.
        p. cm.
    Includes bibliographical references and index.
    ISBN 978-0-465-01935-9 (alk. paper)
    1. Organizational change—Social aspects. 2. Success in business. 3. Motivation
(Psychology) 4. Job satisfaction. 5. Social change. I. Brown, John Seely. II. Davison,
Lang. III. Title.

HD58.7.H334 2010
303.4—dc22
                                                                    2009047323

ISBN: 978-0-465-02876-4 (paperback)
ISBN: 978-0-465-02113-0 (e-book)

10 9 8 7 6 5 4 3 2

Dedicated to the Edge Fellows—cool kids doing edge work

Contents

Preface to the Paperback Edition

Since *The Power of Pull* was first published in 2010, we have been humbled and inspired by the thought-provoking discussions and responses it has sparked. This book, admittedly, was released with extremely lofty ambitions; with it, we sought to showcase the potential to harness pull in order to reshape our lives, firms, and industries. The *Power of Pull* begins with an analysis of the profound long-term shift playing out in the global economy and its implications for the very different practices and institutional platforms required to create value. But arguably the most important part—the actual steps we can take today as individuals and institutions to get from where we are now to where we need to be— comes in the second half of the book. Yet in our time-scarce world, we fear that many of our readers never made it that far, or perhaps, that the magnitude of the change we were proposing did not fully resonate with them at the time.

That is why, with this release, we want to focus attention on the subtitle of the book, *How Small Moves Smartly Made Can Set Big Things in Motion*. We want readers to see, and will underscore here, that although the required transformation is great, it need not be daunting. In fact, we have developed a robust methodology for driving this change in an unintimidating, pragmatic way.

No one will argue with the fact that we live in a world of tumultuous and accelerating change, visible everywhere from the exponential adoption rates of new technologies to our increasingly volatile stock market. It is easy to become overwhelmed by this uncertainty and give up trying to anticipate where the world is headed. It is true that exponential change can be disruptive and destabilizing, but it is during periods of upheaval that the *right* move, one aligned with these waves of change, can achieve far greater results than a *big* move. Simply put, by leveraging the forces driving change, we have the opportunity to achieve much, much more with so much less.

Even though addressing these long-term shifts requires fundamentally different institutional platforms, we have today unprecedented access to the tools and techniques needed to make these huge changes in smaller, more pragmatic steps. These tools and approaches, in fact, have become more pervasive since *The Power of Pull* was originally released. Since then, we have been surprised and delighted by how quickly improvements in the "big four" technologies (cloud, social, data analytics, and mobility) have lowered the barriers of implementing small moves and amplified their potential returns. These new tools can significantly improve the means for and the economics of institutional innovation—making it more feasible to transform even a large, staid institution into a nimble organization able to make the most of, rather than merely cope with, waves of exponential change.

In mapping out the path that institutions can follow to harness the power of pull, we hasten to emphasize that this is not a matter of making a journey from Point A to Point B, from one static point to another. Instead, we suggest that the tools and approaches required to design a pragmatic pathway through the shifting business landscape will set into motion practices and institutional platforms that will continue to rapidly evolve. There is no fixed destination, only a continuing path toward achieving a blend of stability and change that will orient us while propelling us forward into even more change. Instead of striving for a new state of being, firms must reach a new state of *always becoming.*

What, then, is holding firms back today? There are countless examples of skunk works, or top-secret R&D groups, tasked broadly with "innovation." We argue, however, that the mindset required to truly harness the power of pull is fundamentally different than that required to maintain a peripheral R&D outpost, even one that is fertile in generating a continuing stream of innovations. The latter is more about diversification or entering new markets than transformation of the core business. Really harnessing pull is not about seeking incremental growth opportunities that afford periods of stability. In a world of pull, we must reconceive changes as part of a grand adventure and be at peace with fluidity, even though it may defy our natural instinct to reach a steady state. Since the release of *The Power of Pull*, we have done extensive research to understand how firms can use new generations of technology to catalyze change from promising, rapidly scaling "edges" of the institution, which serve as fertile ground for the development of new pull practices and platforms. These edges offer firms early and tangible evidence of how pull can lead to rapid performance improvement, and are a far cry from the lonely outposts of innovation that previous approaches to change championed. Rather than finding promising edges and bringing them back into the core of the business, we suggest pulling more and more people from the core of the institution out to the edge—until it ultimately *becomes* the new core.

But who can make these changes? Who are we trying to reach with our book? When we wrote *The Power of Pull*, we were trying to reach two broad sets of readers. On one level, we were trying to reach individuals from all walks of life who wanted to deal more effectively with mounting pressure and achieve greater impact. Our second target audience was senior executives. From personal experience, we knew they were particularly challenged; even as they coped with the massive changes in business with a set of push-based practices, their institutions were proving less and less effective. And third, although we did not explicitly target them when writing the book, we were surprised and pleased to see how much our book resonated with leaders in the nonprofit sector: foundations, NGOs, educational institutions, and government agencies. By laying out a broad enough framework, we found that all of these audiences could gain insight into the potential of pull to transform lives and institutions.

In fact, we have found that the most positive response to the book so far has come from individuals and leaders of nonprofit institutions. Perhaps this is not surprising, given that these are the two groups that tend to be the most resource-constrained. Without a lot of resources to push around, they are much more open to the potential to harness pull in ways that may help them achieve more impact with fewer resources. These readers are also receptive to the message that passion can be a powerful catalyst for achieving greater impact with pull platforms.

C-suite executives have proven more resistant to the message that their tried-and-true management practices are insufficient in today's business landscape. Our book came out at the trough of the recent economic downturn, a time when near-term pressures seemed insurmountable. Under the scrutiny of impatient Wall Street investors, these executives had little time for discussions of fundamental, long-term changes; significant asset values were under attack at that instant.

Their response was to cling even more tightly to the tried-and-true practices as they searched for stability in a world that seemed to be spinning out of control. With a survivalist mindset, they turned to cutting costs by any means necessary. In fact, firms have reacted with deeper and deeper cuts to headcount during each downturn over the past fifty years—clearly reflecting a classic push mindset. Rather than viewing labor as an asset capable of generating increasing value over time, firms still conceive of talent as a fixed cost that should be pushed and squeezed ever harder.

The re-release of *The Power of Pull* comes at a Cambrian moment in our economy—almost everything is up for grabs and the opportunity to shape the future means rich rewards for those willing to act. As early signs of economic recovery emerge, firms that have been relying on short-term, survivalist tactics now face growing pressure from shareholders to deliver growth as well as profits.

This pressure for growth is mounting at the same that time capital constraints and a sense of risk aversion prevail, making the "big bang" growth approaches of the past—large-scale acquisitions or long lead-time organic growth initiatives—much less attractive. Perhaps this pressure for growth will provide the catalyst for these executives to re-assess the approaches of the past.

New generations of technology coupled with pull-based management practices and platforms provide a promising third path to growth—leveraged growth. Rather than relying on traditional *financial leverage*, it is time to focus on *capability leverage:* mobilizing a diverse set of third-party capabilities to deliver ever more value to the customer. In today's networked world, the ability to leverage the capabilities of third parties has never been greater. Of course, scaling this approach requires mastering the techniques of pull and challenging traditional push-based mindsets, where tight control was the top priority.

In *The Power of Pull*, we help executives and individuals address the questions most relevant at this time of unprecedented opportunity and change: How do we attain ever higher levels of operational efficiency in a networked world? How do we accelerate growth in ways that reduce up-front investment, compress lead times, and amplify long-term growth potential? How do we pursue innovation without putting firms at financial and strategic risk? How can we generate even more value from the talent that we have spent so much time and resources recruiting? What is the business value of new generations of technology, and how can we deploy them in a staged way that does not require massive investment up front?

So we are optimistic that the time is now ripe for senior executives of the largest companies to embrace *The Power of Pull*. Today, even the largest companies are drawn to the message that small moves, smartly made, can set big things in motion. Massive organizational change is not necessary at the outset; there are much more pragmatic paths to help executives stage their way into the changes that need to be made.

To get the most out of *The Power of Pull*, it is helpful to understand how the two pieces of the book fit together. The first half explains the lens through which to view the Big Shift and understand the imperatives and opportunities it creates. The section focuses on reframing our readers' mindsets around the broader context of long-term shifts and helping them see the implications in terms of promising approaches to generate value. The second half of the book focuses on the key question of the pragmatic pathways that can help get us from where we are today to where we need to be. This is where we detail the small steps that can be taken at the individual and institutional levels to begin enacting transformation pragmatically.

In many ways, *The Power of Pull* is more relevant today than when it was first released. As the pace of social and economic change continues to pick up, the pressure on firms and individuals is mounting. Yes, we may all experience some modest relief in the recovery that is ever so slowly gaining momentum, but the desperate hope that we might return to "normal" has now proven to be an illusion. It is time to step back and challenge basic assumptions about how to achieve sustainable impact. If we get this right, we have the potential to move from a world of diminishing returns to a world of increasing returns.

With the release of this new edition, we hope to reach all three audiences—individuals, senior corporate executives, and leaders of a diverse set of noncommercial institutions—at a critical juncture in time. We ask our readers to come in with an open mind, step back, take a look at the longer-term changes playing out in our global economy, and assess the implications for how we might turn stress into success. As you read, we hope that you take both the mindset and the methods in *The Power of Pull* to heart. And we continue to look forward to the stories, feedback, and debates this book will spark. That will help us to focus our next wave of research—there is so much more to learn about the world that is changing around us.

Introduction

‖‖‖‖‖‖‖‖‖‖‖‖‖‖‖‖ ‖ ‖ ‖

They started out as grommets—groms, for short, an affectionate name for kids learning extreme sports. These five were little surf kids, no bigger than a three-foot wave, learning to ride a board on the beach break near the shore, and their names were Dusty, Clay, Wesley, Granger, and Kai. Since anyone could remember, they were always together, either in the living room of Dusty's parents' house, or at school, or down at Hookipa surf break (on Maui's north shore) ripping up the waves. Now in their early twenties, they are all on the verge of making the World Championship Tour, the most elite group of competitive surfers in the world.

It doesn't seem like so unusual a story: Local kids make good. Best pals and brothers have long succeeded together in surfing. The Bronzed Aussies of the 1970s, and the Malibu Crew of the 1960s. The Momentum Generation came up together in the 1990s. The Coolie Kids burst on the scene in the early 2000s, and the Hobgoods and Lopez brothers came out of Florida about the same time.

But Maui has never sent a surfer to the 'CT, as the pro tour is called, let alone produced a champion there. Nobody's quite sure why. Maybe it's because, despite a handful of world-class breaks, Maui generally doesn't have the best surf in the Hawaiian Islands. That honor goes hands down to Oahu, which is surrounded by great waves and historic surf breaks—and which has produced the lion's share of Hawaii's most famous surfers.

So how did the five little groms from Maui, who grew up best pals and stiffest competitors, go from surfing for kicks to winning Junior titles to standing on the verge of making the pro tour?

That question, in its more general form, applies well beyond the world of surfing. Whether it's in online gaming, amateur astronomy, open-source software development, apparel manufacturing, or online music remixing—what is it that makes one set of circumstances right for individuals or institutions to flourish while others yield weak or even depreciating results? How can a group of obscure motorcycle assemblers in China challenge the best Japan has to offer? Why does World of Warcraft remain the most popular online game, despite competing titles that keep coming along to challenge it—and that keep failing? How can a big software company attract into a sprawling virtual community everybody it needs to get a difficult new product adopted quickly? What, in other words, does it take to turn passion into success?

The common dynamic that we see underlying all of these success stories is what we call "pull," the ability to draw out people and resources as needed to address opportunities and challenges. Pull gives us unprecedented access to what we need, when we need it, even if we're not quite sure that "it" is. Pull allows us to harness and unleash the forces of attraction, influence, and serendipity. Using pull, we can create the conditions by which individuals, teams, and even institutions can achieve their potential in less time and with more impact than has ever been possible. The power of pull provides a key to how all of us—individually and collectively—can turn challenge and stress into opportunity and reward as digital technology remakes our lives.

If you want to succeed personally, if you want your company to succeed, if you have grand ambitions about what the world ought to look like, we think we've identified the keys to success that you will need in a world that's changing almost too fast to keep track of. By understanding those fundamental changes, and by grasping how pull works, we think you can be happier working at something you love, build institutions that can act as platforms to catapult change (and create real value while doing it), and maybe even transform the world in necessary and far-reaching ways. We won't lie to you: It won't be easy. But the choice has become that we adopt these techniques and thrive, or we choose to ignore them and face a great risk of failure as passion, talent, and material resources head elsewhere.

||||||||

IF WE ARE GOING TO SUCCEED in this rapidly changing world, we face two challenges: making sense of the changes around us, and making progress in an increasingly unfamiliar world. These challenges are related, of course. On one hand, we can't make progress without first making sense. The myriad of surface changes can quickly distract and disorient us. On the other hand, making sense will not help us unless we can use our understanding to craft a journey that will honor where we are today and help us to make progress in measured and pragmatic steps. This book takes on both challenges—it is our goal to help you make sense and to help you make progress.

To begin to understand how pull helps and enables individuals, groups, and institutions to thrive, we visited the living room of Wendell and Lisa Payne's Lahaina home in Maui. Not just any living room turns out to develop world-class athletes, of course. So what made this one different? On the surface, the Paynes' living room looks much like any other: There's a sofa, an easy chair, a scrapbook on the side table (with a one-word title: "Dusty"), a television, and a book shelf. But this living room also became a place where Dusty and his friends, without realizing it, were tapping into deep processes that have lessons for all of us.

More often than not, these processes start with a simple question: What interests us? What are we passionate about? As eight-year-old Dusty squinted into the sun in the backyard of the small family house in Haiku, Hawaii, his father asked him, "What do you want to do?" Dusty, who had already gotten tired of stick and ball games such as baseball and soccer, thought for a few moments and said, "I want to surf."

From that moment on, Wendell and Lisa immersed their young son—and themselves—in the world of amateur surfing, becoming heavily involved with the Hawaii Amateur Surfing Association and eventually the National Scholastic Surfing Association, where they met the Larsens, the Marzos, and the Bargers—the parents of other promising groms who were as hooked on surfing as Dusty was. Most years at Thanksgiving they flew over to the Rell Sunn Menehune Surf Contest on the beautiful beach of Makaha in Oahu, where in 2001 a record sixteen kids from Maui showed up, families in tow, an early foreshadowing of a new generation of top surfers.

In the midst of all this activity the Paynes' living room became a focal point, a clubhouse, a place of retreat and reflection following the day's experiences out in the surf—the calm center in the middle of a growing intermingling of influences, contests, people, and interactions that together launched five of the most promising young surfers of their generation.

Dusty and his friends would surf all day and then—gathered in front of the Payne family's VCR, enthralled by the prodigious romance and athletic daring of the older generations of surfers—devour the latest surfing movie at night (and don't picture Gidget, either; these movies featured footage of top surfers as they pushed the limits of the sport). "Every time a new movie came out they'd watch it a hundred times," Wendell recalls, "dissecting how this guy did that move or some other guy did something else, analyzing it in the living room and then going out the next day to try those moves on their own."

Before long the young surfers were videotaping each other, using the cheap video cameras that had just arrived on the market and iMovie editing software on the Payne family's iMac. They'd break the movies down frame by frame, examining each other's techniques, saying, "If only you'd slid your foot a bit further forward on that move," or, "If you'd rotated your head a little more to the left." Then they'd go out and try to incorporate those moves into their repertoire, practicing again and again until they became second nature. In this way, they came to capture hundreds of little maneuvers, each of them made in response to the unpredictable movements of the waves.

Most times these adjustments were routine. Occasionally, however, they represented performance breakthroughs accomplished in spontaneous (and often unconscious) reaction to the demands of the moment and the unforeseeable dynamics of the wave.

If one of them just happened to have grabbed the edge of his board at a certain moment—say, right before landing a jump—he was able to review just what he'd done with his buddies while sitting around eating pizza that night in the Payne family's living room. Then they could replicate it, and maybe even refine it. As video became an indispensable part of their development, so did the many surfing websites that began to appear, which served to amplify the effect. The youngsters no longer had to wait for new surfing movies to come out. Instead, they could access footage of just about any pro surfing competition and even watch the pros (and prominent "soul surfers")[1] as they were free-surfing. Often the footage would appear the same day it was shot. Dusty and his friends would break these videos down just as carefully as their own, analyzing the subtle nuances of technique and learning from surfers they'd often neither met nor, in some cases, even heard of. They also started posting their own videos to the web for others to watch and learn from.

And it wasn't long before the surf world took notice, most notably in the form of Matt Kinoshita, perhaps the preeminent board shaper in Maui, who became a coach and mentor. Surfers and board shapers (who are often prominent surfers themselves) have a long history of working together and spurring one another to new heights of performance. Professional videographers also took notice of the talented, photogenic kids and began following them around and posting clips of their exploits. This in turn attracted sponsors such as Volcom and Body Glove that clamored to place their logos on their boards and hats. Standing in the Payne's unassuming living room, flipping through the pages of the scrapbook Dusty's parents kept about him, we marveled at how the world of sun, sand, and waves could so closely resemble what we were learning about pull in so many other, very different places, contexts, and people.

WHAT TO EXPECT IN THIS BOOK

Pull is about expanding our awareness of what is possible and evolving new dispositions, mastering new practices, and taking new actions to realize those possibilities. It's about figuring out how to be systematic in how we combine work and life to pursue our passions, how to find others who share our passion but bring different experiences and perspectives to challenging performance needs, and how to create conditions where we're more likely to happen upon interesting people, resources, and opportunities—even as we contribute the same chances to others. We all pursue some of these techniques—searching, tapping into networks of one kind or another, connecting with people who share our passions—but almost none of us do it systematically or even consciously. And few of us know how powerful these ideas and techniques, properly deployed, have the potential to be.

Pull is really about harnessing the same techniques and attitudes that allowed Dusty to excel, but doing it systematically and consciously. *Pull* starts by exploring three increasingly powerful levels of pull—access, attract, and achieve. We will describe in detail the techniques, approaches, and practices required to most effectively harness these levels of pull, drawing on examples of individuals and companies that have been successful applying them. In developing each of these levels, we will also describe the deep changes underlying them. The distance yet to be traveled, individually and collectively, may feel daunting. Make no mistake, this will be a difficult (and yet exciting) journey.

Accordingly, we've written the second part of the book to reflect the elements of a successful journey toward pull, the steps we can all start taking. This journey by necessity starts with the individual and then builds out to the institutional level and ultimately to broader arenas—markets, industries, and even society in its entirety. Several crucial "elements of the journey" must be systematically created and put into place: the right *trajectory* (the direction in which you're headed); sufficient *leverage* (the ability to mobilize the passions and efforts of other people); and the best *pace* (the speed at which you progress) to make it all come together in a world that's moving ever more quickly and unpredictably. This is the story of how to get from where you are now to where you

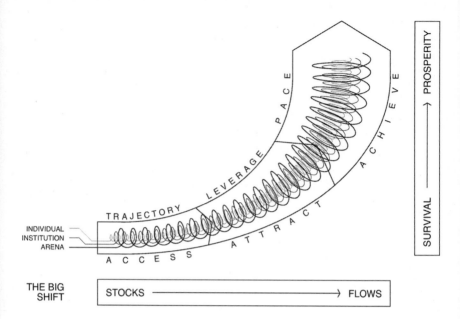

Havilland Studio, Palo Alto, California, and Lahaina, Hawaii

really want to be. It's the story of how small moves can have dispropor-tionate impact. It's the story of how to change the world.

To help keep track of these different aspects of our book, we're in-cluding a "map" showing the three levels of pull (access, attract, and achieve); the three domains in which they apply (individual, institu-tional, and societal); and the three elements of the journey that all of us will follow toward pull (trajectory, leverage, and pace). (See the dia-gram above.) We'll be highlighting aspects of this map in each chapter to help you navigate through the book.

In previous generations of institutional change, an elite at the top of the organization created the world into which everybody else needed to fit. The institutional changes ahead will be quite different. These changes will be driven by passionate individuals distributed throughout and even outside the institution, supported by institutional leaders who understand the need for change but who also realize that this wave of change cannot be imposed from the top down. The new institutional model will involve a complete refocusing: Rather than molding individuals to fit the needs of the institution, institutions will be shaped to provide platforms to help individuals achieve their full potential by connecting with others and better addressing challenging performance needs. The success of institutions will depend on their ability to amplify the efforts of individuals so that small moves, smartly made, can become catalysts for broad impact. Institutions will themselves become powerful pull platforms, helping individuals gain leverage they could never achieve on their own and, as a result, develop their talents more rapidly than they could as independent agents. Rather than individuals serving the needs of institutions, our institutions will be recrafted to serve the needs of individuals. As each of us brings into the workplace the practices we have mastered in our personal lives, the institutions where we work will be transformed, and our professional lives along with them.

Not every one of us will make this leap equally willingly or at the same time. But we believe that in the digital age, as social networking sites, powerful search engines, and the like continue to exert their democratizing influences, the power of pull will become the governing principle for success, and that those who learn how to use these tools and methods most effectively are the ones who will pull their institutions into a new era of higher performance and achievement, often through the use of edge practices at the core. This, in fact, is the thesis of this book, and we will show, in detail, how this new model works and explain how an individual or company can begin to use the pull framework to excel and move into the twenty-first century.

Even though these changes are likely to come from individuals and build up organically, today's institutional leaders have a crucial role to play as well. Their success or failure will increasingly depend on the extent to which they can identify and support trail-blazing, early-moving individuals and give them the support and empowerment they need to help accelerate institutional change. Eventually, as institutional arrangements and practices continue to evolve, we foresee increasing potential for both individuals and institutions to use the power of pull to shape broader markets and societies—a future with radical implications for individuals, for institutions, and for the world.

LEAVING BEHIND THE WORLD OF PUSH

To get to pull, first we've got to come to grips with what push is and how it permeates our lives. Push approaches begin by forecasting needs and then designing the most efficient systems to ensure that the right people and resources are available at the right time and the right place using carefully scripted and standardized processes.

Push programs have dominated our lives from our very earliest years. We are literally pushed into educational systems designed to anticipate our needs over twelve or more years of schooling and our key needs for skills over the rest of our lives. As we successfully complete this push program, we graduate into firms and other institutions that are organized around push approaches to resource mobilization. Detailed demand forecasts, operational plans, and operational process manuals carefully script the actions and specify the resources required to meet anticipated demand. We consume media that have been packaged, programmed, and pushed to us based on our anticipated needs. We encounter push programs in other parts of our lives as well, whether in the form of churches that anticipate what is required for salvation and define detailed programs for reaching this goal, gyms that promise a sculpted body for those who pursue tightly defined fitness regimens, or diet gurus who promise we will lose weight if we follow a certain menu or choose from particular foods. Push knows better than you do, and it's not afraid to say, "Do this, not that!"

Pull is a very different approach, one that works at three primary levels, each of which builds on the others. At the most basic level, pull helps us to find and *access* people and resources when we need them. At a second level, pull is the ability to *attract* people and resources to you that are relevant and valuable, even if you were not even aware before that they existed. Think here of serendipity rather than search.

Finally, in a world of mounting pressure and unforeseen opportunities, we need to cultivate a third level of pull—the ability to pull from within ourselves the insight and performance required to more effectively *achieve* our potential. We can use pull to learn faster and translate that learning into rapidly improving performance, not just for ourselves, but for the people we connect with—a virtuous cycle that we can participate in. Perhaps the most intriguing example of this third level of pull in action comes from an unexpected area—the world of online gaming and, in particular, a game that has captured the imagination of nearly 12 million gamers—World of Warcraft.

These three levels of pull go far beyond the "on-demand" focus of the technology industry in recent years. On-demand initiatives generally seek to facilitate the first level of pull, but they have very little to offer regarding the second and third levels of pull.

Chapters 2 through 4 will develop these three levels of pull in much more detail, but for now, let's explore a bit further what each of these levels of pull involves.

The First Level of Pull: Access

The first and simplest level of pull is all about flexible access—the ability to fluidly find and get to the people and resources when and where we need them. As we shall see, this is considerably different from the notion of "pull" that some readers will associate with lean manufacturing. Search engines such as Google or Microsoft's Bing provide perhaps the clearest examples of robust pull platforms that help us to find and access people and resources wherever they reside. More specialized aggregators, such as Orbitz or Travelocity, help people search and connect with a broad range of relevant resources (although the more general search engines are now adding some of this more specialized functionality as well). Note that pull platforms needn't exclusively live on digital networks, although they function most effectively there. They can also bridge the physical and virtual worlds. One example of this principle can be found in Cisco's efforts to connect customers with more than 40,000 specialized channel partners to support their individual needs in a highly customized way. Another is found in the Hong Kong firm Li & Fung, which operates a global network of more than 10,000 business partners to configure customized supply networks for customers in the apparel industry using mostly fax machines and telephones.

Access will become increasingly necessary as competition intensifies and disruptions become more frequent. It used to be that we could rely on "stocks" of knowledge—what we know at any point in time—but these stocks are diminishing in value more rapidly than ever before. Consider the compression of product life-cycles occurring in most global industries today. Even the most successful products fall by the wayside more quickly than the ones that preceded them as new generations come through the pipeline at an ever faster clip. In more stable times, we could sit back and relax once we had learned something valuable, secure that we could generate value from that knowledge for an indefinite period. Not anymore.

To succeed now, we have to continually refresh our stocks of knowledge by participating in relevant "flows" of knowledge—interactions that create knowledge or transfer it across individuals. These flows occur in any social, fluid environment that allows firms and individuals to get better faster by working with others.

To get a sense of the difference between stocks of knowledge and knowledge flows, imagine a car mechanic trying to keep up with the rapidly changing technologies embedded in today's cars. A mechanic falling back on the training she received at the outset of her work life would be hopelessly lost with today's computer systems. Even attending additional training programs or reading manuals would not be sufficient to keep up. There would likely be a need to connect with other mechanics and perhaps even the manufacturer to problem-solve unanticipated issues with the cars coming in for repairs. Without access to these flows of knowledge, the mechanic would soon be out of a job. And a good mechanic would not just wait until a specific problem arose. In one way or another, we all are becoming more active in professional gatherings where we can pick up knowledge through discussions with others that will ultimately prove useful in our work. By getting deeply involved in these groups, we evolve our understanding of the context we are working in; we even learn how to frame really good questions that can be effectively answered when the need arises. For a mechanic, such a group might be an online discussion forum where mechanics gather on an ongoing basis to discuss some of the new technologies entering the marketplace and the challenges they represent.

Or consider again the professional surfing world, where innovations happen quickly and often jump the boundaries from other sports, such as motocross, skateboarding, and snowmobile jumping. As top surfers, Dusty and his friends might already know how to execute a "pop-shove-it," in which you rotate your board 180 degrees while in midair (a move learned from skateboarders), but what about the "superman," where you quickly thrust the board in front of you, at arm's length, while "flying" behind it? When somebody mastered that move on a surf break half a world away, Dusty and the others were some of the first to know about it.

In this case the surfer's "stock" of knowledge—the pop-shove-it—had just become less than the newest thing. Its value had diminished relative to the new *new* thing—the superman—that was getting its own fifteen minutes of fame before something else would inevitably supplant it. And yet these young men knew about it almost immediately. How do they keep up? By heading over to Surfermag.com, Surfingthemag.com, Surfline.com, or TWsurf.com and making sure they've seen the newest surfing maneuvers nearly as soon as they've been shot. Refreshing the stocks of what we know by participating in flows of new knowledge is fundamental to performance improvement, no matter the endeavor, both for individuals and, more broadly, for institutions.

Unfortunately, this represents a significant challenge for our existing institutions, since they have been organized around the proposition that economic value comes from protecting existing stocks of knowledge and efficiently extracting the value that these stocks of knowledge represent. It's not always easy for us as individuals, either, to acknowledge that all those years of education may not be as helpful as we had hoped. We discover that we must compete for employment with talented individuals halfway around the world, in places we may never have heard of before. As a billboard along Highway 101 in Silicon Valley put it, "1,000,000 people overseas can do your job. What makes you so special?"[2] The days when any of us, as workers, could take our job security for granted seem as distant as the genteel era in which surfing pioneers stood ramrod straight on ten-foot-long red-wood surfboards.

It's quickly dawning on us instead that our education was at best a thin foundation that needs to be continually refreshed in order for us to stay competitive. The stress in our professional lives bleeds over into our personal lives as we find ourselves working longer hours and as long-standing relationships are disrupted by unexpected events. We are all becoming heavily reliant on pull platforms in our personal life to help us cope with growing pressure. Everything from car buying to house hunting and investment management has been significantly transformed by the availability of new, technology-enhanced pull platforms. Can any of us imagine a time when we could not turn to search engines to access people and resources that could help us with our needs?

The Second Level of Pull: Attract

We can be systematic in our search techniques and scenario planning, but often we're at a loss for what questions to ask, much less what to look for. In this kind of world, access and search have important, but increasingly limited, utility. Go ahead: Try and search for something when you're not quite sure what it is that you're looking for, what your question really is. Or if you know the elements of what you're looking for but not how they go together or what subject they might fall under. Frustration quickly mounts. Our success in finding new information and sources of inspiration increasingly depends upon serendipity—the chance encounter with someone or something that we did not even know existed, much less had value, but that proves to be extraordinarily relevant and helpful once we find out about it. But it turns out that these "serendipitous" events are not always just chance. Louis Pasteur famously observed, "Fortune favors the prepared mind," but this still assumes that the initial encounter is pure luck and that it is only a question of being prepared for luck when it happens. What if it is possible to shape those unexpected encounters so that we could increase the probability and quality of the encounters?

Consider how Dusty Payne won $50,000 in a contest he didn't even know he'd entered. We could say that we should all be so lucky. But it wasn't luck. The year was 2008, and Dusty was free-surfing at Canguu in Bali, tired from having stayed up late the night before, celebrating his win at the Oakley Pro Junior the previous day, where he'd made a series of stunning aerial maneuvers in eight-foot surf against some of the best rippers in the world. It was the biggest win yet in his promising career, and now he was enjoying some time away from the competition, riding the waves for the joy of it.

In retrospect, it wasn't the perfect wave that he caught that day. But what he did with it was spectacular. Cutting to his right, he made a few quick small turns before launching himself out of the water on his board, spinning 360 degrees above the lip of the wave, and then landing cleanly again in the water. He didn't know it yet, but this "massively tweaked-out frontside air" (as *Surfer* magazine later called it)[3] proved to be the winning move in a year-long contest sponsored by a footwear company called Kustom, which had invited all comers to post videos of themselves online in a winner-takes-all shootout between August 2008 and March 2009. One of the videographers following Dusty's every surfing move caught his "Balinese boost" on film and posted it online, where it attracted Kustom's eye. Even the awards ceremony was a surprise as Kustom representatives leaped out of a closet to give Dusty a jacket festooned with hundred-dollar bills.

The story of the Kustom Air Strike demonstrates the ripple effects of serendipity. One morning Dusty Payne happened to be free-surfing and unleashed a huge move. A videographer caught it and posted it online, where Kustom saw it and decided it was the winning "entry." Dusty wasn't trying to win the Air Strike with that move. He didn't know if the videographer would capture the move, or post it. But he was prepared, and he went out into the morning to have fun and create something new and unexpected.

Serendipity is also one of the secret ingredients explaining the continued growth of "spikes"—geographic concentrations of talent around the world. The Silicon Valley engineer attends his daughter's soccer match and happens to meet another engineer on the sidelines. In the course of their conversation, the engineer stumbles upon an interesting solution to a design problem he had been wrestling with for months. And so on. When talented individuals choose to live in spikes, rather than in, say, small towns or rural areas,[4] they're doing so because it increases their rate of discovery, making it more likely that they'll stumble on what they need. Of course, it's important to choose the right spike. If you're interested in surfing (or your child is), it doesn't do you much good to live in Washington, D.C., even if it might be easier to get there.

Thus aspiring country musicians move to Nashville, while up-and-coming software engineers go to Silicon Valley or Bangalore, screenwriters to Los Angeles, models to New York, and so on. Talented individuals tend to go where they have the greatest chance of running into what they need in order to take the next step, even if they don't quite know or understand what form it will take or who might inspire it.

Serendipity also generates congregations of complementary talent in virtual communities of like interests, from mothering to survivalism. Online communities are perfect for bringing together far-flung people who have common interests. If you want to find out what it is you don't know that you don't know, you need to hang out with other people who might already know it.

Online social network sites, such as Facebook or LinkedIn, play an interesting role in all of this. They help people stay in touch with their existing friends and colleagues, but, increasingly, they also provide environments for serendipitous encounters with friends of friends, or colleagues of colleagues, even people whom one has never before met. Social scientists call these "weak ties"[5]—people we barely know who can connect us to rich networks of relationships in domains completely different from ours. These tools are helping to make our activities and interests broadly visible to enhance serendipitous encounters brokered by those on the periphery of our social networks. Ironically, these online social networks have very primitive search capabilities—as of this writing at least—but when used skillfully they can allow one to attract people from unexpected directions.

By phoning up the videographer beforehand, as Dusty did, even if we don't know what good might come from it; by moving to Silicon

Valley or some other spike of complementary talent; by being appropriately open with our personal and professional information on social networking sites—in all these ways we can enhance the potential for attracting serendipitous encounters. In other words, we can shape serendipity rather than waiting passively for it to occur. Following Louis Pasteur's advice, we can work to prepare ourselves. We can reach out, make interesting connections—often for their own sake. But doing this requires an understanding of the areas where the most valuable new ideas, insights, and experiences are likely to surface so that we can position ourselves for serendipity. For many people, it also requires overcoming the terrifying sense that we'll get it "wrong" when we use digital media like Facebook or Twitter. Maybe we'll say too much, or what we say won't be interesting, or we'll be ridiculed for posting an idea that we haven't really thought through.

Meeting new people and finding new ideas can be fun in and of themselves. But attraction—and the serendipity that arises from it—takes on increasing value as we look to attract and retain the attention of people who exist at the edge of our areas of interest and to increase the probability of serendipitous encounters at the most relevant times. Edges are places that become fertile ground for innovation because they spawn significant new unmet needs and unexploited capabilities and attract people who are risk takers. Edges therefore become significant drivers of knowledge creation and economic growth, challenging and ultimately transforming traditional arrangements and approaches. The sociologist Vanina Leschziner, for instance, tells the story of how chefs go to other cities—particularly cities with leading cuisine scenes, such as Paris, New York, and San Francisco—to pick up fresh ideas from other restaurants about combining ingredients and creating appealing restaurant ambiance.[6] If we want to participate in serendipitous environments, we need to pay special attention to environments and practices that can attract edge players. These practices often involve creating the right incentives, whether they're economic incentives or something personally rewarding and meaningful to the recipient, such as status points in a social network. Since it takes us beyond our comfort zone, going to the edge may not always give us a sensation of safety. But the "productive friction"[7] generated by unfamiliar circumstances can be surprisingly beneficial, as can surrounding ourselves with people whose ways of perceiving the world and solving problems differ from our own.[8]

Note that while serendipity often occurs in social networks, where we unexpectedly encounter friends of friends or even total strangers who prove helpful, we're not simply talking about old-style networking, where you "work" a party or a conference for anybody and everybody who might prove useful to you. We're not talking about the mutual back-scratching of the old-boys' network, either, to fix parking tickets or an embarrassing situation with a relative. Nor are we talking about pulling strings behind the scenes, or making Machiavellian use of information. Anyone approaching pull in a mercenary, "what's-in-it-for-me" fashion is likely to get burned. In fact, he or she will not really be practicing pull at all, as they will offer no reciprocal benefits to the people and institutions with whom they interact. Pull is a way of creating value, period, not just extracting a bigger piece of some mythical pie for yourself.

The Third Level of Pull: Achieve

Individuals can use the techniques of access to find what they need, and can use the techniques of attraction to draw new people, ideas, and information to them. Institutions can abet individuals in this by providing them with platforms that allow them to reach out. But pull goes beyond these basics.

We can use these pull techniques to attain new levels of performance and, having achieved these levels, to immediately begin exploring ways to get to the next level. Like Olympic snowboarders practicing moves in 2009 that were undreamed of in 2006 (such as the double-corked 1260—a spin cycle of three and a half rotations and two off-axis flips), or competitive surfers learning the next aerial maneuver, they know that today's level of achievement will not be sufficient tomorrow. You might think that such goals are only for performers at the highest levels—Olympic athletes, CEOs, best-selling recording artists. But in truth they're for everyone. In fact, one of our examples, Malcom McLean, who changed the way the world shipped everything with the introduction of the shipping container in 1946, started off driving a truck for someone else.

It is no accident that these early examples of performance improvement come from various edges, because it is exactly at the edge that the need to get better faster has the most urgency. Incumbents at the core—which is the place where most of the resources, especially people and money, are concentrated, and where old ways of thinking and acting still hold sway—have many fewer incentives to figure out the world, or to discover new ways of doing things, or to find new information. They're on top, and they're ready to keep doing what got them there. But simply accessing or attracting static resources no longer cuts it. Accessing and attracting have little value unless they are coupled with a third set of practices that focus on driving performance rapidly to new levels. These practices involve participation in, and sometimes orchestration of, something we call "creation spaces"—environments that effectively integrate teams within a broader learning ecology so that performance improvement accelerates as more participants join.

Creation spaces allow large numbers of participants, often in the millions, to come together to test and refine the practices required to master this third level of pull—achieving their potential more effectively. You can see these creation spaces coming into being in a wide range of activities at the edge. Although from a distance it may look like they are emerging spontaneously, self-organizing in response to the needs of the participants, a closer look reveals that creation spaces are carefully crafted by their organizers, especially in the early stages, to engage the right kinds of participants and foster specific types of interactions, all within environments that unleash the potential for increasing returns.

In fact, these creation spaces may change the way the "experts" look at business strategy. The "experience curve," first popularized by Boston Consulting Group in the late 1960s, has proved remarkably accurate in describing how performance improves in industries as diverse as semiconductors, toilet paper, and beer. It has been a foundation of business strategy for decades. Yet in all these industries experience curves are also diminishing returns curves—the more experience an industry accumulates, the longer it will take to accumulate enough experience to deliver a comparable increment of performance improvement. By making the most of the techniques of pull that we outline, creation spaces may deliver a very different form of performance improvement curve—one that rises even more rapidly as more and more people join the effort, demonstrating a powerful increasing-returns effect. We call this a *collaboration curve* to highlight the central role of new forms of collaboration in delivering higher and higher performance levels. Collaboration has always been central to value creation, but harnessing these three levels of pull will amplify the power of collaboration, producing increasing returns that previously have been beyond the reach of most collaboration efforts.

These creation spaces are emerging outside our existing institutional boundaries. As they gain force on the edge of current institutions, they will provide some sense of the fundamental institutional changes required to harness this third level of pull more effectively. Today's institutions—including the company where you work, or the one that you run—will require widespread changes to make the transition from push to pull.

Creation spaces differ in at least two ways from the "learning organization" approaches pioneered a couple of decades ago. First, they emerge as ecosystems across institutions rather than within a single institution, so they reach a much more diverse set of participants. Second, they are not primarily focused on learning—their goal is to drive more rapid performance improvement, and learning occurs as a byproduct of these efforts.

The moral of the story? To get better faster at whatever it is you do, you've got to be supported by a broad array of complementary people and resources from which you can pull what you need to raise your rate of performance improvement. Dusty Payne, Clay Marzo, Kai Barger, and the Larsen brothers would have been just another set of guys who loved to surf if it hadn't been for the Paynes' living room and the creation space of sponsors, board shapers, surf movies and videos, and competitive contests in which they grew up. They are the product of their environment, and that environment is a creation space.

When people chase what they love, they will inevitably seek out and immerse themselves in knowledge flows, drinking deeply from new creative wells even as they contribute their own experiences and insights along the way. (Remember, just as you're seeking out people on your edge, others are looking for you.) A powerful virtuous cycle begins playing out as more and more people enter creation spaces in their quest to learn faster. In the process of engaging and participating in knowledge flows, they begin to generate new knowledge flows that create even richer environments, attracting the next wave of participants.

It is no accident that most of these early examples of creation spaces are initially attracting individuals rather than institutions. Passionate individuals (that's you) naturally seek out these creation spaces to get better faster, while most institutions are still deeply concerned about protection of knowledge stocks and do not yet see the growing importance of knowledge flows in driving performance improvement. As passionate individuals engage and experience the performance benefits of participation, they will help to drag institutions more broadly into relevant creation spaces, becoming catalysts for the institutional innovations required for effective participation.

PUTTING PULL TO WORK

The three levels of pull explored in the first half of this book represent a powerful new approach to value creation in our personal and professional lives. In the second half of the book, we will explore how both individuals and institutions can put the levels of pull into practice. Embarking on the journey toward pull is something that will require significant changes in dispositions, in practices, and, ultimately, in how our institutions work and how they're structured. It will certainly not happen overnight, and it won't be easy. In fact, it can rapidly become overwhelming, prompting skeptics to question whether such profound transformation can ever be achieved. We can make this journey feasible and even see it yield pragmatic benefits along the way by beginning the transition as individuals, rather than seeking to transform our institutions at the outset, and by engaging on relevant edges first, before seeking to confront and transform the core. It is a journey that many have already started, and we will explore some of the lessons learned by those pioneers.

We're going to explore this journey at the level of the individual (Chapter 5) and at the level the institution (Chapter 6) and then explore how it might play out in broader economic and social arenas (Chapter 7).

That said, you can start on your journey now. There's no reason to wait. You know what your passion is. Find like-minded souls and get moving. As you begin, focus on three broad imperatives corresponding to the elements of trajectory, leverage, and pace described earlier.

Make Your Passion Your Profession

Dusty Payne told his dad, "I want to surf." This simple declaration gave Dusty and his family a directional heading for their journey; it gave them the right *trajectory* for where they wanted to go. It's hard to decide what course of action to take if you haven't first identified your passion. Once your direction is clear, however, much can fall into place. Dusty started off with a longing to surf. Now he's doing it for a living. Many former surfing pros stay in the industry, editing magazines, coaching, shaping boards. Many "retired" executives continue to work—on boards of directors, for example—simply for the joy of working. Their passion is their profession.

Those of us who continue to toil at jobs we don't love will find ourselves nonetheless toiling harder as our competition continues to intensify. We'll find it increasingly difficult to cope with the mounting stress or to put in the effort required to raise our performance. We need to marry our passions with our professions in order to reach our potential. As we'll discuss later, this isn't just about the select few who surf for a living; it's something that all of us need to purposely set out to do. Passion in this context refers to a sustained and deep commitment to achieving our full potential and greater capacity for self-expression in a domain that engages us on a personal level. We often develop and explore our passions in areas such as sports or the arts outside of work, but we rarely integrate our passions with our professions.

As we make our passions our professions, we may find our dispositions shifting, too. Rather than viewing change as a threat and something to be feared, we will find ourselves embracing change, recognizing its potential to drive us to even higher levels of performance. Stimulated by our passion, we will eagerly search for ways to more effectively achieve our potential, and this will lead us to master all three levels of pull.

Harness Your Ecosystems

For many of us, pursuing our passion will draw us toward the geographies in which similarly passionate people live. These spikes are places where talented people cluster around shared interests and passions: Think Silicon Valley and technology. Our passions will draw us to these spikes and motivate us to explore their richness as we seek out people who can help us to get better faster—further building the leverage that constitutes the second key element of our individual journeys. What we gain from living and working in spikes enhances all three levels of pull—access, attraction, and achievement. Dusty and his friends helped to catalyze a growing spike of surfing talent in Maui even as they regularly journeyed over to the spike of big-wave surfing on the north shore of Oahu. They enthusiastically used video and digital technology to extend and amplify the rapidly evolving social networks spawned within their local spikes. They worked hard at extending their personal social networks until they embraced and were embraced by a powerful ecosystem of world-class surfers, fans, sponsors, and board shapers from around the globe.

As our passions become our professions, we begin to see how social networks can provide us with an unparalleled opportunity to achieve our potential by allowing us to access resources and attract people who can help us while we help them. We construct our own personal ecosystems, an interesting blend of local relationships and global relationships, and a mutual leveraging occurs.

The core of our networks—the relatively small number of people with whom we maintain deep and rich relationships—will always remain important. But in using the digital infrastructure, and especially the social media tools now available, we discover that we can extend the edges of our social networks more effectively than ever and explore these edges in ways that were simply not feasible before.

The edges of our social networks represent the weak ties that connect us to people who can provide us with access to new insights, experiences, and capabilities that provoke us to improve our own game. Our passions will motivate us to extend and explore the edges of our networks more actively than ever as we pull relevant people and capabilities to us. We will not only explore—our passions will lead us to move quickly from conversation to shared creation initiatives that will help us to build much more meaningful relationships on the periphery. Dusty and his gang travel the world and, wherever they go, they are quickly immersed in the scene at the local surf breaks, comparing notes with local experts and their fellow traveling pros about the unique characteristics of each break and what they mean for surfing it.

Over time, we will discover that many of these edge connections become part of our core network, in the process transforming that core in deep yet unexpected ways. Dusty and his friends idolized Bruce and Andy Irons from afar as the two brothers from Oahu burst onto the surf scene in 1999. Later on, the Irons brothers became important friends and mentors to the Maui kids, and they continue to offer their help to this day. In fact, the complex interplay between the strong ties in our core network and the weak ties at the edges of our networks helps us to pull more value out of both types of relationships. In the process, we may have to master new types of communication—ranging from blogs and twittering to visual presentation and mobile presence—and get more comfortable appropriately sharing our personal selves online, even when our online networks include professional colleagues. As we do, we will generate the leverage that allows us to amplify our own impact and that of others—the second crucial "element of the journey."

Maximize Return on Attention

As the people and resources that we can access through these spikes and broader virtual social networks proliferate, we will also be motivated to adopt tools and services that can help improve our return on attention—the value we get for the time and effort we invest in focusing on someone or something. In fact, we'll have to adopt these tools. The speed, diversity, and force of the knowledge flows involved might otherwise easily overwhelm us as we lose the signal in the noise. Our progress can be materially slowed by the time it takes to sort through the noise to find the signals that can guide us. If we are to achieve the pace we need to keep up with, much less get ahead of, the changes unfolding around us, we need to make return on attention a top priority.

Although search tools will play an important role in improving return on attention by helping us to connect with resources that we are actively looking for, serendipity tools will become even more important. In a rapidly changing world, we become less confident that we even know what to look for. We welcome the help of others who know us deeply and can use that knowledge to introduce us to people and resources that we were not even aware existed, yet could assist us in pursuing our passions even more effectively.

These tools work in both directions. Besides helping us find what we need, they also help give greater visibility and "findability" to the creations we generate, allowing these creations to come to the attention of people who could provide us with useful feedback regarding their value and ways to improve their value even further. Just as we are bombarded with more and more requests for attention, we must find ways to attract attention from the people who matter the most to us. That, too, will help us to pick up the pace on our journey.

PULLING FROM THE TOP

As individuals begin making their passions their professions, they will in fact exert enormous pressure on institutions of all types to help them more effectively achieve their potential. Any institution that cannot provide a powerful platform for talent development will find its most talented people fleeing their cubicles and corner offices for other "homes" (or perhaps even literally setting up business from home). What can institutional leaders do to respond to this growing pressure, the demands of ever more powerful talent and customers to have a dynamic and passionate experience in their field or endeavor, and use it as a catalyst for institutional innovation? Again, they will find themselves on a journey mixing the elements of trajectory, leverage, and pace.

Defining a Trajectory for Change

Most institutional leaders today will maintain with great conviction that developing talent is one of their highest priorities. Yet, as the continuing popularity of the *Dilbert* comic strip and the television series *The Office* shows, the stultifying effect of our work environments is very real. There is a wide gap between rhetoric and reality. Institutions designed for push cannot easily accommodate pull.

The difficult transition these organizations must undergo begins with redefining the talent challenge. Rather than focusing on attracting and retaining talent, as they do today, institutional leaders must shift their attention to accessing and developing talent. Though at first this may sound like meaningless rhetoric, it actually is a reframing of the issue that is critical. It sets the institution on a new heading, a new direction. It provides a new *trajectory*. This new conception of the firm helps align it with the sweeping new power that pull gives to individuals, in their roles both as employees and customers, and recognizes that unleashing the creative talent that resides, largely untapped, in all individuals will be the primary source of corporate profitability in the digital age. Any corporate "vision" that fails to put talent development of individuals at the heart of its strategy will surely fail.

Of course, this insight drives much of the current interest in open innovation. "Open innovation" means reaching out to take advantage of talent beyond the firm (or responding to such outreach opportunities), but most of these efforts at this time involve only narrowly defined, short-term transactions—for example, posting a problem and offering a reward to individuals proposing an effective solution (or responding by offering that solution). This is a powerful technique, but it misses the opportunity to build longer-term, trust-based relationships that can be used to engage diverse teams in tackling more diffuse and broadly framed challenges. This latter approach, the focus of our third wave of pull, has the potential to create cumulative waves of performance improvement and talent development for all participants.

Creating Leverage

Institutional leaders will not be able to prevail in the transformation of their institutions in this new environment without substantial leverage from passionate individuals, both within and outside their institutions. Push can be driven from the top down, but pull will quickly crumble unless it has widespread support from all constituencies involved. The challenge for the institutional leader will be to quickly attract and mobilize passionate individuals wherever they reside within the institution (or even if they're outside the institution). These individuals are often the most talented and motivated people in the organization, but they are also often the unhappiest—they see the potential for themselves and for the institution but feel blocked in their efforts to achieve this potential. Institutional leaders must encourage the mechanisms and structures needed to help connect these individuals with each other as well as with the institutional leaders, who must serve as both champions and resource procurers for these people. These dynamics will in some cases reverse the way mentoring commonly occurs: Institutional leaders will need to seek out "reverse mentors" among (often younger) individuals who can help them understand and master edge practices.

As these groups of individuals coalesce, they can begin to target and address specific institutional initiatives to harness pull that require fairly limited investment but have the potential for significant near-term impact. Rather than seeking massive change at the outset, these groups will focus on defining pragmatic paths to institutional change in ways that deliver near-term value to strengthen champions of change and neutralize resistance of entrenched interests.

Accelerating Pace

Passionate people supported by a committed institutional leader can accomplish a great deal. But it is often only a matter of time before the forces wedded to traditional push approaches mobilize resistance to the efforts to remake the institution in the name of pull. The forces of change need to move as quickly as possible to demonstrate impact and rally more people to their side. Technology can play a key role in all of this by making the pull platforms that support and organize people's activities and interactions possible. In truth, though, much of the existing technology infrastructure stands as an obstacle to pull initiatives. It's too focused on forcing employees to comply with a set of policies and automated processes, the better to improve efficiency. But as institutions begin investing around platforms supporting collaboration and talent development across institutional boundaries, leaders can amplify the efforts of the passionate people they are attracting and mobilizing. In practice, this means embracing the technology platforms that many individuals, especially the younger generation of employees, are already using to connect with their colleagues across institutional boundaries. The technology allows connections with talent wherever it resides, helping to amplify the efforts of those within the institution.

Too many companies now block access to these tools—social networking sites, in particular—on the logic that they distract employees from the jobs they've been assigned. Institutional leaders will have to come to grips with the fact that these tools aren't a waste of time but rather a key part of reaching out to talent outside the firm. Of course, it is not just technology that can help to accelerate pace. Our individual dispositions represent a far "softer," but ultimately more powerful, accelerant of our own transformation. When institutional leaders help to pull core participants of the institution out into relevant edges and celebrate the most passionate workers and their contributions, employee attitudes and dispositions will begin to evolve, with more and more individuals embracing change and seeking out new challenges to test and expand their performance horizons.

HARNESSING PULL TO CHANGE THE WORLD

As we will see in our final chapter, the power of pull can be used to reshape major markets and industries on a global scale. Malcom McLean,

Victor and William Fung, Dee Hock, and Shai Agassi are just a few examples of individuals who have done this in such diverse arenas as transportation, apparel, financial services, and computing. They're using (or have used) pull to change the world.

To have this kind of impact, one must use what we call "shaping strategies." Shaping strategies represent pull with its broadest reach and on its biggest scale. By creating positive incentives and by flipping perceptions of risk and reward, we can open up massive creation spaces where the three levels of pull come together. In this way we can access resources on a global basis; create incentives that attract and influence very large ecosystems of people and institutions; and define challenges that will motivate people and institutions to more fully achieve their potential. The incentives created through the use of shaping strategies pull participants into very large ecosystems galvanized by a passionate "shaping view," encouraging them to invest in ways that amplify the investments of all the participants involved, including the shapers themselves. For example, look at the investments made by railroad, trucking, and shipping firms, not to mention port operators and distribution centers, to accommodate containerized shipping. As more and more companies adopted the new container standards and technology, the technology became more and more valuable, enabling the companies to avoid costly and inefficient packing and unpacking of cargo. The cost of shipping dropped by an order of magnitude as containers were more easily moved from one type of transport,vehicle to another. These strategies ultimately benefit from increasing returns, but they focus on the key challenge of quickly gathering a critical mass of participants. Although shapers disproportionately reap the rewards from these strategies, all institutions mastering the techniques of pull will find that they enjoy increased rewards by supporting them.

This is the most significant potential of pull. And it is a natural outgrowth of our efforts to master the power of pull at the individual and institutional level, enabling us to achieve much broader impact in economic and social arenas. As we become more comfortable with our ability to achieve our potential at these levels, we will begin to see more and more opportunities to amplify our potential even further by reshaping broader and broader arenas. We will also have more insight into, and experience with, the pull techniques required to pursue shaping strategies.

Don't think these strategies are only for CEOs or other leaders who wield enormous influence and resources. They're for you. Shaping strategies show how small moves, smartly made, can have an impact far beyond the initial resources and effort invested.

Chapter 1

The Diminishing Power of Push

To understand how fundamentally important pull is, we first have to go back and understand the world of push—how it works, where it came from, and why it is rapidly failing. We'll introduce you to a concept we call the "Big Shift," a fundamental reordering of the way we live, learn, socialize, play, and work that is now taking place, driven by a new technology infrastructure and public policy changes. The Big Shift is redefining what success means in a wide range of endeavors for both individuals and society. In this context, we can see why the old techniques of push won't work even as we begin to understand the new techniques that will allow us to succeed.

This Big Shift is so important that every one of us—even those who are already successful, perhaps earning six or seven figures a year—will have to either understand it and embrace it, or be left behind. Maybe you're at the top of your game, reading this in the CEO's executive suite. Maybe you're passionate about what you do professionally. Or maybe you run a big NGO, or have a powerful government role, or live simply on very little money, enjoying the fabled four-hour work week.[1] You did all the right things to get where you wanted to be, and you may be asking, "Why should I change my formula for success?"

There's one short answer: The world is transforming around you. The truth is, the things you did to get there will no longer work to keep you there. Some of the changes are highly visible while others are occurring in the deep background, barely discernible unless you know where to look. Factors that seemed marginal just fifteen years ago have accelerated with impressive speed as the digital infrastructure came to penetrate our daily lives. More than just bits and bytes, this digital infrastructure consists of the institutions, practices, and protocols that together organize and deliver the increasing power of digital technology to business and society. And new products and services are cascading out of this digital infrastructure at a dizzying rate. Taking communications technology as an example, think of Skype, the iPhone, Android, and Google Voice as just a few of the breakthroughs that have been made in recent years. These products have changed the way we communicate. Those who have figured out how to use the new communication tools to best advantage have a leg up on the competition. Yet many of us—especially those who have achieved success—tend to believe that the approaches we used in the past will continue to work in the future. We hold onto assumptions about the path to success that we developed along the way, often without bothering to make them explicit or testing to see if they still hold true. In fact, things are radically different from the way they used to be. We no longer live in the industrial economy of the 1950s, or even that of the 1970s. And the techniques we used to master those worlds are no longer effective.

At a certain level, most of us already know this deep down. We don't search for jobs the way we used to. We don't look for information in the old ways. We don't try to reconnect with friends in the old ways, either. Or at least not *just* in those ways or even primarily. We have new ways of carrying out these activities. But we've yet to realize that these changes in how we search for things or people are only the very beginning of more far-reaching changes—not just in how we search, but in how we attract resources and achieve goals as well. Most of us, in our minds and in our behavior, have yet to put it all together, to realize the full implications of the Big Shift. We need a systematic framework for how these changes fit together, a map for the journey.

We need to know what we must do to adapt to the changes, not just to survive but to thrive. We need to make sense of how the world is changing around us, getting our bearings, before we can begin the journey and make progress. That's the opportunity we're offering in this book: a look at where we've been as a society, and where we're going, in this Big Shift, and what it will take to be part of it in a way that will benefit you in myriad ways.

This Big Shift is affecting every aspect of society. Companies are discovering that their best employees leave in dissatisfaction if the company is not in tune with the changes taking place; their customers prove ever less loyal to their brands as new brands emerge with exciting new features. Our educational institutions are grappling with the need to move from being institutions of learning to learning institutions that rapidly evolve in response to the quickly changing learning needs of students and that find ways to extend the learning process well beyond the walls and semesters that define courses today. Our governments are racing to adapt to a world where social and economic changes far outstrip the ability of legislatures and even dictators to maintain control. It's a different game now, and many of us have yet to learn to play it. Those who fail to do so will, as individuals, feel increasing stress. Institutions will see their current performance declines deepen and become more difficult to reverse.

There's a new paradigm in town, and it's called pull. To grasp the power of pull, it helps to think carefully about the power of what it replaces—push—and what that power arose from. If we dive below the surface events that garner so much attention—from journalists and bloggers alike—we begin to discover that our foundations are profoundly shifting, generating a set of dynamics that is shaping everything else. The world is changing in unprecedented ways, and we must change with it.

Now, to some, this may seem reminiscent of the claim in the 1990s that the Internet would change everything. The evangelists of Internet-driven revolution forgot that change takes time to play out. New technology infrastructures take time to evolve and get adopted. Personal and management practices and social norms take even more time to adapt in response to the new capabilities that are becoming available.

As we shall see, the initial results may in fact be deterioration in performance, and it may take quite some time to discover and accept new approaches.

WHAT IS PUSH?

Since the beginning of the industrial revolution, entrepreneurs, educators, real-estate developers, politicians, media barons, technologists, financial wizards, and industrialists have been in thrall to the philosophy whose time is approaching an end: the philosophy of push. Our description of the world of push may sound pretty familiar. That's because we've all been living in it our entire lives.

"Push" describes a method and means of organizing activities and actions. Push operates on a key assumption—that it is possible to forecast or anticipate demand. Based on this assumption, push works mightily to ensure that the right people and resources are delivered at the right place and the right time to serve the anticipated demand. Companies build up inventory in advance of demand—for instance, a shirt maker accumulates inventory of shirts in the warehouse, and retailers on their shelves, in anticipation of demand. Car dealers stockpile automobiles on their lot before you arrive there to buy. Developers build houses and commercial properties on spec. Universities push the curriculum at their students, comfortable in the belief that they know what sort of education the students will need to have had in the years to come. Corporations hire employees with the confidence that they can predict the company's future needs for labor—after all, they've developed detailed five-year plans outlining their specific resource needs for this period. Cable and television networks broadcast programming when they think audiences will want to see it.

What are these methods and means? Push approaches are typified by what might be called "programs" or "routines"—tightly scripted specifications of activities designed to be invoked by known parties in predetermined contexts. Think of the thick process manuals in most enterprises, or standardized curricula in most primary and secondary schools, not to mention the programming of network television, and you will see that institutions rely heavily on programs of many types to deliver resources in predetermined ways.

Push models treat people as passive consumers whose needs can be anticipated and shaped by centralized decisionmakers. Push programs represent a top-down approach to dictating activities. These programs tend to specify activities or procedures in detail. Variances from the plan are deeply suspect and great efforts are made to eliminate them.

Because of the work required to specify, monitor, and enforce detailed activities, push programs tend to be restricted in terms of the number and diversity of participants. This is especially true beyond the boundaries of a single institution; complexity increases exponentially as the number and diversity of participants (and interactions among them) grows. This is a key reason why most large companies have worked so hard to reduce the number of suppliers in their supply chains. Even within a single institution, push programs specify the type of participants, their roles, and the sequence of their involvement in the activities covered by the program.

The tight coupling of the procedures in these programs tends to make companies rigid and inflexible. After all, every time you modify one part of a push program you cause (often unanticipated) disruptions and difficulties in other parts of the program. You can't change the way you shelve items in the warehouse without also changing how your customers display them at retail or how, where, and when your suppliers deliver items to your warehouse—all with commensurate changes to paperwork, IT systems, processes, routines, and, often, contracts and other legal agreements. These difficulties multiply with the number of facilities and participants involved. For this reason, designers tend to approach modifications very cautiously and bunch them together into major reengineering efforts. Local experimentation or improvisation becomes deeply threatening.

Push programs tend to treat all relevant resources as fixed and scarce quantities—after all, that is one of the rationales for a push program to begin with: to ensure that scarce resources are deployed to the highest-priority needs. If one participant gets the resources or the rewards, other participants must do without. In this sense, push programs operate with zero-sum reward systems for their participants.

Often there is intense political maneuvering to gain privileged access to resources. As the availability and movement of resources are dictated from above, the political maneuvering focuses on influencing the center. The key planning instruments of push programs are forecasts of demand, budgets (for financial resources), and materials requirement plans, or MRPs (for physical resources), and these are the primary arenas in which the politics play out. In push, perceived limits and scarcity cause people to focus on the control of domains and resources and the wielding of managerial power.

In the push system there is a hierarchy, with those in charge offering rewards (or punishments) to those lower down the ladder. The reward systems tend to concentrate on extrinsic rewards—for example, money, promotions, or grades. The people participating in push programs are generally treated as instruments to ensure that activities are performed as dictated. Their own individual needs and interests are purely secondary, if relevant at all. These programs default to extrinsic rewards as a way to motivate participants.

Push programs lead to a curious combination of boredom and stress among participants.[2] Participants are performing repetitive, tightly scripted roles, and they must suppress much of their natural curiosity or individuality in order to integrate into the push program. Nearly all of us have worked in such a situation, or still do, and know that it isn't much fun. As companies boil their business operations into routinized practices, they suppress many of the creative instincts of their workers, who become standardized parts of a predictable machine. Push-oriented companies not only suppress the creative instincts of their workers, they ultimately suppress the individuals themselves—except perhaps for the inner political animal, which gets a chance to thrive, often with non-value-adding (and sometimes destructive) results. For example, individuals find infinite ways to game virtually any top-down performance-management system so that they can advance their own agenda—whether it is a salesperson "sand-bagging" orders into the next quarter or the call-center manager framing questions in customer-satisfaction surveys to show high satisfaction rates. Push-driven programs require standardization and predictability. But individuals, especially passionate ones, are ultimately unique and unpredictable.

Summarizing the philosophy of push, we might tally the following instincts, assumptions, and beliefs:

- *There's not enough to go around.* If you win, I lose.
- *Elites do the deciding.* In push systems, small groups of people make the decisions on behalf of passive recipients who consume the output.
- *Organizations must be hierarchical.* How else can elites maintain their command and control?
- *People must be molded.* As employees and as consumers, people are expected to follow certain patterns in ways that support predictable production and consumption of the goods and services that are created and delivered through push programs.
- *Bigger is better.* Companies can reap efficiencies by getting ever bigger, so that economies of scale yield lower and lower unit costs on products and services.
- *Demand can be forecast.* If consumers can be molded to consume what's given to them, then it follows that business can forecast demand. Similarly, school systems can foresee what sorts of knowledge and skills students will need after graduation.
- *Resources can be allocated centrally.* This might smack of command economies, but the difference here is that it's the center of the institution that's allocating the resources.
- *Demand can be met.* If demand can be forecast, and resources allocated accordingly, then it follows that companies can build processes and programs delivering resources to the right place at the right time and in the right quantities to meet that demand.

THE ORIGINS OF PUSH

The philosophy of push came of age at the beginning of the last century as the world was turned upside down by new communication and transportation infrastructures. It seems distant now, but when the telephone arrived people no longer had to go to a centralized telegraph office and wait for trained workers to laboriously tap out dots and dashes when they wanted to communicate quickly with someone outside their local geographical area. Instead they could sit in the privacy of their own homes and offices and carry on extended conversations with other people who were in *their* homes and offices halfway around the world.

A similar opening up of possibilities occurred with the advent of electricity, the internal combustion engine, and the airplane, each of which made it progressively easier to move ourselves and our products, more quickly and at lower cost, across great distances, and to scale up our commercial activities. As road systems and airports multiplied, we gained more and more flexibility and speed in travel, making it seem as if the most distant towns were just around the corner.

It didn't happen overnight, of course. The infrastructures to support these new technologies took time to build and spread. It took even longer for individuals and firms to figure out how to use these infrastructures most effectively.

In her book *Technological Revolutions and Financial Capital,* where she examines the patterns associated with the deployment of new technologies in society—including the steam engine, electricity, and automobiles—Carlota Perez outlines three phases of change that must occur.

First, there is the innovation of the technological building blocks themselves. Second, the innovation causes a society to engage in a rethinking of the infrastructures required to deliver these new technologies most effectively to everyone. "Infrastructures" refers to the methods of organizing the technology as well as the institutional arrangements that help others to access the technology. For example, in the early years following the invention of electricity, companies operated their own power generators—until it became apparent that it was far more efficient to generate electricity from centralized facilities. By building an electricity grid, a city or region could capture economies of scale. Methods were developed to distribute electricity across large distances.

As infrastructures begin to harness the power of the new technology, the third phase of change kicks in. In this phase, the rest of society works on discovering the best way to use the new technology in their professional and personal lives. The best of the new methods spread and become common.

Each stage of this dissemination of a new technology takes time to play out. Participants at each level explore and experiment with approaches to figure out how to deliver even more or perform even better. In the twentieth century, the Great Depression ended up being a key catalyst for change. As individuals and firms wrestled with rapidly intensifying performance pressures, they began to embrace the capabilities of the new infrastructures of their day—and to rethink how they did things accordingly.

The twentieth-century firm scaled rapidly as a result of these efforts. The business historian Alfred Chandler ably documented the key characteristics of these companies.[3] They were built on the premise that the primary role of the firm was to arrive at lower costs by getting bigger—to make the most of the scale economies available through the new infrastructures of the day, what we call "scalable efficiency."

Thanks to the long reach of the railroad, and, later, containerized shipping and airfreight, large-scale manufacturing operations could be centralized and concentrated into fewer facilities and deliver lower-cost products on a national and eventually a global scale. The scale of manufacturing operations led inevitably to efforts to build comparable scale in marketing operations: If companies were going to mass-produce products, then they needed mass markets to consume them. The rise of the mass media in the form of magazines, radio, and television helped to make mass marketing a viable proposition.

These push programs proved enormously successful and spread rapidly across the business landscape. First, during the Depression in the 1930s, business leaders in major developed economies around the world were motivated to exploit the capabilities of new communication and transportation infrastructures more effectively to harness scalable efficiency and compete during a period of stagnant or declining demand. Second, during the 1950s, another generation of business leaders broadened their horizons to scale push programs beyond national boundaries to take advantage of trade liberalization and to serve global markets.

It is no coincidence that the famous British economist Ronald Coase wrote his path-breaking essay, "The Nature of the Firm," in 1937.[4] He effectively captured the primary thrust of institution-building during this period, arguing that firms existed to reduce the transaction costs that made coordinating activity across independent entities difficult. For this insight, he won the Nobel Prize in Economics.

As firms deployed these new push-based approaches, other institutions underwent similar transformations. Educational systems were rationalized through push-based programs of their own—standardized curricula—that were designed to mold students into predictable participants in the workplace. A new generation of labor unions emerged to help negotiate standardized and predictable contracts with workers so that firms could minimize unanticipated disruptions in the workplace. Building on early initiatives during the Progressive Era, the New Deal made significant strides in rationalizing government institutions and programs to more effectively support the needs of large firms in scaling their operations. The national government expanded its powers relative to state governments, in part to provide a uniform public policy environment for national firms to scale their operations.

Push reigned supreme across all institutional domains, helping to create enormous wealth. Such success helped to shape mindsets, and many key assumptions about the value of push became so ingrained that following the push methods seemed to be the obvious best choice. No other option even merited discussion—these ways of doing things were, after all, common sense.

A CAUTIONARY TALE

Institutional elites still try to use push to control the masses. But can people still be molded the way they were by Edward Bernays, the first person to employ "public relations" techniques systematically to mold consumer habits? Maybe. But it's getting more difficult for them to do so.

Consider how, during the "Saffron Revolution" in Myanmar in 2007, a pair of blood-soaked flip-flops came to increase the pressure on one of the world's most repressive military juntas. The image of a pair of bloody sandals lying in the street—along with other photos and videos showing troops firing on unarmed civilians and shooting tear gas into elementary schools—were taken by ordinary Burmese citizens and monks, using their cellphones, during a series of escalating street protests in Yangon, the capital of Myanmar. The images generated an intense international outcry and condemnation from the UN Security Council.

The protests were eventually put down, at heavy cost to human life, but not before the flow of images and video had overwhelmed the attempt by Burma's foreign minister to convince the United Nations that the demonstrations were "small protests hijacked by political opportunists."[5]

Burmese citizens may not have yet succeeded in winning their freedom, but thanks to the new digital infrastructure they are no longer isolated. Despite the best efforts of the junta to limit Internet access (and thanks to the efforts of a few determined individuals both inside and outside of the country), Burmese citizens maintained rapid, real-time *access* to the world around them through which to make their plight known. What a contrast to previous eras, in which the flow of information from the country was at best a time-lagged trickle.

As access increases, individuals gain power and institutions have a harder and harder time exerting control. In Burma the repressive junta now has greater difficulty controlling its citizens and manipulating international opinion.[6] In Iran a similar dynamic unfolded in 2009 as Iranians took to the streets to protest the allegedly fraudulent reelection of President Mahmoud Ahmadinejad (more about that in the next chapter). Videos taken with cellphones documenting the demonstrations went viral on Facebook, LiveLeak, Twitter, and other social media and were quickly picked up by the mainstream media. A heart-rending video taken of the last moments of a young woman's life, just as she'd fallen to the street from a sniper's bullet, became a rallying cry in Iran and around the world.[7]

The point may not be as dramatic in other circumstances, but, as we shall see, it generalizes broadly. Individuals in nearly every walk of life have increasing market and political power as a result of the new digital infrastructure. And institutions still following the old rules are struggling.

THREE WAVES OF THE BIG SHIFT

The Big Shift: A world in which citizens gain political power relative to political institutions. A world in which talented employees capture economic value relative to the firm. A world in which consumers have increased market power relative to vendors. A world in which corporate performance is in decline. The Big Shift captures the fundamental shift from a world of push to a world of pull that has been playing out for decades and will continue to unfold for decades more. In a profound way, it enables far more robust and scalable pull techniques to come into play while at the same time generating pressures that will make pull an imperative, rather than an option.

What form, exactly, will the Big Shift take as it plays out in our economy and lives? Our research suggests that the Big Shift is emerging in three waves, each with distinctive characteristics. These waves capture the focus of action at any point in time, but they are not strictly sequential. We can see evidence of the second and third waves beginning to gather force even as the first wave is still washing across the globe, leaving rapidly evolving infrastructures in its wake.

The first wave involves the rapid, unflagging evolution of a new digital infrastructure and parallel shifts in global public policy. These foundational forces, playing out over the past five decades, catalyze and contextualize the many other changes occurring in nearly every domain of contemporary life.

The First Wave: Infrastructural Shift

The breakdown of push began with the introduction of two key technological innovations. First, three separate groups delivered a first-generation microprocessor to the market in the early 1970s. These three groups—Intel, Texas Instruments, and Garrett AiResearch—independently succeeded in bringing together all the functions of a central processing unit (CPU) into a single integrated circuit, setting the stage for Moore's Law to drive rapid increases in processing power. Technically, Moore's Law observes that the number of transistors on a single integrated circuit tends to double every two years. In economic terms, this suggests that the price/performance ratio of microprocessors has been increasing exponentially and shows little sign of slowing down, even after almost forty years of experience.

The second key technological innovation involved the introduction of standards for packet-switched networks. Previous generations of communication networks had involved circuit switching. In these earlier networks, any communication required the establishment of a dedicated circuit across the parties that wanted to communicate. This circuit would be completely dedicated to the parties involved until they were finished communicating, even if the circuit did not have a lot of traffic at specific points in time.

In contrast, packet-switched networks, enabled by digital technology, broke down longer communications into discrete packets of data that could be sent across shared networks. This represented a far more efficient use of network capacity. Although the concept of packet switching as an alternative technology for communicating had emerged in the early 1960s, it was not until the mid-1970s that researchers began to define the TCP/IP standard (Transmission Control Protocol/Internet Protocol) that ultimately provided a foundation for connecting a wide variety of digital networks together. In parallel with this technological advance, significant innovations in optical-fiber technology led to the formulation of a "fiber law" by George Gilder, who observed that the number of bits that can be piped down a single optical fiber tends to double roughly every nine months, leading to corresponding increases in price performance over time. This performance trend has been driven by a variety of innovations involving the ability to send an increasing number of frequencies through a strand of fiber and to switch frequencies much more efficiently through photonic switching. Once again, this rate of performance improvement shows little or no sign of slowing down.

A similar pattern of improvement in price/performance ratios is playing out in digital storage with a series of technological innovations involving different storage media, methods of compressing data more efficiently onto storage media, and techniques for accessing data. In fact, a "storage law" anticipates that storage capacity on a single disk doubles roughly every twelve months.

These technologies are the foundations of the new digital infrastructure that is transforming our business and social landscape. Just as the telephone, automobile, and airplane reshaped our society in the first half of the twentieth century, the new digital infrastructure is beginning to reshape institutions in the twenty-first.

There's a key difference, however, between this technology revolution and previous ones. In past technology revolutions, a new technology or cluster of technologies emerged in a burst of innovation, experienced rapid performance improvement for a short period of time, and then quickly began to experience a flattening of the performance-improvement curve. This pattern enabled a process of stabilization to follow the initial disruptive innovation. As the performance curve of the technology began to flatten, it provided an opportunity for infrastructure to stabilize once innovators discovered the best way to organize the infrastructure to deliver the distinctive capabilities of the new technology. Similarly, as the infrastructure stabilized, it helped the rest of society to stabilize as well—once it discovered a new set of practices to harness the potential of the new infrastructure. Everyone could take a deep breath and play catch up.

For the first time in history, we are dealing with a technology that shows no sign of stabilization in terms of price/performance ratio improvement. In fact, the exponential rate of improvement of the three building blocks of digital technology—processing, storage, and transport—is likely to continue for an indefinite period of time. It's getting faster and faster, leaving us no time to play catch up. Of course, exponential rates like these cannot be sustained forever, but for the foreseeable future the technologists driving innovation in these domains see scant evidence of a flattening of performance-improvement curves for key digital technology components—even if other advances in the labs today, such as quantum computing, might eventually leapfrog today's technologies altogether.

The absence of stabilization in the core technology components suggests that we are not likely to see stabilization in the digital infrastructure either. More than thirty years into this technology revolution, we are just now beginning to explore the contours of cloud computing. The cloud-computing approach suggests that the most efficient way to deliver digital technology is through big centralized data centers that can flexibly deliver computing, storage, and transport services to users. Given all the recent hype surrounding this new development, it is sometimes difficult to keep in mind that only a tiny fraction of the total digital technology resources is today delivered through this kind of infrastructure. Most of our digital technology resources are distributed out to the user's premise rather than concentrated in large, centralized facilities. It will take many years and perhaps even decades for this new innovation in digital infrastructure to be broadly adopted. In the meantime, can anyone doubt that the continued exponential improvement in the digital-technology building blocks will lead to additional disruptive innovations in digital infrastructure?

A second fundamental trend is playing out in parallel with the deployment of a new digital infrastructure. Over the past sixty years, there has been a global trend in public policy toward greater liberalization in terms of removing barriers to the movement of people, products, money, and ideas across national boundaries and within national economies. Public policy shifts removing barriers to movement have magnified the impact of the first trend regarding broader deployment of a more powerful digital infrastructure by making it easier for people to use the capabilities of this infrastructure more fully. To be sure, this policy trend has not been uniform, with some countries and some industries moving more rapidly in this direction than others. There have even been reversals of this trend in specific countries. Yet, the overall trend is striking and has been sustained over many decades.

Although this trend may not continue—as we write, in the midst of a global economic downturn, public support for protectionist policies is growing in many parts of the world—these public policy trends have reinforced the profound social and economic effects of the new digital infrastructure. Together, they are the powerful catalysts setting the Big Shift into motion.

Economic Impact

The Big Shift is still at an early stage of its innovation and dissemination process, but already-visible patterns are nearly certain to persist as digital technologies systematically and substantially reduce barriers to entry and barriers to movement on a global scale. It is now possible for even the smallest vendors to reach a global market of customers using digital networks. The digital infrastructure makes outsourcing more feasible than ever, and this in turn makes it easier for small companies to access and use world-class capability to deliver more value to their markets and to respond more rapidly to unanticipated changes in markets. Customers and companies can more easily switch from one set of vendors to another.

That's the first-order effect. The second-order effect is that competition is intensifying on a global scale. The structural barriers that dampened competition are now rapidly eroding as companies face new competitors from unexpected quarters and as companies discover that even their most innovative moves are more rapidly copied by competitors. Digital technologies are also increasing the power that all of us have as customers. We can now access a much broader range of vendors and obtain much more detailed information about the quality of their goods and services. As customers gain power, they capture greater value from vendors, who now must deliver even more value to customers or face losing them to even more aggressive competitors. One small indication of this is the fact that the ability of strong brands to charge a significant price premium for their products has eroded substantially over the past several decades. In effect, this means that everyone is competing with everyone else—or nearly so.

There's a third-order effect as well. As competition intensifies, instability and uncertainty increase. Stock prices are more volatile. Consumers are more fickle in their tastes, as shown by declining customer-loyalty measures in the 2009 Shift Index.[8] Executives keep their jobs for shorter durations. These are all indicators of a less stable world.

The instability is reinforced by the continuing exponential improvements in the underlying price performance of the digital technology components that make up the digital infrastructure. Just as soon as any of us begins to feel comfortable that we have figured things out or discovered some form of competitive advantage, we find out how quickly it erodes.

This instability and uncertainty has an important implication. Push programs are built upon one key assumption: the ability to accurately forecast demand in order to ensure that resources can be pushed to the right place at the right time. As instability and uncertainty increase, the ability to forecast accurately begins to decline, and the efficiency potential of push programs begins to erode as well. This sets the stage for a far-reaching transition in how we mobilize resources and, indeed, how we conceive of what a company is. As the Big Shift takes hold, companies are no longer places that exist to drive down costs by getting increasingly bigger. They're places that support and organize talented individuals to get better faster by working with others. The rationale of the firm shifts from scalable efficiency to scalable learning—the ability to improve performance more rapidly and learn faster by effectively integrating more and more participants distributed across traditional institutional boundaries.

Performance Results

The economic impact of the Big Shift has had a dramatic impact on performance results of firms and other market participants. Consider firms, where corporate performance, despite steady gains in labor productivity, has steeply declined over the past four decades. The economy-wide return on assets (ROA) in the United States has fallen to nearly one-quarter of its 1965 levels, even as business's reliance on physical assets to generate a profit (asset intensity) has dropped 40 percent.[9] Moreover, the gap between the most and least successful businesses has increased over time, as measured by both ROA and shareholder value creation. This doesn't imply a simple averaging out, in which big winners are being dragged down by a few big losers. The "winners" in aggregate are barely maintaining their previous ROA levels, while the losers are experiencing bigger and bigger losses. Our research shows that this is a long-term pattern that was established and that was sustained well before the "Great Recession" began in 2007.

It's no surprise then that the "topple rate," measuring loss of position in ROA rankings, has more than doubled since 1965. Companies that outperform their peers do so for ever-shorter periods of time. There's lots of churn as one company after another takes the lead in any given industry. Perhaps the topple rate would be even higher if not for an interesting consequence that arises in the quest for "scalable efficiency." Twentieth-century firms have been remarkably successful in pursuing this quest, so much so that we are now wrestling with the public policy issues associated with scale. In particular, we have developed in the United States (and likely in most developed economies) a view that many companies are now becoming "too big to fail." This public policy posture means that many of our largest companies are insulated from the full force of competitive intensity by safety cushions that get deployed in times of crisis. As a result, the companies most in need of confronting a fundamental reorientation of their firms are precisely the ones most protected from the increasingly dysfunctional consequences of pursuing their traditional quest for scale. In fact, some perverse incentives have set in: Companies are motivated to continue pursuing "scalable efficiency" because this helps to ensure that governments will intervene to protect them against the gales of creative destruction that are gathering force on the horizon.

Underlying these performance declines is the fast-moving digital infrastructure that is spreading rapidly throughout the world, reshaping societies as distant as Iran, Ghana, and Myanmar. In the United States, the exponentially advancing price/performance capability of computing, storage, and bandwidth is driving an adoption rate for the digital infrastructure that is two to five times faster than adoption rates were for previous infrastructures, such as electricity and telephone networks.[10] As the price/performance ratio goes down, new capabilities emerge faster than before and disruption occurs frequently rather than in isolated episodes.

Fueled by this new digital infrastructure—and public policy changes that overwhelmingly have reduced barriers to entry and movement—U.S. competitive intensity is more than twice what it was in the mid-1960s.[11]

Declining ROA rates, even as labor productivity rises, suggest that firms are unable to hold onto the financial benefits created by steady gains in labor productivity. Who is capturing the rewards instead? Our metrics suggest that creative talent is one beneficiary—for example, computer engineers, health-care professionals, architects, and managers, whose total compensation has more than doubled during the past five years.[12]

Consumers are also benefiting, thanks to increasing access to ever-growing numbers of products and services and to information (such as comparative price information) about them and the vendors that offer them. Consumers are no longer limited by what's carried in the local store.

Just like the Myanmar junta that found its ability to control its citizens reduced, today's corporations are finding it more difficult to "control" their employees and citizens. Control is the essence of push, and push is breaking down.

Personal Implications of the Big Shift

Similar implications are playing out in our personal lives. We find we are no longer limited by physical geography in terms of the friendships and relationships we build. No matter what our areas of passionate interest—whether it is sports, art, business, or world affairs—we can find others who share them, even if they are in remote parts of the world. Global competition is also intensifying pressure in our individual professional lives as we begin to realize that we are vulnerable in our jobs to being replaced by someone who just happens to have the requisite skills even though they live in a completely different country. We discover, to our dismay, that the significant investments we made in education in the early part of our lives was just the beginning. In order to stay successful in a world of accelerating change, we need to find ways to learn faster, often in areas that we once viewed as quite peripheral to our professions.

We can sum it all up with the following statement: Push is no longer the dominant paradigm in business, education, or civic life. Welcome to the foundational change that makes pull the dominant paradigm in our lives.

The Second Wave: Knowledge Flows

If the Big Shift's first wave is all about lowering barriers to entry and movement, the second wave shows what happens when those barriers go away: Capital, talent, and knowledge start flowing increasingly rapidly across geographical and institutional boundaries. By our estimation, developed economies today are somewhere in the early part of the second wave of the Big Shift, with the third wave yet to come. Firms have yet to make a meaningful transition into the digital age. The long-running performance declines revealed by the 2009 Shift Index show that corporate performance has gotten steadily worse as digital technology has penetrated the economy.[13] The fact that richer knowledge flows and even elements of creation spaces—which are characteristic of the third wave—are now becoming visible on the edge demonstrates the overlapping, rather than sequential, nature of how the Big Shift is unfolding.

In *The Power of Pull*, we're aiming to help individuals and their institutions understand the first wave (it's the world many of us are now living in, so it's incumbent upon all of us to make sense of it), to use the techniques of pull to surf the second wave much more effectively, and to take advantage of the significant opportunities available in the final and third wave.

In this second wave, the sources of economic value move from "stocks" of knowledge to "flows" of new knowledge. "Tacit" knowledge becomes more valuable than "explicit knowledge" as the edge transforms the core.

From Stocks to Flows

In markets and industries that were relatively stable in the past, a given stock of knowledge—whether it was a proprietary technology or a unique insight into how to organize production or marketing activities—could be relied upon to generate economic value for an indefinite period. The only challenges were to guard against others appropriating this knowledge and to design and execute the most efficient and scalable ways to extract value from this knowledge.

We saw in the introduction how competitive surfers must keep pace with new maneuvers as they're developed. The same applies in the business world. What we knew yesterday—either as employees or in terms of what our institution as a whole knows about its business—is proving to be less and less helpful with the challenges and opportunities we confront today. Growing topple rates (the rate at which companies lose their leadership positions) gives powerful testimony that stocks of knowledge, no matter how valuable at the outset, are diminishing in value more rapidly than before. Across many industries, product lifecycles have begun to compress—early success with a blockbuster product has become harder and harder to sustain. Said differently, the "clockspeed" of products has increased—as MIT professor Charles H. Fine put it in his book of the same name. Fine also found that the rate of change has been rising for processes and organizations. The industries with the fastest clockspeeds included personal computers, toys and games, athletic shoes, semiconductors, and cosmetics.[14]

As clockspeed increases, companies must continually refresh the sources of their success: their knowledge stocks. This means precipitating and participating in a broader range of knowledge flows, which in turn requires finding people, particularly people on the edge, interacting with them, and building reciprocal relationships with them over time. Edge players are more likely to introduce us to new insights and to help us more rapidly develop new knowledge stocks.

This new way of operating is not without its challenges. Push mindsets and practices are tightly grooved to a world where knowledge stocks mattered and knowledge flows were at best a peripheral event. We must accelerate a shift to a very different mindset and to practices that treat knowledge flows as the central opportunity and knowledge stocks as a useful by-product and key enabler. Increasingly, strategic advantage for corporate institutions will hinge on privileged positions in relevant concentrations of high-value knowledge flows and the adoption of practices required to participate in and profit from these knowledge flows.

We are certainly not saying that knowledge stocks have no value. It's a question of balance. No one will be able to effectively participate in relevant knowledge flows without possessing useful knowledge stocks of their own. People who reach out to connect with others to simply take knowledge will find that these interactions quickly dry up as others begin to realize they have little to gain from these connections. As in all relationships, reciprocity is essential. Knowledge stocks thus become both a means and an end to participation in knowledge flows.

Many companies wrestle with the challenges of expanding knowledge flows within their own siloed organizations, but confront even greater difficulties when reaching out beyond the four walls of their enterprise. Even when they are successful in tapping into a more diverse set of knowledge flows, companies tend to concentrate on flows involving transfers of existing knowledge rather than creation of new knowledge. I read your white paper. You show me your well-polished and tightly scripted PowerPoint presentation. We certainly gain value from exchanging this knowledge. But we are able to create even more value if we can bring people together across different companies to engage in deep problem solving around a performance challenge so that they are creating new knowledge. Now we are not simply accessing knowledge that already exists, but driving performance to new levels that could not be achieved without distinctive new knowledge.

It used to be a lot easier: We just hoarded information, compiled it, indexed it, and added to it as new discoveries were made. Life inside the corporation, while not exactly easy or simple, had a concrete and powerful logic: Protect that which is proprietary. Breaking out of that logic will certainly be difficult and often painful, requiring us to overcome deeply ingrained instincts, but it's necessary.

Knowledge flows in our personal lives. Until relatively recently, most of us believed we had to invest considerable time and effort early in our lives navigating an educational system designed to transfer stocks of knowledge to us. As a reward for our diligence and persistence in school, we believed, these stocks of knowledge would serve us well throughout our lives. Of course, we might have to acquire some additional knowledge along the way—a training program here, an adult education course there—but the bulk of our knowledge would be acquired through the educational system. If this was ever true, it certainly has rapidly diminishing validity today.

Our schools can barely keep up with the knowledge that is developing in the world today. Even when they succeed at this level, what we learned in school does not help us keep up to speed with rapidly evolving knowledge flows once we've graduated. To some degree, we can compensate for this by signing up for adult education courses and a variety of other training sessions, but, like companies, we run into the problem that these programs mostly focus on transfer of existing explicit knowledge, rather than on the creation of new knowledge, or even on giving us the necessary learning skills to tackle knowledge flows. For example, how many training programs have you been in that focused on how to frame productive questions, rather than simply cramming facts and data into your head? And, like companies, we are individually facing increasing global competition in terms of the talent we offer. To maintain an edge in this intensifying talent race, we must find ways as individuals to precipitate and participate in knowledge flows involving the creation of new knowledge.

Knowledge flows on the edge. Certain types of knowledge flows are more valuable than others. Knowledge flows within the core—which, you'll recall, is the place where most of the resources are concentrated and where the old thinking and behavior still hold sway—are certainly important and can help firms in the core to perform better in the face of intensifying competition. Yet, these knowledge flows pale into insignificance relative to the importance of precipitating and participating in knowledge flows emerging and evolving on relevant edges. As we have seen, the core is under intense profit pressure and struggling to keep up, while edges provide attractive opportunities for profitable growth.

Knowledge flows naturally flourish on the edge. Why? Because, by definition, participants on these edges are wrestling with how to match unmet needs with unexploited capabilities and all the uncertainty that implies. Edge participants therefore focus on ways to innovate and create value by connecting unmet needs with unexploited capabilities and then scaling these opportunities as rapidly as possible. In the process, they create significant new knowledge. But there is a problem—this knowledge is not easily accessible.

What we're focusing on is tacit knowledge—the "know-how" rather than the "know-what"—that we often have difficulty expressing. Much knowledge starts as tacit knowledge. A good part of it is eventually codified into explicit knowledge, although all knowledge ultimately represents some blend of explicit and tacit knowledge, for not all tacit knowledge is codifiable. Imagine instructing someone on how to ride a bike—something that you learn by doing, rather than by reading a set of instructions. This is not a left-brain task. Or imagine trying to perform brain surgery after having read all the books you can find on the subject. The books are the explicit knowledge telling you what to do—which is eminently necessary—but knowing how to perform this kind of surgery critically depends on an extended apprenticeship process in which tacit knowledge gets communicated through observation and participation on the periphery of these operations. That's the whole raison d'être of apprenticeship, including the medical residency: learning by doing under supervision.

Another example of tacit knowledge in action is brewing beer. A brewer recently explained to us how he moved from using kits in the early 1990s to following recipes shortly thereafter, while keep logs of the process. Then he started tinkering with the recipes (still taking notes), experimenting with different mixes of hops, yeast, and so on, still carefully noting the process and the results. Now, after twenty years of experience, he simply throws together new mixes, based on the results he'd like to see. "Throws together" is too informal a phrase. He's basing his recipes on deep, tacit knowledge of both the process and the ingredients. He could probably explain what he was doing and why, but the recipe he'd produce might not turn out exactly as he would have planned because of all the little personal touches and techniques he employs that he's not aware of. As he said at the end of the conversation, "Forget it. Just come over on Saturday afternoon and I'll *show* you."[15]

As knowledge emerges, it displays an interesting characteristic. All knowledge represents some mix of explicit and tacit knowledge— some of it can be easily expressed and quantified, while a lot of it remains deeply embedded within each of us and we struggle to express it. If the mix includes a large amount of tacit knowledge, it becomes very hard to share with others, except when we work together over long periods of time. Early-stage knowledge tends to have a much higher tacit component, but in a rapidly changing world this is often the most valuable knowledge—it provides us with early insight into emerging opportunities. So there is a dilemma—the most valuable knowledge is often the most difficult to express and share.

To access this kind of knowledge, we need to make another kind of shift. In the core, we have become used to acquiring knowledge assets in transactions. We buy patents. We post difficult research problems and give rewards to those who can offer solutions. But what about tacit knowledge? How do we access it? Accessing this kind of knowledge typically requires long-term trust-based relationships. Trust is necessary because of the inevitable fumbling that occurs as we try to express and share tacit knowledge. Without trust we may lack the respect for the other needed to stay with them as they fumble. Trust also fosters the shared understanding that makes it easier to access tacit knowledge. This suggests that one key dimension of the Big Shift is a movement from a world where value is concentrated in transactions to one where it resides in large networks of long-term relationships.

Since much of the most relevant knowledge on the edge is tacit knowledge, edge participants naturally place a heavy emphasis on building diverse networks of relationships that will help them to collaborate more effectively with others in the creation of new knowledge. For this reason, conferences and other gatherings where participants can share stories and experiences, learn from each other, and identify potential collaborators become particularly prominent on edges.

Edge participants also often reach out to participants in the core in an effort to build relationships and enhance knowledge flows. But those efforts are often frustrated—or, at best, marginalized—because core participants are too busy concentrating on defensive strategies within the core, trying to protect their profits and position, to understand the true growth opportunities represented by relevant edges. Core participants tend to focus on transactions rather than investing in the long-term effort to build sustainable, trust-based relationships on the edge.

For this reason, especially, the few core participants who understand the full potential of the edge—and are able to reach out and connect into the rich knowledge flows occurring on the edge—will be in the best position to create economic value. They will be able to respond to increasing margin pressure in the core by helping to scale innovations on the edge and participating in the rich new sources of profitable growth arising there. Unfortunately, most core participants, to the extent that they recognize the increasing importance of knowledge flows at all, tend to focus on knowledge flows within the core rather than making a concentrated effort to identify and participate in relevant knowledge flows on the edge.

In this context, the link between individuals and firms is a powerful one. Tacit knowledge is held by individuals, so if firms want to enhance their participation in tacit knowledge flows, they must find ways to expand and enrich the social networks of their employees, helping them to connect with other individuals on relevant edges.

Edge Transformation of the Core

Edges often have a transformative effect on the core. Consider how trendsetting inner-city kids on the cultural edge started wearing their jeans tightly belted below their butts, boxer shorts flapping around for everyone to see, and the following year suburban kids were doing the same (to their parents' dismay).

Fashion might seem a trivial example, but the edge-transforms-the-core pattern goes much broader and deeper than just how you wear your pants. A few short years ago, India and China (on the geographic edge) were marginal players in the global economy. Now they are central ones. Not long ago the Internet (on the technology edge) was a specialized communication platform for scientists. Now it's a center for commerce and advertising. Only yesterday, it seems, teenagers (on the demographic edge) stayed in touch outside of school on the telephone or at the mall. Now they use mobile devices to log on to a growing number of social networks. Until lately, derivatives and hedge funds (on the institutional edge) were marginal actors in the financial marketplace. By 2008 they were at the center of a jarring financial crisis. These examples together point to an important new locus for economic value creation: the edge.

This process might seem threatening. But edges and cores need each other. Unless they eventually become part of the core, edge players can never get past the margins of society and culture, and they can never gain access to the money and connections they need to go from dive bars to stadium tours. The core of society likewise needs innovations from the edge to continue refreshing and regenerating itself. In business terms, edge companies need resources to scale growth, and core companies need new growth platforms to compensate for increasing competitive pressure in the core.

Notice that the edge transforms the core through *flows*. (Therefore the most valuable flows first emerge on the edge.) In surfing, for example, a videographer captures the first "superman" on film (itself a flow of images) and posts it online, where it streams (or flows) to another surfer's computer, and then another and another, until surfers around the world are trying the move—even if they're mostly wiping out in the process. The edge has transformed the core.

Edges have always been engines of transformation, but, until recently, one could notice something emerging on the edge and—because it would take so long for its effect to be felt in the core—safely ignore it. There was comfort in the knowledge that one could lead a long and productive life without having to master the practices emerging on the edge.

We are now in a different era, one where edges emerge and rise up with astonishing speed to catalyze changes on a global basis in less time than ever before. This is occurring for several reasons: (1) thanks to the new digital infrastructure, people on the edge now have unprecedented access to what they need to establish a business, such as contract manufacturing, logistics services, or complex analytic equipment; (2) knowledge flows connecting the edge and the core are proliferating; and (3) businesses in the core of our economy are experiencing growing economic pressures, which causes them to look to the relevant edges for new ideas. One significant indication of this speed is the rate at which individuals around the globe have adopted the Internet, which is perhaps the best single embodiment of the new digital infra-structure. They're doing so at a rate that's from two to five times faster than the rate at which previous infrastructures were adopted.[16] We can no longer afford to wait around in the core for edge ideas to arrive. We have to seek them out by going to the edges—wherever they are—ourselves.

The Internet has spawned the growth of businesses at a rate never seen before. Amazon and Google became billion-dollar businesses in a few short years. Facebook acquired more than 400 million users glob-ally within years of its founding on the Harvard campus. There are more billionaires under forty than at any previous time in history. The speed at which the edge transforms the core has become compressed.

The Third Wave: Institutional Innovations

The third wave is the world that will be created by the forces driving the evolution of the Big Shift. As we all adopt pull techniques, as individ-uals and institutions we're going to start radically transforming the way the world works. All of those small moves will add up to something en-tirely new. In this wave, push-oriented institutions will fall by the way-side as more pull-based companies learn to harness the first two waves of changes through innovations to institutional architectures (such as the ability to foster and participate in creation spaces where perform-ance accelerates as more participants join). Over time, these innova-tions will enable firms to develop and adopt new ways of creating and capturing wealth in the digital era. Shareholder value and ROA may initially deteriorate, but these things will eventually improve as firms harness the foundational and flow forces of the first two waves of change and accelerate their rate of performance improvement.

We hope that you now understand that we're in the midst of a rad-ical transformation—the Big Shift. But to surf the wave of change, we must do more than acquire a new understanding of the foundations of our economy and our lives: We must adopt new techniques. We used to live in silos—closed communities that existed largely because some elite organized our lives that way. No more. Closed, push-based organizations—what the writers of *The Cluetrain Manifesto* called "fort business" more than ten years ago[17]—simply cannot take advantage of the forces that add up to the Big Shift. We—the individuals who make up our organizations—can take advantage of them, and some of us are, even now, beginning to do so. In the following chapters, we'll lay out systematically how the three levels of pull work, so that you can start taking advantage of them too.

Chapter 2

Access in an Unpredictable World

‖‖‖‖‖‖‖‖‖‖‖‖‖‖‖‖

I t was June 12, 2009, in Iran. Voters poured into the polling booths around the country. They were about to elect their next president. The incumbent, Mahmoud Ahmadinejad, an Islamic hardliner, was being challenged by Mir-Hossein Mousavi, a longtime Iranian politician who had emerged as a spokesperson for reformist forces in the country. Emotions ran high on all sides.

By the next morning, the official Iranian News Service had announced that Ahmadinejad had won by a landslide, garnering 63 percent of the votes cast, while Mousavi, the leading opposition candidate, appeared to have received only 33 percent of the vote. The reformists reacted with dismay. Charges of voter fraud quickly surfaced from opposition forces. Mousavi encouraged his supporters to protest the election results and, within hours, throngs headed into the street, voicing their support for Mousavi and demanding a recount. The protests built throughout the day. The Arabic news network Al Jazeera reported on what it called "the biggest unrest since the 1979 revolution." By the next day, at least two protesters had died in the rioting and tens of thousands of others were gathering in Tehran. On the following day, June 15, hundreds of thousands, some say even millions, of protesters joined forces in a massive rally to hear Mousavi speak. The demonstrations were spreading throughout the country and rapidly gaining momentum.

Leaders of the protest were using a variety of social media and mobile technologies to mobilize forces and coordinate their activity as the government began to crack down on the protests. They were able to quickly reach out to a very large number of Iranian citizens and engage their participation in specific protest actions—sometimes coordinated shouting and chanting, sometimes sitting in the middle of the street in an attempt to block the passage of the notoriously thuggish Bassij militia. Seeing the power of these social networks, the Iranian government moved quickly to shut down, one by one, the various social media networks in an effort to undermine the ability of members of the opposition to stay in touch with each other.

Within a few short days, only one social network remained operational—it was Twitter—and the opposition used it to great effect to reach out to people across their country who shared their concerns. Tens, maybe hundreds of thousands were brave enough to venture out into the streets and plazas to express their opposition to the government's actions in the election, but they knew it was only a matter of time before the government, using sophisticated filtering technology supplied by Western vendors, would find a way to block usage of this network too.

Meanwhile, Dan Kaminsky, a well-known hacker who in 2008 coordinated the largest synchronized security fix in Internet history,[1] had been feverishly working to come up with—and had found—a way to post messages to Twitter that would make it virtually impossible for the Iranian government to monitor and stop the service. Dan, in his eagerness to support the protest movement's right to free expression, was about to broadcast the script on Twitter to make it as broadly and as quickly available as possible.

On the other side of the world, another well-known technologist, by the name of Joichi Ito, was in the middle of a late-night instant-message conversation with his friend Sean Bonner in Los Angeles. They were discussing business ideas and blog postings about the events in Iran when Sean told Joi about Dan's intentions to release the script—any minute now—in a tweet. Joi reacted with concern. Wasn't the Iranian government actively monitoring Twitter streams? Surely the government would be quickly alerted to the existence of this script. Agreeing that this was a big risk, Sean reached out to Dan and within fifteen minutes had set up a three-way Skype call bringing the three of them together. It turned out that Dan's hack was amazing and robust—and the Iranian government might never have been able to crack it—but Joi wanted to buy as much time as possible to support the free expression of the protesters. Dan quickly agreed to pursue a better way of getting the script into the hands of the right people—a way that would not alert the Iranian government to its existence.

Joi (pronounced more like "Joey" than "Joy") was prominent in the tech world as a company founder, venture capitalist, and guild master in World of Warcraft. Having grown up in both the United States and Japan, he was renowned for the size and diversity of his personal network, which spanned the globe and included artists, musicians, moguls, magnates, diplomats, academics, journalists, and geeks. Thanks to his recent relocation to Dubai, Joi was now getting increasingly involved in human rights issues. As for Sean Bonner, his website proudly proclaims: "It's rather difficult to say what Sean Bonner does exactly." Let's just say that Sean is a well-known web publisher and cultural curator as well as an inveterate Internet troublemaker.

With his deep technology background, Joi knew there had to be a better way to disseminate this script. Within minutes of the Skype chat with Dan and Sean, he began reaching out to select people in his network through a combination of cellphone text messages, e-mails, and tweets. He quickly found relevant people at Human Rights Watch, WITNESS, Global Voices, Harvard Law School's Berkman Center, and other organizations—people he knew shared a common concern over the deteriorating situation in Iran and a passion for preserving human rights and free speech in a country that was moving quickly to suppress them. He started querying them about people who might know people in Iran who could help with the dissemination of the script. At the same time, Joi reached out to people he knew who were creative technologists who could help devise approaches for preserving the integrity of this hacked Twitter script.

Joi set up a group online chat, and a few hours later, now very late into the night in Japan, many of the people he had contacted logged on to discuss exactly how to modify the script and the tool to make it more secure and easier to spread, and how to disseminate it thereafter. Two very diverse worlds were represented in the group that gathered online, the human rights movement and the technology world. Some of the people knew each other, but many of them didn't—Joi was the only one who knew everyone taking part in the group chat. They represented a broad range of experiences, skill sets, and personal networks. The Berkman folks were experts in the analysis of online filtering. The participants from Global Voices represented a network of well-placed bloggers sharing a desire to protect human rights. Human Rights Watch were on-the-ground researchers and had the most active connections in Iran, and WITNESS had considerable experience using technology to assist human rights organizations. The various participants were distributed around the world: New York, Los Angeles, Dubai, Taiwan, and Japan were among the locations represented.

Exhausted but energized by the shared passion of the group, Joi moderated the discussion. New people, responding to messages from Joi, kept joining the chat, and the earlier participants quickly briefed each newcomer regarding the situation. Everyone felt the sense of urgency, the spirit of collaboration that bridged the diverse backgrounds and perspectives of the people in the chat. The discussion was focused and productive, melding together lots of different ideas. Within a few hours, the group devised an ingenious approach to distributing the script. They then dispersed and used their own networks to connect with the right people around the world to put the plan into action. A website was quickly set up to provide resources to support the script. Within forty-eight hours after the group chat, the most popular Iranian tweeter had privately acknowledged receipt of the code.

The result of this rapid mobilization of relevant people from around the world was that the Iranian protest movement gained a powerful weapon to sustain their freedom of expression. In short order, the movement within Iran was able to attract public attention as the ferocity of the government's crackdown became more and more evident. The future of the Iranian protest movement is still to be determined. But one thing is clear: Without Joi's diverse and widespread personal network, and his resulting ability on the spur of the moment to reach far and wide into that network to identify people who shared his passion and concern about the situation in Iran, this promising technological weapon to support the protest movement's right to free expression could have been neutralized. As of the writing of this book, a wide range of human rights workers and reformist protesters are still armed with this technology; the script is still a secret from the public; and, as far as we know, the Iranian government has yet to get its hands on the details of the technique. Joi had achieved a level of access that served him well at a time when unexpected developments were rapidly playing out with life and death consequences for many people in a faraway country.[2]

SCALING WHO KNOWS WHOM

Who-knows-whom networks are as old as human society. They're the conduit through which many things flow: introductions, information, knowledge, capital, influence, opportunities, cooperation, and collaboration (not to mention more shadowy elements, such as discrimination and corruption).

Most of us have put our own networks to use at one time or another, perhaps by calling a close friend, relative, or business associate who might be able to help with an unexpected problem. Or maybe we've made friends with a friend of a friend or gained introduction through colleagues or associates to someone we wanted to meet to advance our career prospects.

That's one kind of network, but there's another one that's likely just as old—even if, in the Big Shift, it's now gaining in scope, scale, and importance. This second type of network is based less on mutual interest—what each person can get out of their connection to the others—and more on mutual *interests*—what each participant is passionately interested in and values. These mutual passions and interests create an environment in which the participants can move with considerable speed to meet unexpected challenges when they arise. The people who came together around Joi in June 2009, for example, were each passionately interested in protecting and preserving human rights. Together they moved quickly to advance their cause.

Networks based on passions and interests have always been with us, of course, but we are seeing them proliferate in the Big Shift. People are seeking out others for mutual support around common interests and passions more actively than ever before. What's also different now is the reach and scale of these networks—their actual size as well as the diversity of participants they attract and mobilize. Anthropologists believe that in the absence of digital technology, there is a limit to the number of people with whom we can maintain social relationships. It is roughly 150—Dunbar's Number.[3] Beyond that we begin reaching diminishing returns. That number may rise from time to time, but when it does we grow apart from certain friends or relations until the total number of people with whom we have social relationships reverts back to about 150. That number of relationships, which might prove smaller for the more introverted or bigger for the more extroverted among us, doesn't connect us to a lot of people, even if we are reaching out to friends of friends. It's simply too much for any one individual to juggle, keep track of, and nurture a larger number of connections with people—there's simply not enough time to do so, and our attention must be focused on other matters that take priority. It's just not physically possible to stay in touch with more people.

Yet digital technology removes some of these physical-world complaints. Digital technology enables these networks to "scale"—to get bigger with little extra effort and still prove useful—in some ways, more useful than ever. With digital technology, Dunbar's Number may not go away, but it likely becomes much bigger. For the first time, abetted by digital social networks such as Facebook, LinkedIn, and Twitter, we can increase the number of people with whom we maintain social relationships.

The richness of our interaction with them on a digital social network may not be the equal of face-to-face interactions. But they are, on the other hand, more frequent than face-to-face interactions, and the combination of photo sharing (of our children, perhaps, or our motorcycle vacation through the Smoky Mountains), link publishing (to that new article in *The Atlantic* or to the YouTube video of that presentation you gave at last week's conference), e-mail, and chat is a far richer, more efficient way of keeping up with friends, acquaintances, and colleagues than previously less-integrated digital methods such as e-mail and instant messaging (IM), which were silo'd and one-to-one rather than one-to-many. Relative to nondigital technology like pen and paper, and to related networks like the postal or telephone system, maintaining social relationships with these new technologies is far easier. The story of how Joi Ito united a diverse group of technologists and human rights advocates, all of whom he knew personally, indicates just how useful and efficient these digitally integrated methods can be—as, indeed, does the use of Twitter by Iranian citizens to organize themselves in the face of oppression.

As the number of people we can connect with expands, our ability to pull from that network the resources and people we require to address unexpected needs expands along with it. Using the tools and platforms emerging today, any of us can now find a person in a remote part of the world who just happens to have the knowledge or expertise required to help us out. This goes beyond the reasonably straightforward search engines with which we're all familiar. Those engines are tremendously helpful, but they mostly help us access information. Today's search engines are far less adept in connecting us to people or to products. (One of us has a friend from childhood named Jonathan Smith. We'd love to reconnect with him, but a search-engine query yields more than 46 million results.) Search engines are rapidly deepening their capabilities, and knowing how to narrow the search with key terms can help. Meanwhile, we can supplement these broad search capabilities with our own social networks to find what we need when we need it. This is the first level of pull, as shown in the diagram on the next page.

Joi Ito experienced this principle firsthand not long ago while traveling. Joi, as it happens, is about as experienced a traveler as they come. In his multiple roles as successful entrepreneur, adviser to big companies, angel investor, gamer, guild leader, and CEO of Creative Commons, Joi is rarely in one place for more than three days at a time.

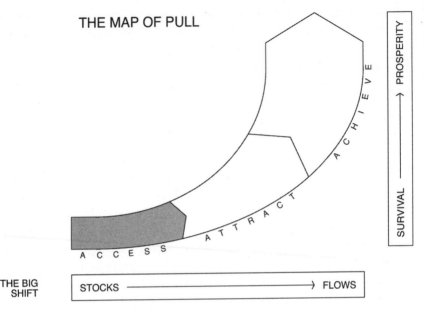

Havilland Studio, Palo Alto, California, and Lahaina, Hawaii

Now he's in Dubai, rubbing shoulders with Pakistanis. Then to Milan for a public debate with a distinguished lawyer who had recently called him a "pirate" in an Italian newspaper—and who will be a friend by the time Joi leaves town two days later for Tokyo. Then to San Jose for a stretch, and on to Amman to meet with Princess Rym Ali of Jordan.

Seasoned as he was, Joi wasn't prepared for what happened the first time he visited India. He'd arrived in New Delhi at 3 A.M. for a conference. When he got to the hotel, he found that it was in a sketchy area of town. If he hadn't been so tired, Joi might have reversed course before he even got out of the taxi. Now, standing on the sidewalk, he turned around to look for it but the driver had already left. The lobby clerk, after Joi finally managed to wake him up, handed him half a bar of soap and a padlock for the door of a filthy room. There was no drinking water. Nor were there any towels, or a broom for the rat droppings in the corner, for that matter. Needless to say, the power outlets didn't work, either. Joi was, by his own admission, getting nervous as he fired up his Nokia GPRS with the last of his batteries. He signed on to his Internet Relay Chat, which at the time averaged about a hundred people logged onto it at any given time. Minutes later, two guys living in New Delhi asked him where he was and advised him not to go outside until morning. Then, they told him, take a right out the hotel and a left on the following street—walking neither too fast nor too slow—and soon he should be able to find a cab the heck outta there, and over to the right hotel on the other side of town.

Joi has never met the two guys, either before or after they helped him. But that night in New Delhi they were just what he needed.

Who and What We Need

Joi's difficulties in New Delhi and his efforts to support the Iranian protesters' freedom of expression were two very different problems in two very different contexts. But he solved both of them the same way: by using his network to access the people and information he needed when he needed it. These weren't problems he could have solved without being able to reach out to, and through, his network. That's what the first level of pull—access—is about.

Access involves the ability to find, learn about, and connect with resources (people, products, and knowledge) on an as-needed basis to address unanticipated needs. In the Big Shift, this capability becomes increasingly central to our survival, much less our success. In the previous chapter, we discussed how foundational elements—the convergence of digital infrastructures and public-policy regimes supporting economic liberalization—were leading to intensified competition and growing economic pressure. In particular, this first wave of the Big Shift increasingly undermines our ability to forecast demand, requiring very different approaches to resource mobilization. Rather than pushing resources based on reasonably accurate demand forecasts, we must find ways to access a broader range of resources in shorter periods of time to respond to unanticipated events as disruptions become ever more frequent. From something that was nice to have, access is becoming essential to survival in an increasingly unpredictable world. This is equally true at the level of the individual as we find it harder and harder to plan our careers or even to anticipate the opportunities and challenges that we will face in the months ahead. We are often disappointed to find that the education we invested so much time and money to pursue has failed to prepare us for the lives we are now leading.

Access has become more central to our daily personal and professional lives, and social networks are evolving to help us enhance access in both arenas. Access is particularly challenging in the business world, where institutional boundaries have tended to limit visibility and the ability to connect with needed resources. Pull platforms can help us to overcome institutional barriers in the business world as well as to expand our reach in our personal lives. Later in this chapter we'll address some of the common misconceptions that executives have about pull platforms and explore two examples of pull platforms that emerged on a global scale to help companies connect more flexibly with valuable resources. But first, we'll look in more detail at how access works and the promise of pull platforms for both businesses and individuals.

To a certain extent, we have always had limited ability to access what we needed when we needed it. Think of the objects around your workspace—the jar of sharp pencils, the portable flash drive, the bar of dark chocolate, the squeeze toy, the stapler you're ready (if you're a certain Silicon Valley CEO of our acquaintance) to throw at a subordinate when things go wrong. All of them are standing by at a moment's notice, to be pulled in to help with the task at hand—even if the task isn't sanctioned by your local HR representative.

But we haven't ever had the scalability of access that we have today. Consider how, pre-Internet, if you were looking for a particular book passage, but couldn't remember which book it appeared in, you could only flip through the books on the shelf hoping to come across it. If you couldn't find what you were seeking in your own books, you might have walked next door to see if your colleague had it. From there your search might have taken you down the hall to the common library maintained by your department or function. Failing to find it there, you'd have then headed off for the library across town, where the librarian might have been able to help you out.

Such a scenario almost seems quaint now. It's easy to forget just how different things were prior to the advent of search engines. And yet not all of our practices have caught up. Just the other day one of us had the odd sensation of walking to the office bookshelves, trying to find an elusive passage, and suddenly recalling, as he stood there staring at the spines of all the many books, that there was a search function he could use to make the task easier: It was the one to be found back on the desk, Google Books. Soon he was staring at the passage on the computer screen as the hardcover itself gathered more dust across the room.

That's what we mean by the scalability of access. We're no longer limited simply to the 150 people we can maintain physical-world relationships with, to the books on the shelf across the room, or even those at the local library.

But for all their power, today's search engines have their limitations. They work best when we know what we're looking for and when we're looking for publicly available data presented on the Internet. They work far less well if we don't know what we're seeking or if what we seek proves to be part of the "dark" Internet, stored behind firewalls or other protective barriers designed to keep out search-engine spiders. Today's search engines also have difficulty providing us with information regarding products and people. Social-networking platforms such as Facebook, LinkedIn, and MySpace are beginning to address the latter need, but, as anyone who has tried to navigate through these platforms can tell you, their search capabilities need considerable refinement. Of course, once you succeed in finding a person who can help you, not only do you get their initial response, but there's opportunity then for a back-and-forth that may result in something unexpected. That's why, ultimately, the most valuable search is the one that connects us to people; they often are the best sources of information and knowledge, especially new tacit knowledge—know-how relating to new fields of endeavor or new activities on the edge.

Pull-based access services are also emerging in more specialized domains. Travel services such as Orbitz and Travelocity have made it easier to search for specific routing and fare options as we plan our trips. Increasingly, these services are also layering in traveler evaluations of specific hotel and other travel options, so that we can find even more information about potential services. Rearden Commerce provides a robust access service for employees seeking to connect with a variety of vendors providing services that are relevant to their jobs, including package delivery services, travel services, and conferencing services. HomeExchange and similar services help travelers who want to trade their own home for a vacation at the home of somebody who wants to do the same.

Still other search engines help users find products and services in particular areas of knowledge that are further from the beaten track, allowing them to search, for instance, U.S. federal legislative records, or biographies, or medical information. We'll discuss a company later in this chapter that provides help to apparel designers in finding and connecting with highly specialized supply-network service providers around the world. Cisco helps its customers find and connect with service providers in a network of more than 40,000 partners to get more value from the networking equipment they purchase. By developing a detailed understanding of their customers' needs and the capabilities of diverse providers, these access services move beyond simple directories and search engines to offer advice tailored to individual users that is designed to help them find and connect with the most appropriate providers.

These services are quite different from traditional distribution and retail businesses. Of course, customers can go into a large retailer, search through a very broad selection of products, and "pull" the right product off the shelf to meet specific needs. More specialized retailers might even offer personalized advice based on a detailed understanding of the individual customer to help the customer find the right product. But these distribution and retail businesses have vast infrastructures designed to push products through complex logistics networks to be available at the right place at the right time to meet anticipated customer demand. The access services that we are describing here do not attempt to forecast demand in advance—they are set up to help customers find and access products and services when the need arises.

What we have access to has grown considerably, as has our ease of accessing it. Moreover, our newly scaled access can help us follow our interests and passions in new ways. We can use new tools and platforms to access people who share our interests and hobbies, no matter how esoteric, and build sustained relationships with them over the Internet that often spill over into "real life."

Access Beyond Institutional Boundaries

There's no Dunbar's Number for institutions. But big corporations, government agencies, and the like have an obviously tough time scaling their relationships, too. For a variety of reasons, most prefer to keep the number of business partners with whom they interact to a minimum. For most big institutions their very size works against them: Scale becomes a barrier to access, not an enabler.

Anybody who's worked in a big company knows how hard it can be to find "the right someone" on short notice to help address a question that arises. As Lew Platt, the former CEO of Hewlett Packard, famously observed, "If HP knew what HP knows, we would be three times as profitable."[4]

The problem compounds once we contemplate the truism that there are a lot more smart people outside any particular company than within it. How do companies connect with them efficiently and effectively? For most of us, our ability to connect with relevant expertise within our own institution—let alone beyond it—is at best sporadic and episodic rather than systematic.

But some companies are beginning to figure it out. They're building scalable networks to access capabilities beyond their boundaries. One of them, SAP AG, has a significant outpost in Silicon Valley, just down the road from where we live, even though its headquarters are in Walldorf, a small town in rural Germany. Founded twenty-five years ago by a group of former IBM engineers, SAP has grown to become the fourth-largest software company in the world, creating the big company-wide software applications that today's firms use to run most of what they do.

The software industry started to go through a wrenching change earlier in this decade as it moved from large, complex, tightly integrated application software to much more loosely coupled modules of software embedded in service-oriented architectures. To its credit, SAP, whose success had been driven by the previous generation of software, embraced this next wave of software architecture, introducing its NetWeaver platform in early 2003—a nifty piece of software that fit on top of and around its existing enterprise applications, helping them talk to each other and to non-SAP applications.

In so doing, however, SAP ran into a classic chicken-and-egg dilemma: The product's full potential wouldn't become apparent until customers began using it and discovering what it could do. Yet customers might not adopt NetWeaver—which SAP was essentially giving away as part of its applications—until they could grasp its potential.

Even NetWeaver's early adopters—typically among the most tech-savvy of its customers—were struggling with its basics. Yet SAP had neither the reach nor the resources to train and teach its entire customer base—let alone educate tens of thousands of systems integrator consultants.

That's when SAP executive board member Shai Agassi came up with a great idea: Why not let all of SAP's customers, systems integrators, and independent service vendors teach each other about NetWeaver, peer-to-peer, as they learned to use it? The result was the SAP Developer Network (SDN), a broad ecosystem of participants interacting in discussion forums, wikis, videos, and blogs. In one fell swoop, SAP went beyond the limitations of its own resources to access a broad network of talented and passionate participants who proved to be crucial to the platform's success. The SDN community grew quickly and powerfully and, as it did, SAP established NetWeaver with its customers and third-party vendors. SAP's Developer Network and its related ecosystem initiatives have created a rich network of 1.3 million participants contributing to more than 1 million separate topics of conversation.

Of course, what SAP's managers accomplished wasn't easy. It required considerable confidence in their product, a willingness to receive criticism about NetWeaver, or about the SDN itself, and an operational ability to respond in a timely manner to inquiries, complaints, and commentary so as not to appear standoffish or as if they were stonewalling. All too many companies underestimate the difficulties these challenges present when they set up online communities and discussion forums.

The SDN was a success in no small part because it provided ample opportunity for nearly everybody involved to become more productive in what they do. Independent software developers could improve their coding chops. SAP's in-house code-writers could learn more quickly which of the features they wrote worked for their users—and which did not. And SAP itself could get a lot more value from its customer service people: As the SDN began taking care of more routine and entry-level customer questions, SAP could focus on the more difficult ones.

FROM PROGRAMS TO PLATFORMS

Pull approaches to providing access to resources are fundamentally different from push approaches, as the SAP story illustrates. The way of organizing resources is different, and the management techniques are different—very different.

A key to the pull approaches is the use of "platforms" that are designed to flexibly accommodate diverse providers and users of resources. SAP's Developer Network is one good example. These platforms are open-ended and designed to evolve based on the learning and the changing needs of the participants. "Platforms" in the literal sense are tangible foundations; here we are using the term metaphorically to describe frameworks for orchestrating a set of resources that can be configured quickly and easily to serve a broad range of needs. Think of Travelocity's travel service, or the emergency ward of a hospital, and you will see the contrast with the hard-wired push programs. Emergency wards, of course, exist to help only in dire situations. Yet they demonstrate the feasibility and value of pull-oriented approaches in more traditional settings. In the emergency room, the medical personnel make skilled decisions as to the time necessity of their interventions and are ready to pull from and mobilize a wide variety of resources that are on hand to help who-ever comes in with a problem.

The contrast between push programs and pull platforms is quite stark. Pull platforms tend to be much more modular in design. Of course, push programs can also be modular, but the modules are spec-ified for the benefit of the provider and usually tightly integrated. On pull platforms the modules are for the convenience of the participants in the platform. For example, many "open university" initiatives allow students to take courses (which are "modules" in a degree-granting program) online whenever they choose, in different sequences and groupings, giving maximum flexibility to the student. Modules are created to help to make resources and activities more accessible in flexible ways, since the core assumption of pull platforms is that the needs of participants cannot be well anticipated in advance. Pull plat-forms are designed from the outset to handle exceptions, while push programs treat exceptions as indications of failure. Most companies in fact spend considerable effort trying to eliminate exceptions—such as when an order bounces out of an automated order processing sys-tem because of a customer request for unusual financing terms, or for shipment of the order using an unanticipated delivery method.

In pull platforms, the modules are designed to be loosely coupled, with interfaces that help users to understand what the module con-tains and how it can be accessed. Because of this loosely coupled mod-ular design, pull platforms can accommodate a much larger number of diverse participants. In fact, pull platforms tend to have increasing returns dynamics—the more participants and modules the platform can attract, the more valuable the platform becomes.

In our personal lives, many of us have become accustomed to cre-ating our own highly personalized music experiences by leveraging pull platforms such as Apple's iTunes store. We use photo-storage sites such as Flickr to pull together photos into diverse virtual photo al-bums, and we construct our own tailored video experiences by as-sembling videos into sequences that address our individual needs.

In many cases, pull platforms are initially deployed to serve a spe-cific need, but, because of the flexible design, these platforms rapidly evolve in unexpected directions and end up serving a broad range of needs. Instant-messaging networks were initially deployed to help teens and hackers to communicate more rapidly, but they are now actively used by financial traders who want to gain an edge in rapidly moving financial markets. The design of these platforms is emergent, shaped by the participants themselves as their own needs evolve. This kind of organic growth is very appealing, on the one hand, because it makes the most of a company's initial investment as other participants contribute. It's somewhat scary, on the other hand, for managers who are used to controlling what takes place. Who knows? Perhaps the community will start talking about or even recommending competing products. Yet SAP's example shows that companies can influence and shape the direction in which the community goes—so that it creates the most value for all the participants— without over-controlling things.

Because they're more modular, pull platforms are enhanced much more frequently than push programs. These enhancements can occur at multiple levels. Modules may be recombined in innovative ways to serve new needs. Activities and resources within modules may be reconfigured through improvisation and experimentation to serve needs more effectively. Because these modules are relatively self-contained, this improvisation and experimentation does not introduce as much risk of widespread unanticipated adverse effects as in tightly specified push programs. You can change one thing without having to change everything. Finally, enhancement can occur through the addition of new layers to the platform as participants discover entirely new ways to add value by leveraging the capabilities of deeper layers.

Pull platforms make it easier to assemble participants and resources on an ad hoc basis to problem-solve unforeseen issues or situations. As a result, they enhance the potential for productive friction as people with different perspectives, skills, and experiences come together to try to find a solution for a specific problem. In contrast, push programs view all friction as an inefficiency that must be eliminated. The purpose of tightly specified programs is to eliminate wasteful debate and disagreement, especially at the point of execution.

Since pull platforms are designed to easily accommodate new participants and to create new value in innovative ways, they tend to generate positive-sum reward systems for participants. The innovation of each participant enhances the overall value of the platform, creating a larger pool of rewards that can be distributed among the participants. As pull platforms attract additional participants, they also encourage more specialization of capability so that diverse niches emerge and evolve, reducing head-to-head competition and commoditization. Positive-sum reward systems reduce the perceived need for political maneuvering, and the opportunity to connect on a peer-to-peer basis with resource owners diminishes the role of the center as a focus for resource allocation.

Because pull platforms can be flexibly configured to serve the individual needs and interests of each participant, they provide much greater opportunity for intrinsic rewards as a key motivator for participation. Look at the rapid growth of Wikipedia, the online encyclopedia emerging from the contributions of thousands of volunteer participants. These contributors participate based on interest, and they are motivated by the desire to contribute and share their interests with others. Of course, extrinsic rewards will still play a prominent role in many pull platforms, but they will be balanced by a much more significant opportunity to pursue intrinsic rewards as well.

There are some downsides to pull platforms—at least if you're highly wedded to push programs. After all, push programs were created in the belief that the world was relatively stable and predictable and that long time periods pass between disruptions. Many people have an understandable nostalgia for a time when economic and social events were more stable and predictable. So they hold onto the push mechanisms to try to maintain that stability. But longing doesn't make it so. The world is changing around us, thanks to our new digital infrastructure. In the Big Shift era, it's not a question of whether or not to give up push programs—we've already lost them, at least in the sense of their being effective.

Blurring Creation and Use

Pull platforms tend to allow us to perform the following activities, with a blurring of the boundaries between creation and use:

- *Find.* Pull platforms allow us to find not just raw materials, products, and services, but also people with relevant skills and experience. Some of the tools and services that pull platforms use to help participants find relevant resources include search, recommendation engines, directories, agents, and reputation services.
- *Connect.* Again, pull platforms connect us not just to raw materials, products, and services, but also to people with relevant skills and experiences. Performance fabrics[5] are particularly helpful in establishing appropriate connections. The mobile Internet is dramatically extending our ability to connect wherever we are.
- *Innovate.* Pull platforms provide much more flexible environments for participants to innovate with the resources made available to them. This innovation could take many forms, including creative ways of orchestrating resources—for example, recombining and remixing—to deliver more value. The innovation may involve creation of entirely new resources or more modest improvisation and tinkering with existing resources to enhance their functionality and performance. Participants in pull platforms rarely just use the resources made available to them—this isn't a one-time, quick, finite relationship. Instead, participants become actively involved in modifying the resources to more effectively serve their needs. It therefore becomes easy to cross-pollinate an idea that's established in one domain of expertise and apply it to another to good effect.
- *Reflect.* Although reflection is feasible in push models, it tends to occur in a much more centralized and episodic fashion in push models than in pull models. Pull models are designed to enable the distributed participants to reflect on the performance of resources available to them and then to recombine or improvise, with much more rapid feedback regarding the impact of these efforts. The musicians participating on ccMixter get to add their "sample" of music onto the site and then see how others react to it (through comments or through the addition of their own music to the sample). Perhaps one person will suggest remixing the original sample to bring the vocals forward relative to the

piano, and another will suggest adding more reverb. The distributed participants have a much richer and nuanced understanding of the local context of their performance than they could if they were performing in an isolated push context and are therefore better positioned to develop appropriate approaches to improving their performance. In addition to local reflection, analytic tools designed to help participants identify patterns in performance can help to enhance reflection on the performance of broader elements of the pull platform and support broader-based innovation initiatives.

Pull platforms are emerging as a response to growing uncertainty. Instead of dealing with uncertainty through tighter control, pull models do the opposite. They seek to expand the opportunity for creativity by local participants dealing with immediate needs. To exploit the opportunities created by uncertainty, pull platforms help people to come together and innovate in response to unanticipated events, drawing upon a growing array of highly specialized and distributed resources. Rather than seeking to constrain the resources available to people, pull platforms strive to continually expand the choices available while at the same time helping people to find the resources that are most relevant to them. Rather than dictating the actions that people must take, pull platforms provide people with the tools and resources (including connections to other people) required for them to take initiative and creatively address opportunities as they arise.

Common Misperceptions of Pull

When we talk to people about pull platforms, we sometimes run into the misperception that pull is somehow manipulative, below-board, taking place behind the scenes in a smoke-filled room. But this is not your father's old boys' network. Academics often harbor the same assumption, figuring that pull involves the classic "broker" who, for his own gain, acts as an unreliable, duplicitous go-between among unsuspecting innocents. Shakespeare's plays are full of such characters: Othello's "friend" Iago, to name one. Some academics call such a broker *Tertius Gaudens*, "the third who benefits." Instead, we're talking about what David Obstfeld has named *Tertius Iungens*, "the third who joins"—and who in so doing creates value for all concerned.[6] The model of behavior we're interested in is *Iungens*, not *Gaudens*.

In talking to executives about pull platforms, we often encounter two additional misconceptions. First, they tend to think of large companies such as Toyota and Dell, companies that have mastered lean supply-network management to pull resources into their manufacturing operations as needed, rather than relying on large accumulations of inventory to buffer unanticipated shifts in demand. Second, they often assume that we are talking about technology platforms. Both of these misconceptions miss the significance of the changes that are unfolding around us.

Beyond the Supply Network

The lean manufacturing systems of companies such as Toyota and Dell do represent an important transition away from more conventional push-driven supply-chain approaches. For example, Toyota operates its assembly lines with a "just-in-time" philosophy. The company's workers pull resources into the assembly line just as they are needed, rather than allowing large inventories to accumulate at various stages of production. In its Japanese operations, Toyota is not quite at the point of attaching a customer's name to each car entering the production process, but it is much closer to executing a true "build-to-order" system than U.S. car manufacturers are. In all these respects, Toyota and other lean-manufacturing practitioners have begun a move to pull models of resource mobilization. Think of what this does for the motivation of the workers on the assembly line.

Yet, in other respects, even the lean-manufacturing practitioners continue to rely on push. For example, to make their just-in-time manufacturing work, Toyota limits the number of suppliers that it deals with and tightly integrates its operations with these suppliers, often requiring colocation of facilities to reduce cycle times and enhance the potential for rapid problem solving. Activities throughout its operations are highly specified and standardized. In other words, Toyota has been able to achieve high flexibility in its operations by closing its system and limiting the diversity of participants.

While some of the pioneers of pull systems and lean manufacturing have used these techniques to solve difficult managerial and operational problems, most of their followers focus more on efficiency than learning, missing entirely the crucial collaborations with business partners that can yield new tacit knowledge and push the performance edges out.

We are suggesting the need for more scalable pull platforms that will reach out to and connect vast numbers of participants on a global basis. Pull is not about controlling suppliers. As competition intensifies and uncertainty increases, the scale and diversity of participants will increasingly make the difference between success and failure. There is an opportunity to learn from early efforts to build scalable pull platforms and identify the key principles that seem to enhance the potential for scale.

Not Just Technology

The second big misunderstanding executives have about pull platforms comes from the tendency to equate "platform" with "technology." There is no doubt that the new digital infrastructure described earlier is making it more feasible to build and manage scalable pull platforms, and it certainly makes it easier for individuals to connect with one another. But equating platforms with technology misses some significant elements of pull platforms. Scalable pull platforms depend upon the definition and adoption of standards and protocols for interaction. Although some of these standards and protocols are technology related, others simply focus on helping people and companies to connect more flexibly when the need arises. In fact, one of the most successful pull platforms emerged and evolved with minimal use of technology. At the center of pull, remember, are people.

THE LI & FUNG STORY

Li & Fung operates in a variety of industries, but it got its start in the apparel industry. It was there that the company initially developed an operating model that it is now extending into other industries. In the apparel industry, Li & Fung's customers are apparel designers in the United States and Europe. It works with these customers to define their needs in terms of apparel production and then configures supply networks that are not just customized for the individual customer, but customized down to the individual item of apparel.

Li & Fung does not perform any of the supply-network operations itself. Instead, it works with more than 10,000 business partners in more than forty countries around the world to ensure that exactly the right capability is deployed to support each item of apparel. For example, the participants required to produce a high-end wool sweater might be quite different from the participants required to produce a low-end wool sweater. Li & Fung has a deep understanding of the capabilities of each of its partners. Its role is to identify the appropriate partners, define and sequence their roles in the supply-network process, and perform quality checks to ensure that each customer is getting exactly what it needs. Everything else—all raw material sourcing, production activities, and logistics activities—is performed by Li & Fung's partners.

In effect, Li & Fung has organized a global pull platform for apparel designers. In sharp contrast to traditional supply-network managers, who have focused on limiting the number of supply-network partners and creating tightly integrated operations, Li & Fung is rapidly expanding the range of participants to provide an even broader range of specialized capabilities that can be flexibly "pulled" by individual customers to serve their specific needs.

The scalability of this global pull platform critically depends upon the sophisticated techniques that Li & Fung uses to define and deploy standards and protocols for coordinating complex activities across multiple levels of production operations. Li & Fung invests considerable time and effort in specifying modules of activity in apparel supply-network operations. Rather than specifying the activities to be performed within each module, it focuses on defining the outputs required from each module. (Note how easily this philosophy can be translated to the human relations aspect of big-company life. Netflix, for example, has no limit on the paid time off that its employees can take or any "face-time" policy specifying how much time workers must spend in the office. Employees do have to get their work done, and they often exceed expectations, but, like Li & Fung, Netflix is counting output, not specifying input.)

Li & Fung has created a robust set of standards for specifying what its expected outputs are. Every participant in its network knows, for example, that when Li & Fung specifies a color, that color is exactly what must be delivered. Li & Fung has also established a set of protocols for hand-offs across modules so that each participant knows how to interact with other partners in the supply-network process.

These standards and protocols help Li & Fung to quickly bring in new partners to their network and to reconfigure partners in a particular supply-network process to respond to unanticipated needs. In the apparel industry, where time, cost, and quality requirements can be very demanding and customer demand can change radically in a matter of days, the company has built a global network that can respond instantly and effectively to the needs of its customers. And yet, from a technology viewpoint, Li & Fung, until quite recently, has relied on only the most basic technology—telephones and fax machines—to coordinate the activity of its supply-network partners. The power of its pull platform is certainly not in the technology; rather, it is in a deep understanding of how to orchestrate complex supply-network activities through standards and protocols governing interactions among its global partners.

Li & Fung has been highly successful. Generating $15 billion in revenue, Li & Fung has been growing at a double-digit rate annually over the past twenty-five years, a considerable feat in the low-growth global apparel industry. It is also highly profitable, typically enjoying double-digit return on equity—again, an impressive accomplishment in an industry known for razor-thin margins. Clearly, pull platforms can be scalable and highly profitable. But they can never have a chance to succeed unless executives overcome their fears and adopt new practices.

Skeptics will suggest that this is an isolated example. Some point to Li & Fung's base in China and speculate that this is only possible because of the personal, trust-based networks of relationships that Chinese culture fosters. The implication is that these same management approaches could never work for Western companies, even though the vast majority of Li & Fung's partners operate outside of China—many of them in the West. Other skeptics observe that the apparel industry is a relatively simple industry, but perhaps these skeptics are unaware of the degree to which sophisticated synthetic fibers are making increasing inroads into this "simple" industry. The fact is, Li & Fung has done well despite intense competition, not just hanging on but continuing to grow while maintaining very high financial returns, especially relative to other apparel companies.

THE PORTALPLAYER STORY

Perhaps the skeptics of pull power would be convinced by the example of another platform that emerged about ten years ago in an emerging high-tech sector—the budding digital music player market. PortalPlayer was founded in 1999 by a group of former National Semiconductor executives. It received very little public attention, but it played a key role in the introduction of Apple's iPod product line. The founders of PortalPlayer set out from the beginning to organize a global pull platform to help it design and develop technology to meet very demanding performance specifications, including a small form factor, low power consumption, high audio quality, and low manufacturing cost. PortalPlayer focused on designing the core MP3 decoder and controller chip with related software that made it easy to incorporate technology from a broad range of other companies. This became the centerpiece of PortalPlayer's pull platform.

From the outset, the company was organized as a micromultinational with its own operations based in both San Jose, California, and Hyderabad, India. PortalPlayer invested significant efforts in building a global network of technology companies with complementary capabilities to support MP3 development. These companies included some U.K. technology providers, such as the microprocessor company ARM and Wolfson Microelectronics, a specialized provider of digital-to-analog conversion technology. From the United States, participants in the PortalPlayer network included Texas Instruments and Linear Technologies, a small company specializing in power-management integrated circuits. From Japan, PortalPlayer recruited Sharp to provide flash memory, Sony for battery technology, and Toshiba for hard-disk-drive technology. In Taiwan, PortalPlayer developed close relationships with both United Microelectronics Corporation (UMC) and Taiwan Semiconductor Manufacturing Company (TSMC) to access silicon-foundry capabilities. In effect, PortalPlayer had deployed a pull platform to drive rapid iterations of innovative MP3 designs by accessing and connecting with world-class capabilities from specialized companies around the globe.

When Apple came up with an idea for a new MP3 product line coupled with an online music store, it approached PortalPlayer to mobilize its global design network; as a result, Apple was able to enter the market with its iPod just nine months after the initial product approval. Apple focused on the external design of the iPod and the user interface design, leaving the rest of the design to PortalPlayer and its design network, and for many years PortalPlayer was the key source for the innovative MP3 functionality embedded in the iPod product.

||||||||

FLEXIBLE ACCESS to people and resources can be enormously powerful in a world driven by changes that, more often than not, lead us in unanticipated directions. We all need to master the pull platforms that can help us to do this—both personally and professionally. Many of us will create significant new businesses by developing and deploying pull-based platforms that help to make people and resources even more accessible.

Access through pull platforms is a significant opportunity today. But it is increasingly becoming an imperative. Those of us who remain wedded to push-based institutions and practices will find it more and more difficult to succeed. Even the most carefully crafted forecasts often mislead us. If we do not master the ability to access people and resources as needed, we will risk becoming progressively marginalized by those who understand and embrace the foundational changes playing out on a global scale.

Rather than relying on financial leverage, we need to become more adept at "capability leverage"—finding and accessing complementary capabilities, wherever they reside in the world, to deliver even more value. Though this certainly applies at a corporate level, it also applies at a personal level. Especially in the United States, we have used financial leverage to access what we want. Pull platforms provide us with an opportunity to access what we need and to create even more value for ourselves and for others.

And this is just the beginning. So far, we have discussed only the first level of pull—access. As we will discuss in the next couple of chapters, there are two more levels of pull—attract and achieve—that will help us to thrive in the Big Shift era.

BRINGING IT HOME

- Can you identify the fifty smartest or most accomplished people who share your passions or interests, regardless of where they reside?
- How many of these people are currently in your professional / personal networks?
- How many of these people have you been able to engage actively in an initiative related to your shared passions or interests?
- To how many of these people would you feel comfortable reaching out and mobilizing in a new initiative related to your shared passions and interests?
- For these fifty people, how effectively are you using social media to increase your mutual awareness of each other's activities?

Chapter 3

Attracting What We Need

||||||||||||||||||||

O nly when the apple fell from the tree did Sir Isaac Newton begin pondering the nature of gravity. Only by setting sail for India did Christopher Columbus find America. Only by going to a conference to hear presentations on the future of the Internet did Google founders Sergey Brin and Larry Page meet Israeli entrepreneur Yossi Vardi, who later gave them an important key for monetizing search results.

The innovation Yossi suggested was deceptively simple: Divide paid search results on the right-hand third of the page from free search results on the left-hand two-thirds of the page.[1] This small alteration instantly made the integrity of Google's search results visible and apparent by making it clear which results advertisers had paid to display and which results were free. The change instantly set Google apart from its primary competitors at the time, which did not distinguish between paid and free search results. "Yossi invented for us the magic formula," Sergey Brin later told a conference audience. "He told us to devote two-thirds of the [Internet] page to original results, and a third to advertisements, and that is what we did."[2]

The uses of serendipitous encounters and discoveries could fill a whole book. In fact, it already has—Robert K. Merton and Elinor Barber's wonderful *The Travels and Adventures of Serendipity*.[3] Yet most of us, despite the role serendipity has played in our own lives—introducing us to our future spouse, perhaps, or informing us of a job opportunity—tend to think serendipity occurs on its own, a function of fate or maybe blind luck. "But serendipity doesn't just happen in a serendipitous way," says Yossi Vardi. "You have to work for it."[4] Serendipity can be methodically, systematically shaped by our choices, behaviors, and dispositions. In this chapter on the second level of pull—attract—we'll show you how.

THE SUPER-NODE

Yossi Vardi founded his first company in 1969 when he was twenty-seven years old. Since then he's been an investor in, or godfather to, more than seventy Israeli tech companies. Perhaps his biggest success was as founding investor of Mirabilis, the company behind the first instant-messaging technology, ICQ ("I seek you"), which AOL bought for $400 million in 1998.

Yossi is also one of the best-connected people in technology. "Yossi is a super-node," British Technology executive Gary Shainberg told *Business Week* in 2008. "He connects people and companies from around the world to leverage the world-beating technology innovation in Israel."[5]

Like other people we discuss in this book—Joichi Ito, Ellen Levy, Jack Hidary, and Tara Lemmey—Yossi is thoughtful about how and where he meets people and personal and warm-hearted about how he cultivates and maintains his relationships with them thereafter. You might think of him as a "connector," but he's much more than that. He's not just a point in a network graph that connects other points, but someone striving to amplify and expand the passionate efforts of many other people. In fact, people often become connectors precisely because, as they pursue their passions (in Yossi's case for technology-driven innovation), they find themselves reaching out to anyone and everyone who might share this passion. In the process, while pursuing specific initiatives or projects, they end up connecting people in new and unexpected ways. Passion leads to pursuit, which creates connections.

Though his approach may be at least partially systematic, it is far from cold or calculated: Yossi is famously a good-humored and open-hearted man—a "soft touch," according to *Business Week*—who avoids business plans and instead invests by instinct and according to how much he likes the entrepreneur. "My wife, Talma, who keeps me connected to the ground, tells me it doesn't make sense that every kid with shining eyes walks away from a meeting with me with a check," he says. "But I tell her if I lose the money at least it goes to nice people and allows them to follow their dreams. Who wants to give money to jerks?"[6]

Because he's pursuing his passion for technology-driven innovation, because of his successful track record, because of his approachability, affability, and intelligence—and because of his willingness to invest in young people and their entrepreneurial ideas—Yossi Vardi has the ability to attract people and resources to him that he was not even aware existed. As people seek Yossi out, Yossi himself becomes aware of people he hadn't met before who prove to be relevant and valuable to him.

Yossi exemplifies a second level of pull—attract—that is playing a critical role in the Big Shift (see the diagram on the following page).

Although the word "attract" has many broader meanings, we are particularly focused on techniques for drawing people or resources to us that we were not even aware existed but that prove to be relevant and valuable. Though we were not looking for them, once we encounter them we recognize this value and marvel at our good fortune. But was it really a matter of luck? We think not, and research supports this skepticism. Instead, attraction is often the result of something we did, whether consciously or unconsciously. Serendipity can be shaped: We can make choices that will increase our ability to attract people and resources to us that we never knew existed, leading to serendipitous encounters that prove enormously valuable to us. This chapter explores serendipity and its growing importance in our personal and professional lives. It makes the case that one particular form of serendipity—unexpected encounters with people—is ultimately far more valuable in the era of the Big Shift than other forms of serendipity—for example, an unexpected result in an

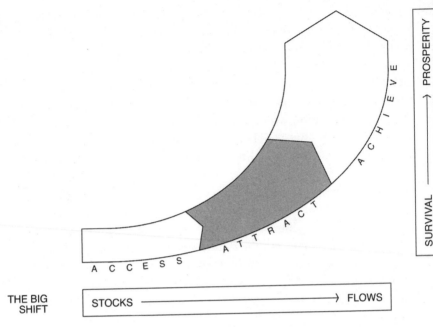

Havilland Studio, Palo Alto, California, and Lahaina, Hawaii

experiment, or the unexpected discovery of some information that proves helpful in a project.

We will look at the specific environments, practices, and preparedness that can help us to increase both the number and quality of unexpected encounters with people. Our particular focus is on managing the "funnel" of serendipity—on the one hand, increasing the scope of relevant serendipitous encounters; on the other, ensuring that each serendipitous encounter is as productive as possible.

Serendipity has always been an important part of our lives. Why is it becoming even more critical to our success now? To answer that, we need to return to the second wave of the Big Shift described in Chapter 1. As you will recall, we discussed a first wave of the Big Shift, focusing on the convergence of two key catalysts of the changes we see going on around us—the proliferation of an ever more powerful digital infrastructure combined with the growing adoption of public policies favoring economic liberalization. These events in turn are leading to a second wave of the Big Shift, which is generating a growing diversity of rich knowledge flows on a global scale. Many of the most valuable knowledge flows are concentrated on relevant edges that become the seedbeds for the next set of innovations that will disrupt our social and business landscape. These innovations percolate on the edge, unseen by most of us, until they erupt suddenly and quickly transform the cores where most of us live. We need to find ways to attract relevant innovators and edge participants so that we can discover early windows into the developments that will end up transforming how we live and work. Sure, serendipity has always been important, but in a world of near-constant disruption, it becomes essential to survival. Without the pleasant surprises of serendipity, we will instead have to cope with the unpleasant shock of unanticipated disruptions that undermine all that we have worked to achieve.

The first level of pull—access—is very powerful. But in a world of near-constant disruption, its value is limited. We increasingly find that we no longer even know what to seek, even with the growing power of search. While it's great that all sorts of information is indexed and sorted on the web, even a daily tour through one's Facebook newsfeed reveals many new people and resources that could be relevant. How do we find out which ones? How do we specify, when we go to Ask.com, Bing, or Google, the areas of knowledge and expertise that would be most valuable? "Show me the stuff that I really need that I don't even know exists," isn't much of a search string. Nor can you type in, "Take me to the edge!" Access only truly works when we know what we're looking for. At times like these, the cursor blinks in the search engine's textbox, mocking us, asking the existential question: Do you even know what you are looking for? And even if we think we do, it's guaranteed that "unknown unknowns," as Donald Rumsfeld memorably called them, are waiting for us, both as opportunities and as barriers.

We must supplement search engines and their equivalents by exploring additional ways of pulling *people* and their knowledge to us, particularly people on the edge. To address this challenge, we will need to master the techniques of attraction in both our personal and professional lives—and learn to harness the power of serendipity.

While most all of us already know how to attract something toward ourselves when it's something or someone we've already encountered, few of us seem to realize that we can shape serendipity to attract the people and things we need but didn't realize we were searching for.

As we begin to engage with this level of pull, we'll foster encounters with people who can be helpful in expanding our horizons and creating the new knowledge that enables us to achieve new levels of performance. Yet brief encounters are typically of little value. You have to do more than have a brief conversation or e-mail exchange: You have to invest time and effort and build trust-based relationships if you are to access the knowledge that is most valuable. Building these relationships requires reciprocity: We must be willing to give if we are to receive.

THE NATURE AND IMPORTANCE OF SERENDIPITY

"Serendipity," according to the Brazilian writer Glauco Ortolano, "is the faculty of finding things we did not know we were looking for."[7] This means finding more than things—it also means finding people, and the knowledge they carry with them.

"Serendipity" is actually a relatively new word. It was coined in the mid-eighteenth century by Horace Walpole, a British literary figure. Walpole was inspired by an old Persian fable, "The Travels and Adventures of Three Princes of Sarendip," in which the princes of the title set out on a journey and along the way discover a whole series of clues that they had not been looking for. "Serendipity" remained a relatively obscure term, largely restricted to literary circles, until the 1930s when Walter Cannon, a professor of physiology at Harvard Medical School, latched onto the term as a way to highlight the role of accidental discovery in science. The term rapidly caught on in scientific circles, and over the next few decades it passed into general usage.

Although many meanings were attached to the term, early uses of "serendipity" focused on the unexpected discovery of items such as obscure books in antiquarian bookstores. Cannon expanded the usage to the discovery of new insights or data that were the unintended consequences of scientific experiments focusing on something entirely different. Early use of "serendipity" treated the discovery as an end in itself. But Cannon focused on serendipitous encounters that catalyzed whole new avenues of inquiry and thus were just the beginning of, rather than an end to, a discovery process. More recently, the term has been used for unexpected encounters with people. For us, it is this expanded usage of serendipity that is the most relevant to our exploration of attraction.

We need serendipitous encounters with people because of the importance of the ideas that these people carry with them and the connections they have. People carry tacit knowledge. You can't learn brain surgery just from a text. Nor can you learn how to make tasty home brew without watching someone else carry out the process. In both cases, you've got to stand next to someone who already knows and learn by doing. Tacit knowledge exists only in people's heads. As edges arise ever more quickly, all of us must not only find the people who carry this new knowledge but get to know them well enough (and provide them with sufficient reciprocal value) that they're comfortable trying to share it with us. This helps to explain a contemporary pattern taking place in new areas of human endeavor: Conferences spring up to accommodate the desire of participants to share stories about their experiences with like-minded people. Whether it is the Internet, biotechnology, or alternative technology, just to name a few current examples, conferences abound. As of this writing, there are eight conferences alone scheduled during the next twelve months specifically on the use of Twitter as a social-networking platform. It is no accident that our friend Yossi Vardi participates in or organizes thirty to forty conferences per year in areas relevant to his interests.

Conferences in emerging arenas are a great example of how serendipitous encounters can work—and of how we can shape them. There, we interact with people we never knew before who were drawn to the same venue because of similar interests and experiences. Conversations that begin in the hallways and dining rooms of these conferences often are the starting point for relationships that, as they build, help us to access the tacit knowledge of people who are exploring similarly uncharted territory. This process can unfold entirely unexpectedly. "It was a casual meeting at a conference," Yossi recalls about how he later came to invest in a company called FoxyTunes. "And the whole relationship started from there."[8]

In this context, serendipitous encounters with people prove to be far more fruitful than an isolated encounter with new objects or data. We not only have the opportunity to access the tacit knowledge other people have gained from their experiences—and to share our own— but can begin to create relationships that may themselves spawn new tacit knowledge as we begin to collaborate on areas of shared interest. Serendipity becomes much more than a one-time encounter or an end in itself: It becomes the crucial means of access to rich flows of tacit knowledge both now and in the future.

From our perspective, attraction is particularly powerful when it leads to serendipitous encounters with people on the edge—and then to long-term relationships with them. This form of attraction offers privileged access to tacit knowledge and rare insight into new opportunities. It also lowers our risk. Think about it: If you're exploring a new territory—an edge—it's very helpful to learn from the experience of others in similar contexts. Serendipitous encounters thus help amplify our efforts by connecting us with our fellow explorers— exactly the people who can help us in our own explorations. Maybe you've been hired as the "change agent" at a traditional corporation, with your role to help the company expand its understanding—and use—of social media. You're bringing the edge to the core. But to you, at least, the core in this case will, paradoxically, have "edgy" characteristics that will be new to you. How do they do things around here? How do decisions get made? How can you best build momentum toward the new? One way would be to look for external conferences attended by people who are exactly in your situation: the "Change Agent Conference."[9] That could help with the more generalized versions of your questions. Another way would be to draw toward you the "renegades" within the corporation who have, in their own roles, been trying to steer the corporation toward the new. It is likely they will have valuable tacit knowledge for you to learn from and questing dispositions that may help you on your own quest.

Simply by registering for a conference in a given area of interest, we are increasing the probability of a serendipitous encounter that will prove both relevant and valuable to us. We still cannot anticipate whom we will meet or what they will know, except in the broadest possible terms, but we have increased the probability of serendipity. We have filtered the population at large down to those most likely to share our interests and passions—and those most likely to carry the tacit knowledge we need and to need the tacit knowledge we carry. Even in the earliest examples of serendipity—the bibliophile entering an antiquarian bookshop—the beneficiary of a serendipitous encounter was shaping the probability of such an encounter by entering the bookshop in the first place. The likelihood of a serendipitous discovery of an unknown book would be materially lower if the bibliophile were in a butcher shop. This observation may seem self-evident, but there are lots of people who, despite having dropped their car keys in the dark parking lot, are still looking for them under the lamp.

All of which raises a primary point: Serendipity can be shaped, at least within limits. There will always be an element of luck and the unexpected, but our actions can materially alter the probabilities of valuable encounters. Given these requirements for making attraction an effective form of discovering the things we didn't know we didn't know, a problem arises: How can we possibly have enough time to put this into practice? There are only twenty-four hours in the day. Worse yet, the more effective we are in attracting the attention of large groups of people, the more challenging it becomes as these people seek us out and want to interact with us. We can easily become overwhelmed with the throngs lined up at our door. We will be consumed in meetings and communication and never find the time to build on the new insights and knowledge we are encountering. How do we avoid getting so overwhelmed by what we've set in motion that, like Garbo, we only want to be left alone?

To master attraction, we need two elements to come together in a powerful and reinforcing way. First, we need amplifiers that can help us reach and connect to large groups of people around the globe that we do not yet know (and may not even be aware exist). These amplifiers relate to our choice of where to live, what gatherings we attend, how we conduct ourselves online, and what we do to draw the attention of others. Second, we need filters that can help us to increase the quality as well as the number of unexpected encounters and ensuing relationships that are truly the most relevant and valuable. These filtering techniques help separate the wheat from the chaff in our interactions with others and become ever more crucial as we begin serendipitously drawing more people toward us. By simultaneously amplifying (to increase the sheer number of unexpected encounters) while filtering (to spend time only on those interactions that yield value to us and to others), we can shape serendipity in order to attract from the edges of our fast-moving world the people and knowledge we need in order to thrive.

SHAPING SERENDIPITY: ENHANCING THE PRODUCTIVITY OF ATTENTION

Mirabilis, the company in which Yossi Vardi was a founding investor, invented ICQ, the first global instant-messaging application. Ironically enough, however, you won't find Yossi actually using ICQ—because of what happens when he becomes visible there.

Yossi is so well known that as soon as he sticks his head up on ICQ he can do nothing else but reply to the many messages he receives. "When I open ICQ I get so many messages that I have to hide," says Yossi, who does respond to all his phone and e-mail messages. "I am known by too many people and I simply cannot manage it. It's invasive."[10]

Few of us are as well known as Yossi Vardi. But it's not hard to imagine any of us, as we seek out multiple relevant edges and try to build relationships there, becoming consumed with random encounters that yield only limited value and, at the extreme, becoming so distracted that these encounters become scourges rather than boons.

We need to find ways to enhance the productivity of attention, increasing not just the number but the relevance of our serendipitous encounters. Earlier in this chapter, we suggested that we can shape serendipity rather than treating it as a matter of pure chance. Of course, there will still be the completely unexpected encounters that we did nothing to promote, but there is much that we can do to increase the probability and quality of these encounters. In a world where attraction and return on attention—defined as the value gained relative to the time and attention invested—are becoming increasingly important, those who master the techniques required to shape serendipity will likely profit far more than those who simply wait for it to surface.

Pull is not a spectator sport. The choices each of us makes about the environments we participate in and the practices and behaviors we choose to pursue once we're there will make a crucial difference in what we'll experience and the extent to which we can shape these experiences or simply let random experiences shape us.

Shaping serendipity requires bringing together three elements: environments, practices, and preparedness. Appropriately orchestrated to control the interactions between them, these elements can yield a much higher productivity of attention than we can achieve without them, especially as we focus on the following goals:

- Choosing environments that increase our likelihood of encountering people who share our passions
- Becoming and staying visible to the people who matter most
- Influencing their endeavors so they amplify our own
- Discovering and interacting with the right people at the right times (timeliness)
- Making the most of every serendipitous encounter (relevance).

These goals suggest a serendipity funnel that can be managed to make a diverse group of potentially relevant parties aware of one's efforts while simultaneously filtering the actual encounters, so that the probability of a high-quality serendipitous encounter goes way up. If the funnel is not wide enough at the start, we risk failing to become aware of potential encounters that could be extremely high in value. If the funnel remains too wide at the other end, we run the risk of becoming inundated with encounters that have only marginal value. In either case, our productivity of attention suffers. Managing the balance across the funnel is key to shaping serendipity so that productivity of attention rises. Greater productivity then enables us to scale serendipity by increasing our availability for a larger number of the serendipitous encounters that deliver the most value.

You can't just attend a conference and expect pull to occur. You'll likely have to change your approaches and practices, not to mention your mindset (or what Lucy Kellaway creation Martin Lukes calls your "headset"[11]). Yossi doesn't just engage in idle chat about the weather or the football league tables or politics. He uses "deep listening" to draw out and uncover the big issues and difficulties the other person is wrestling with, then he shares his own. If there's a fit between them, Yossi and his discussion partner quickly get into mutual problem solving, into a knowledge-creating mode, just as if they were two home brewers discussing how long to roast the hops. The subject of the discussion might be anything. How best to interest a group of relevant investors in a browser extension that just might make everybody millions of dollars. How to create a heavy tremolo effect in a music remix with just the right amount but not too much reverb. How to best wean the world from hydrocarbons. In each case, if the right combination of pull approaches is practiced, a kind of scaffolding emerges between the participants in which everybody learns faster and the performance of everybody involved goes up at a more rapid rate that it would have for any of them alone.

Serendipitous Environments

Through most of human history, people were prisoners of their environment. People were born in a specific geography and, with few exceptions, lived there throughout their lives. As transportation costs and travel times steadily declined, people began to move more freely, and today many of us live in a number of different places over the course of our lives. Some of us, such as Yossi Vardi and Joi Ito, have become perpetual nomads, moving restlessly from one city to the next, rarely stopping long enough to catch our breath, much less settle in. In an interesting reversal, an increasing number of people appear to be reverting to the hunter-gatherer lifestyle of our distant ancestors. Only this time, rather than limiting themselves to one forest or even continent, this new generation of hunter-gatherers operates on a global scale. And they're looking for new relationships and knowledge.

Unlike our ancestors, we have increasing flexibility to choose our virtual environments and can amplify our ability to connect with people globally in ways that even the most dedicated road warrior could not hope to replicate. In one of the many paradoxes of our digital era, the growing availability of rich virtual environments has combined with increasing mobility across physical geographies to create powerful reinforcing loops. Rather than diminishing the need or desire to travel, our digital infrastructures appear to be accompanied by significant increases in travel activity.[12] Conversely, increases in travel activity appear to spur more virtual connectivity as we seek to maintain contact with the people we encounter in our travels. It is no accident that constant travelers such as Yossi Vardi and Joi Ito are deeply immersed in selected virtual environments. The physical and virtual worlds are not an either/or proposition but rather a question of how best to structure both environments to shape serendipity. One enhances the other—they're complements, not replacements.

Geographic spikes. Let's start with physical environments. Here's a paradox: The world is getting flatter by the day as the digital infrastructure helps us to connect with any person or resource wherever it exists in the world. At the same time, though, the movement of people into large urban areas is accelerating. In fact, last year we passed a significant global milestone. More people now live in large urban centers than in any other part of our vast globe. Major new geographic spikes of specialized talent surface with greater frequency and expand at a faster rate than ever before, especially in rapidly developing economies such as China and India, where cities like Bangalore, Shenzhen, and Chonqing are attracting more and more talented people. If distance no longer matters, in this digitally connected and flat world, why is this happening?

In a world of intensifying competition, people seem to be seeking out environments where they can get better faster. These geographic spikes offer a wealth of employment options where ambitious and passionate employees can quickly change jobs and find employers more willing than the previous one to develop their talent. These cities also become geographic gathering spots for specialized service providers and other resources that can help talented people become even more successful.

But there is something else more subtle at work here. These geographic spikes become rich environments for increasing the quality and probability of serendipitous encounters. If you are a talented software engineer, would you be more likely to run into someone who shares your passions and aspirations in Fort Shawnee, Kansas, or in Silicon Valley? If you are an aspiring actor, are you more likely to run into a producer or director in Los Angeles or in Oshkosh, Wisconsin? People intuitively realize that serendipity operates much better in relevant geographic spikes. This may help to explain why, as our 2009 Shift Index documented, the top twenty creative cities in the United States are growing at a much faster clip than the bottom twenty creative cities in the United States.[13] So, this is one important choice that will have a significant role in shaping serendipity—choosing where to live.

Serendipity can be even further increased by identifying complementary geographic spikes around the world and consciously seeking to spend more time across these spikes. This principle, for example, helps to explain the flow of people across three very diverse geographic spikes—Silicon Valley, Bangalore, and Tel Aviv—each focused on a somewhat different dimension of software development. These people, in turn, are spending an increasing amount of time in places such as Seoul, Shenzhen, and Helsinki where wireless hardware access devices are being spawned. Yossi Vardi chooses to live in Tel Aviv for personal reasons—it's where his heart is at home. Fortunately for his career, it also happens to be a hotbed of technology entrepreneurship. But it's not the only one. And that's why he travels so frequently and seems to be especially drawn to other spikes of entrepreneurial and technological talent around the world.

Note that what brings people together in a geographic spike is a shared passion. That's the unifying force. Shared passion, however, does not imply uniformity. Spikes in fact consist of considerable cognitive diversity: different ways of seeing the world, solving problems, and so on.[14] Take Silicon Valley, where we live, for example. Geeks and nerds abound, all drawn to the area by a shared passion for technology. Yet they came from different parts of the country, and even the world (over half of the entrepreneurs in Silicon Valley were born outside the United States). They went to many different schools. They are working on very different technology problems, ranging from how to fit more transistors on a silicon chip to user experiences in virtual environments. As a result, the bars and meeting rooms are marked by spirited arguments over the right approaches to difficult technology problems, but the friction remains largely productive because all the participants share a common passion for pushing the technology envelope.

Conferences. The movement to and across geographic spikes can be augmented in another, more transient physical environment—conferences. As discussed earlier in this chapter, conferences become important gathering spots on emerging edges where people perceive an urgent need to come together with others to share experiences and connect, jointly addressing the challenges and opportunities arising on the edge. Of course, as conferences proliferate on the edge, quality becomes very uneven, and relatively few end up being truly valuable gathering spots. Yossi calls them a "moving circus." At the worthwhile conferences, there is certainly substantial value in the way the formal sessions of conferences structure presentations and conversations around common areas of interests—but often, the greatest value of these conferences does not occur in the meeting rooms. Rather, the true value for many participants comes from the unexpected encounters and conversations in the hallway with people who turn out to have very common experiences and interests. These conversations often lead to sustained collaboration well beyond the end of the conference.

Yossi Vardi has this whole conference approach down cold. When he arrives, he walks the halls to try to create possibilities, opportunities to interact with people. "I don't sit in the lecture," he says, "or even in the lecture hall. I just hang around in the lobby, where everybody is saying, 'serendipity should be somewhere here, let's dig for it.'"[15]

Conferences are useful first because the participants have self-filtered, so to speak, by their decision to attend the conference in the first place, and second, by the simple device of name tags, or badges. In everyday life, approaching someone you don't know and have never met requires a very delicate protocol—even if you're sitting next to him or her on an airplane. "You have to get eye contact and you have to do a gesture so that the other person sees that you want to talk to them," says Yossi. Then you have to evaluate the reaction to that gesture and then, only after a very delicate dialogue of body language and other cues, can you talk to them."[16]

At conferences, however, there is a simple way around all that delicate protocol—the name tag, or badge. Badges act as ice breakers between people who don't yet know each other. "The name badge is actually an open door," says Yossi. "It projects to other people an invitation: 'Hey, I'm Yossi, I'm in the conference, and this badge allows you to come up and talk to me.'"[17]

Any of us when we leave a conference receive a jarring reminder of just how open this invitation can be when strangers on the street greet us by name—and we realize we've forgotten to take off the name tag. A friend calls these "mug me" tags precisely for this reason.

So if participants have self-selected, and fastened a name tag to their lapel, does that mean our encounters with them are completely unexpected? At one level, the answer is certainly yes—the specific person or topic of conversation often proves to be completely surprising. At another level, though, the answer is more nuanced. The probability and quality of these encounters was significantly enhanced by the choice of a specific conference to attend. A researcher in physics is much more likely to have quality encounters at a scientific conference than at a tour operators' conference, and vice versa. We can significantly shape serendipity by choosing to attend more conferences—and by carefully choosing the specific conferences we will attend to enhance the potential for the most relevant encounters. In essence, conferences are a filter for the broader world.

Online social networks. Virtual environments also provide potential to shape serendipity. Social networks such as Facebook, LinkedIn, and MySpace have become increasingly helpful environments for serendipitous encounters. Many of us are familiar with the unexpected invitation to join a social network by someone whom we did not yet know but who turned out to be very relevant to our current interests. Other times we discover that someone we know in one context has another set of interests that prove even more valuable. This recently happened to us when a woman we knew as a private equity investor in Silicon Valley turned out to also have deep experience and insight into Chinese social-network practices. Our discovery of this other dimension occurred through a casual comment she posted on one of our social-network profile pages, reacting to an observation we had made about network practices of Chinese businesses. Similarly, we have also had the experience of reviewing one of our friend's profile pages and running across a particularly insightful comment from one of his friends whom we had not yet met; once the initial discovery had been made, we introduced ourselves and explored areas of mutual interest.

These serendipitous encounters multiply as more people join social networks and contribute richer and more textured knowledge, comments, observations, and other content, all of which give us increasing clues regarding their potential relevance. Furthermore, because the leading social-network platforms are expanding their capability to engage participants on a broad range of third-party websites, the scope of serendipitous encounters is expanding significantly.

The downside to all of this, as mentioned earlier, is that as the number of participants increases, the potential for low-productivity serendipitous encounters grows as well, creating a need for more tools to manage the quantity and quality of these encounters. We do have some such tools: Reputation systems and social-network analysis tools, for example, might provide us with important indicators regarding which initial contacts to pursue and which ones to ignore or to only marginally invest in.

We can also shape serendipity by carefully choosing the social-network platforms we join. Most of today's online social networks are broad and relatively undifferentiated. As they expand and evolve, they will most likely begin to specialize around specific interests, spawning a whole new generation of more focused online social networks addressing the needs of specific segments of the population. (Indeed, the social network Ning allows members to create subnetworks around their passions and interests.) These will in turn establish a loose federation with other complementary online social networks to enhance the potential for connections across domains. The surfers will cross-pollinate with the snowboarders. The foodies will intermingle with the oenophiles. Just as with conferences, we want to seek out the online social networks that help us enhance the relevance of serendipitous encounters.

Connection platforms. Online social networks generally start with the assumption that they are attracting people in existing networks of relationships—relationships that were formed in the physical world—while at the same time offering the prospect of being able to expand one's network, after joining the online social network, through serendipitous encounters. Another type of environment, what we call a "connection platform," begins with a different assumption. Connection platforms help people connect serendipitously around needs.

Most electronic markets—from Amazon.com to eBay—would fit this description of a connection platform, because they bring together people who don't necessarily know each other so that they can enact an economic transaction. But this market-based connection is a very narrow form of serendipity, rarely leading to the kinds of relationships that spawn continuing and unexpected additional value over time for the participants. There are more specialized platforms that focus on connecting people who do not yet know each other. Many open innovation platforms (such as InnoCentive) and a host of open-source software sites—such as SAP's Developer Network—provide a way for people with specific needs or problems to attract the people best suited to solving them, even if these people were completely unknown to each other at the outset and very difficult to find through conventional search.

These sites specialize in building awareness of searcher needs among solvers while providing incentives and protocols to help the most promising solvers to surface and connect with the searchers. As with many serendipitous encounters, the serendipity is one-sided. In these platforms, the solvers deliberately seek out the searchers whose needs they can address. From the perspective of the searcher, however, the encounter is serendipitous: The searcher had no awareness of the solver and is often surprised to discover the source of the solution. Of course, as with conferences, the encounter is not completely unexpected from the viewpoint of the searcher, either. Searchers participate in these connection platforms precisely in the hope that they'll encounter someone who can solve their problem. But they never know for sure if they will encounter that person or not, or who that person might be. Searchers use these platforms to increase the probability and quality of such encounters. Once again, careful consideration is required: Which connection platforms offer the greatest potential of enhancing the probability and quality of encounters? But there is little doubt that these connection platforms can significantly increase this probability and quality.

Although these sites are operated for the broader objectives of corporations, they provide considerable opportunities and benefits for individuals. Many of the participants on InnoCentive's connection platform are freelance researchers making a living solving other people's problems. Connection platforms give the lone researcher greater reach into a rich and diverse set of problems from which to pick and choose those best suited to their skills and passions. SAP's Developer Network also supports the needs of individuals working on their own—such as free-agent software developers—who learn faster and perform better as a result of their participation.

Institutions. We have discussed a series of environments—both physical and virtual—that can significantly enhance the probability and quality of serendipitous encounters. These environments all have elements in common: They engage participants who work at a wide variety of institutions or on their own, and they focus largely on connecting individuals rather than institutions.

What role can institutions play in all of this? Push-based institutions are the antithesis of serendipity. In a world of carefully scripted push programs, unexpected encounters are generally treated as signs of inefficiency and worrisome unpredictability. The enclosed conference room with carefully selected participants and tight agendas presumes to keep people on their assigned tracks.

But there is an alternative. Institutions should aim to themselves become "platforms" to amplify networks of social and professional relationships for their employees. They can not only replicate the virtual platforms described above—social-network and connection platforms—but can make it easier and less expensive for their employees to participate on these external platforms as well. Where necessary, they can become catalysts to form new platforms to engage third parties that would be particularly relevant for their employees—as SAP did with its Developer Network. Many of the technology companies have developed rich virtual platforms to bring together their own software engineers with those of their customers and channel partners, helping them to discover others who can be helpful when they run into software-programming or software-implementation issues.

In terms of physical environments, institutions will need to develop explicit spike strategies, identifying the geographic spikes that exist or are emerging and drawing together pools of talent that are most relevant to the initiatives of the institution. Institutions will then need to develop approaches to participating in these spikes in ways that enhance the potential for serendipitous encounters and the development of appropriate connections across spikes. For many larger firms there is even the potential to help accelerate the formation of an emerging geographic spike in talent arenas most relevant to the institution.

On a different level, institutions will need to develop conference strategies by more proactively identifying the most promising conferences for their employees to attend. Today, most institutions focus on the conferences that can be most helpful for building awareness of their products and services and attracting prospective employees. But when it comes to conferences designed to improve the professional development, capabilities, and performance of their existing employees, most institutions leave it up to the employee to identify these venues and make the case for their participation. While employee initiative is certainly a rich way to identify potential conference venues to enhance serendipitous encounters, institutions can do a lot more to bring the most promising venues to the attention of relevant employees and to encourage these employees to attend.

By recognizing the importance of attraction and serendipitous encounters, institutions can themselves play an organizing and supporting role with regard to serendipity, effectively enhancing their employees' access to physical and virtual environments designed to shape serendipity and helping to integrate them into their lives. As they become more adept at this, they will attract more passionate applicants for new jobs as word spreads. Data from our 2009 Shift Index suggested that passionate employees are far more likely than employees who are less passionate about their work to seek out and participate in environments in which serendipity can be shaped.[18] A virtuous cycle can be brought into play as institutions learn how to help employees participate in these environments. This cycle will attract more passionate employees, whose passion will in turn create even greater levels of participation in these environments, attracting another wave of passionate employees and repeating the cycle.

That virtuous cycle is what this book aims to help people create, and there are practices that both individuals and institutions can pursue to increase the likelihood that virtuous cycles will emerge.

Serendipitous Practices

If online social networks are so terrific, what should we make of the reluctant people who, at the urging of friends, family, and colleagues, finally join a social network, only to abandon it a few weeks later with an abrupt dismissal? It may be that this person had yet to grasp the practices required to harness the potential of the environment, or grasped them but held back anyway. Even those of us who understand the basic norms and behaviors—such as the need for authenticity and reciprocity in postings[19]—likely still have much to learn to find out how we can improve the number and quality of our serendipitous encounters—both on and offline.

Note that this is far from a cold calculus about costs and benefits. Those who truly thrive in social networks have a crucial talent for friendship, an open-hearted authenticity that shines through in their interactions with others. Perhaps more importantly, they have a passion for their endeavors that leads them to actively seek out and use social networks to declare what they love and to expand that passion through their encounters and relationships with people who share their passions.

Attracting attention. A tricky balancing act is required to attract attention in ways that are most likely to draw out the most productive serendipitous encounters. There are real pitfalls here. On one hand, if we attract too much attention, the serendipity funnel becomes too wide, quickly becoming flooded with low-quality encounters that consume scarce resources and distract attention from encounters of potentially higher value. We become like Yossi Vardi when he signs on to ICQ. On the other hand, if we get too narrowly focused we run the risk of diminishing the diversity often required to generate the most productive encounters. A study of InnoCentive's record in connecting searchers with solvers suggested that the solutions were much more likely to come from people in unrelated disciplines than from people in the same discipline as the searcher.[20] This is not just a problem for those at the top of organizations. Think of the power computer user whose reputation draws more and more people to her, making it difficult to get work done as she becomes consumed in mundane questions from more casual computer users.

Segmenting the most promising sources of serendipitous encounters helps both individuals and institutions to determine focused strategies for attracting and engaging people from these segments. Typically the most productive way to attract attention is to start contributing to existing environments where these segments of the population and their influencers spend their time. By beginning to build a reputation for being helpful, either by resolving existing problems or providing insights that suggest new opportunities, individuals can begin to attract attention from people that matter. The goal at this point is not to generate serendipitous encounters; it is merely to draw out the potential for such encounters by becoming known as a helpful and insightful contributor. As one becomes known in that environment, one draws the attention of promising individuals. At this point, the individual attracting attention has little sense of the identities of these other individuals but instead focuses merely on attracting people with promising profiles to pay attention.

Lowering barriers to attention. Attracting attention is heavily influenced by three elements: how much time and effort people must invest to pay attention to us, how much value they receive in return, and how quickly they receive that value. One of the key barriers to attention is findability. If we are hard to find, others will likely soon give up rather than investing the effort required to locate us. Peter Morville's insightful book *Ambient Findability* explains both the importance of findability and the techniques required to reduce the barrier to attention created by low findability.[21] He points out that creators of websites often make large investments to increase the usability of their Internet platforms but ignore that fact that usability matters little if findability is a challenge. Those who cannot find you will not be able to use your resources anyway. The same goes for our accomplishments and endeavors as individuals. If they're invisible to others, they have much less value than if they are on display in some way.

Jack Hidary, who built his career as an entrepreneur in the finance and technology sectors and currently focuses on clean energy technology and policy, likens the notion of findability to "sending out beacons" as if you were on a ship at sea and wanted other ships to find you for some reason. For example, maybe you want to exchange food or information with someone, or perhaps your ship needs a part for repairs. You send out beacons in many directions, and you send them out frequently. A beacon this way. A beacon that way. And so on, until you receive an answer.

"If you've ever been at sea at night," says Hidary, "you know that a ship can have a super bright beacon, but if it's not pointing in the direction of that other ship they're not going to see it. That's why it's really important to have multiple beacons."[22]

Sending out beacons increases our findability. Talking about our passions, in person or online, is one way to do it. Hidary writes a column for the *Huffington Post*. He also puts up simple websites organized around particular topics—such as clean technology—and tries to make them findable by search engines. "We often create websites that are four or five pages, very quick to put up," he says. "It takes us a day or two and we update them every few months."[23] One example is AmericansForCleanEnergy.com. SmartTransportation.org—which focuses on converting the taxi fleet in New York City to hybrid vehicles—is another.

These beacons work. People end up calling in or e-mailing. Maybe they'll prove to be donors. Maybe they'll turn out to be employees, or do something else that is useful. In an age of scalable collaboration, it's essential to attract what you need, and beacons are a great way of doing so. "It's not that they find us through an official government website or something like that," says Hidary. "They found us through our beacon. We put a beacon out there and it's an attractor that brings people to that location."[24]

Another challenge is to structure our interactions with the people we encounter so that our "audience" receives quick and tangible value in return for their attention. This motivates people who have sought us out to continue to return on a regular basis. If the value is negligible or takes too long to receive, people will more quickly leave and be less likely to return. Responding to this challenge requires understanding the needs of the people we want to attract and creative approaches to delivering value quickly. If we do not understand what is valued by the people we are seeking to attract (and it is likely to vary depending on the segment), we will have a difficult time determining how to reward them for their attention. Similarly, if we cannot structure interactions to deliver this value to them quickly, we will suffer low rates of conversion from first-time attention "visitor" to sustained attention "provider."

One of the most effective ways to give value quickly is to offer serendipity to those who pay attention. They may have sought us out in the expectation of receiving one type of value, but we have an opportunity to provide them with some unexpected value as well. We might, for example, refer people accessing our own perspectives online to some third-party content in related areas that these people might not have been expecting. By making explicit the potential relationships between the information we can provide and the information provided by others, we can quickly enhance the value we offer to people without investing significant resources of our own. Thus, by offering serendipitous encounters to those whom we attract, we give them even more incentive to seek us out. Note that this practice has been widely adopted in the blogosphere. Many bloggers simply act as filters for good third-party content, reposting it on their own site without adding much more than a comment to it themselves, if even that.

Focusing and teasing for sustained attention. Sustaining the attention of others, once initially earned, requires communicating with people to show them why they should continue to invest their attention. We devote significant effort to attracting the attention in the first place.

If we are only able to retain that attention for a short period, the investments we put into attracting attention will rapidly outpace the value we receive in return for it. This is not very productive.

To avoid this trap, we must give the people in our network a sense of the long-term payoffs they will receive for offering more attention over time. In particular, we need to communicate clearly and compellingly what we are trying to accomplish over the long term. In doing this, we will give those who are following us a better sense of what the long-term rewards might be for developing the relationship. The combination of rapid and tangible value in the short term, plus a growing awareness of the long-term potential, will motivate people to continue to invest in us with their time and attention in a significant way.

We can also playfully appeal to a person's sense of suspense, giving them teasers. Teasers play a powerful yet underappreciated role in retaining attention. They excite the imagination by offering possibilities without revealing everything—the same way that, for example, a good movie preview makes a movie look interesting without containing spoilers. What we hold back can be the most powerful motivator of all. For example, a company might indicate that it is about to release a new product, but only provide a hint regarding the kind of features it might contain. By exciting the imagination and leaving it to each person to make their own interpretation of the possibilities that might be available, we encourage people to tap into their emotions as well as their minds. We also invite them to participate in imagining outcomes that may be quite different from the ones we intended, thus serving as a catalyst for further innovation. Of course, teasing requires balance. If we have a poor record of delivering on these exciting possibilities, people will quickly become frustrated and leave. But with appropriate reinforcement along the way, teasing can powerfully motivate people to pay close attention over long periods of time.

Influencing without contact. The key to scaling serendipity is to postpone the unexpected contacts until the most productive moment. In the meantime, there are opportunities to motivate the people who are paying attention to undertake initiatives on their own that will contribute to the success of our own initiatives. This is a particular skill of people who have emerged as shapers in various areas of the business landscape.

Bill Gates, the founder of Microsoft, did this extremely well. By understanding what motivated a broad range of participants in the technology web that emerged around the Microsoft operating system, he was able to motivate large aggregate investments in software and services by thousands of third parties to support that system. He was successful in motivating third parties to invest aggressively in ways that made his system more valuable than others. The third parties delivered an ever-expanding array of products and services that could only be accessed with his system. When these third parties had a compelling need, or something particularly powerful to offer Microsoft, they could reach out to Microsoft. This would typically be a high-quality encounter, as Microsoft succeeded in creating an environment that motivated third parties to pursue opportunities without burdening its employees with large incremental investments of time.

Once again, though, this requires balance. Creating an environment in which large numbers of participants can go off and invest and innovate in support of one's own initiatives might minimize one's own investments and provide maximum leverage—but it also reduces, if not eliminates, the potential for serendipitous encounters. Serendipitous encounters are valued because they can often be catalysts for the creation of new knowledge. As a result, influence needs to be managed to encourage encounters when the need or opportunity is great but also to ensure that maximum preparation has been made by the other party before initiating contact and making the introduction. If the other party has made significant investments and learned a lot from experience before contacting the influencer, the serendipitous encounter will offer that much more value to the influencer. Serendipity will also scale more readily, since less time is consumed with low-value serendipitous encounters.

Exposing surfaces. Some serendipitous practices will necessarily push us out of our comfort zone. Jack Hidary thinks about this as "exposing surfaces." The metaphor comes from the Glycemic Index of foods—a measure of how quickly carbohydrates affect blood-sugar levels. It turns out that some foods have a higher glycemic index than others in part because they have more surface area exposed to stomach acids. Thus they deliver sugar faster.

"How many surface areas do you have?" Jack likes to ask.[25] Maybe you're a consultant who works with only one client a year. Maybe you only read science fiction. Maybe you only like French food and rarely try other kinds. Maybe you're politically progressive and never read other political points of view. In all of these cases you've limited your surface area. You're not exposed to a wide range of circumstances and experiences. And your chances of thinking out of the box and spotting trends early are accordingly limited.

According to Hidary, most people become too dependent on one facet of their lives. And when one facet takes up 80 percent of somebody's total exposed surface area, they tend to become defensive around it, protective. They become "experts." They treat what they know as a stock rather than a flow, and they tend to isolate themselves from flows of new knowledge and the people creating them. "Why do people overlook very obvious situations?" asks Jack. "Because people sometimes paint themselves into a corner such that their entire interaction with the outside world is mediated through this one facet. Then they're unable to critically analyze where they are. That's how they end up going down with the ship."[26] In other words, people can be so unaware of their own dispositions that they're victims to their underlying assumptions.

So how do we expose more of our surfaces? We've already seen how Yossi Vardi parks himself in the lobby at big conferences to make himself accessible to the beneficial effects of serendipity. Jack Hidary adds an enhancement to that approach by actually going to conferences— or breakouts within larger conferences—that are devoted to topics he knows nothing about. That's how he ended up getting involved in clean technology. He was attending the Socrates seminars at the Aspen Institute and on a whim wandered into a presentation being made at an Aspen Energy Forum in the same building. At first he sat in the back, listening to what seemed like a foreign language—a set of acronyms and jargon particular to the people familiar with the energy domain. Gradually he began talking to the other participants, learning, making connections between energy and what he knew from other domains. Just a few years later he was co-chairing the renewables track of that particular forum and coining his own additions to the list of acronyms and jargon.

Not that he stopped there. Jack combined what he learned from exposing himself to energy and transportation experts to help Richard Branson and others create a "carbon war room" that acts as a platform for other entrepreneurs to get serious (mostly by donating money) about helping humans go beyond the carbon economy into various forms of alternative energy. This platform combines, in very simple fashion, a number of social media and other resources needed to help mount "guerrilla warfare": the ability to quickly pick battles that matter, to prevail in them—mostly by using social media to, first, sway public opinion, and second, to influence legislators, policy-makers, and big institutions—and then to move on to the next battle. Note that although Hidary is an entrepreneur, this is not an entrepreneurial business or even a business at all. It's not a non-governmental organization, or NGO, either. It doesn't fit neatly into any of the categories we might apply. It's simply Jack, a few twenty-somethings who either code software or perform analysis (for instance, on how many cars it takes to match the emissions of one container ship), a bunch of donors (most of them entrepreneurs), and a handful of websites that help support and organize a "guerrilla warfare" effort that simply wouldn't be possible without the digital infrastructure.

Jack uses social media to mobilize not just donors but also government officials, journalists, Facebook supporters, and NGO staffers behind particular causes, such as the "cash-for-clunkers" initiative he co-organized in the summer of 2009 and the "smart transportation" initiative aimed at getting the New York City taxi fleet converted to hybrid vehicles. The idea for cash for clunkers—in which the U.S. government offered citizens money to trade in their gas guzzlers for more fuel-efficient models—started off as a white paper written by Hidary and a colleague at the Center for American Progress utilizing data from the American Council for an Energy-Efficient Economy, which they then managed to get read by key staffers and influencers on Capitol Hill. Eventually it got signed into law by President Obama.

The lesson? One can cause much to unfold simply by exposing new surfaces. "Just put yourself in a completely different context around people who are deeply expert in their sector," recommends Jack. "Once you're surrounded by them, you're the minority, you are the one who stands out and sticks out and doesn't know anything that's happening. That will get the brain firing and will also lead to all kinds of interesting ideas. You may have a new idea for a new business or a new initiative in your own sector based on the model that you're seeing in this sector."[27]

Beginner's mind. What Jack's doing, in effect, is forcing himself to practice what Zen practitioners call "beginner's mind," an attitude that in Abbess Zenkei Blanche Hartman's words is "innocent of preconceptions and expectations, judgements and prejudices." Hartman wrote: "Beginner's mind is just present to explore and observe and see 'things as-it-is.' I think of beginner's mind as the mind that faces life like a small child, full of curiosity and wonder and amazement. 'I wonder what this is? I wonder what that is? I wonder what this means?' Without approaching things with a fixed point of view or a prior judgment, just asking 'what is it?'"[28]

Practicing this type of awareness involves shutting off some of the distracting and often skeptical voices in our heads that would have us prejudge, preconceive, and turn away from new things before we understand them. We have to be willing to risk looking like we don't know the answer, or maybe even the question. We've got to wean ourselves from overdependence on the expertise we've labored so hard to accumulate. To paraphrase Albert Einstein, we must avoid letting our education interfere with our learning.

Serendipitous Preparedness

We can do everything right in terms of picking fertile, serendipitous environments and refining the appropriate serendipity practices described in the previous section. But if we're not prepared when that unexpected encounter occurs, the encounter will yield only marginal value, if any. By enhancing preparedness, it is possible to further shape serendipity in the sense of maximizing the value generated from every unexpected but potentially beneficial encounter. The first two elements in shaping serendipity—serendipitous environments and serendipitous practices—are primarily focused on ensuring that unexpected encounters, when they occur, have the highest potential quality. The challenge at that point is addressed by the third element—a preparedness designed to take full advantage of the opportunities when they occur. Preparation entails a combination of disposition and skills.

Disposition. Disposition is a difficult concept to pin down. Many people use the term loosely to describe attitudes, worldviews, skills, or propensities to act. We use it more specifically to draw attention to largely unexamined or unquestioned orientations to the world that shape how we approach it. For many people, the unexpected is threatening—it disrupts the perceived order of things and often prevents us from executing our plans. For others, the unexpected is exciting—it represents an opportunity to innovate, learn, and push our performance to new levels. The latter disposition, which in other contexts we have described as an element of the "gamer disposition,"[29] helps people to be open to serendipitous encounters. They're more favorably "disposed" toward the unexpected.

Dispositions are deeply unconscious. In this sense, you don't choose your disposition; instead it is an underlying orientation toward action that evolves over time. But it is possible to become aware of your disposition toward the unexpected and begin to intentionally change the way you respond. One way to speed this evolution is to take yourself to the edge and engage with edge participants in addressing challenging performance issues. Don't simply hang out in the core.

It also helps to pursue a passion. When we pursue our passions, we tend to exhibit questing dispositions. We are constantly scanning the horizon for new challenges to pursue and seek out new problems to solve as a way to deepen our skills in the area of passion. In contrast, when we are simply putting in time for a paycheck, we tend to fall back on a more defensive disposition, regarding any unexpected developments as unwelcome and avoiding risk wherever possible.

Exploration and listening skills. One can be open to unexpected encounters and yet not have the skills to take full advantage of them when they occur. We often form an impression of a person quickly—

too quickly—and jump to conclusions about who he or she is and what, if anything, he or she can offer. We need to resist the temptation to categorize and define boundaries before we have enough information. Many of us lack the skills we need to really listen and draw a person out, finding out about his or her full range of experiences and perspectives. Particularly when dealing with tacit knowledge, which is so hard to express, it is essential to cultivate empathy and respect for the other's experiences while probing beneath the surface to render the tacit knowledge a little more visible. That's what Yossi does at conferences. Note that the conversation that takes place is an especially valuable form of flow in that one participant helps the other get more precisely at what is important to them, and vice versa. A mutual discovery takes place—of the self and of the other. What's discovered was previously below the surface, in the depths—that's one reason we call it "deep" listening. Note that the more we're able to quiet the often cacophonous voices in our own heads, the better we're able to practice this skill. Beginner's mind and deep listening go together.

Relationship-building skills. In this context, we also need to cultivate the skills required to develop shared understandings and to build the trust that can become the foundation for productive, long-term relationships. As we suggested earlier, one cannot draw out the full potential of a serendipitous meeting if it remains simply a short and isolated encounter. We need to learn to view these encounters as simply the opening for a much longer-term relationship, one that will enable us not simply to access existing knowledge but to work together more effectively to build new knowledge. Properly configured, these relationships become fertile seedbeds for sustained collaboration and innovation, amplifying the value of the initial encounter.

KNOWLEDGE FLOWS represent extraordinary opportunity. In a world where edges surface and grow rapidly, these knowledge flows provide the key to continually replenishing our knowledge stocks and exploring new forms of innovation. One challenge in an era of proliferating knowledge flows is to figure out which of these knowledge flows provide the most value. We often are not even aware of the full range of knowledge flows available and therefore cannot effectively use search tools and other mechanisms to access the most rewarding ones. We must master a new set of techniques designed to shape serendipity and attract attention in the most productive way possible. These techniques are the key in turning the challenge of knowledge flows into the rich opportunity of knowledge flows. Rather than a source of value destruction, they become a source of value creation.

Once we harness the second level of pull—attracting attention—we can begin to move significantly beyond the rewards of the first level of pull. At the same time, though, this level of pull becomes a foundation for an even greater opportunity—the third level of pull, in which one achieves one's full potential. That is the subject of our next chapter.

BRINGING IT HOME

- Is your current place of residence (city and neighborhood) the most promising place to generate serendipitous encounters with people relevant to your passions or interests?
- What are the five places in the world that would offer the richest opportunities for serendipitous encounters with people who share your passions or interests? How often have you visited these places in the past year?
- How many serendipitous encounters have you had over the past year in the online social networks you participate in? What actions could you take to increase the likelihood and quality of serendipitous encounters in these networks over the next year?
- What effort have you made to build sustaining relationships with the people you have met in serendipitous encounters over the past year? Do you give at the same level you receive?
- Of the people you met serendipitously in any venue over the past year, how many of these people have you actually engaged in some joint initiative related to your passions or interests?
- To what extent do the institutions you work for or with help to increase the likelihood of serendipitous encounters within the institution? Across other institutions?

Chapter 4

Achieving Our
Potential—The Highest Level of Pull

‖‖‖‖‖‖‖‖‖‖‖‖‖‖‖‖ ‖ ‖ ‖ ‖ ‖

I n the 1920s, the Wright-Patterson Air Force Base outside Dayton, Ohio, was the manufacturing center for a number of iconic World War I–era airplanes—including the 90-horsepower Curtis "Jenny" that a generation of barnstorming daredevils made famous after the war.

Examining the production data for the Jenny and other planes, a small group of analysts noticed an intriguing trend: The amount of time it took to build a plane was declining by a certain percentage with each doubling in the cumulative units of aircraft produced. The more the engineers and manufacturing teams built, the better they got—and in a predictable way. A variation of this learning curve had actually been first described by Hermann Ebbinghaus, a German psychologist, in the nineteenth century, who focused on the time required to memorize nonsense syllables. The Air Force analysis, however, was the first known effort to apply this concept to commercial activity. In subsequent years, analysts identified other products, such as semiconductors, that seemed to follow a similar pattern.

In the late 1960s, Bruce Henderson, a business strategist and the founder of Boston Consulting Group (BCG), led an effort to systematically quantify this relationship across a broad range of products, including beer and toilet paper as well as machinery and industrial components. The relationship proved remarkably consistent, although the specific rate of performance improvement did vary, ranging anywhere from about a 10 percent to a 30 percent reduction in cost with each doubling in performance. Rebranding this concept as "the experience curve," BCG spelled out the wide-ranging implications of this relationship for business strategy, including the economic importance of market share and the opportunity to build balanced portfolios of business initiatives to effectively leverage the economics of the experience curve.

The idea caught on in a big way among the large corporations that dominated our twentieth-century push economy. Thanks to the experience curve, managers could now conceptualize a relationship between the size and the efficiency of their operations: The bigger a given operation got, the more efficient it became. Scalable efficiency soon became something of a secular religion, with the experience curve as its creed.

Consistent with the focus on scalable efficiency, the experience curve measured cost reduction as the key dimension of performance. It was simple and powerful. But it had one troublesome characteristic. Every experience curve was in the end a diminishing returns curve. The more experience accumulated in a specific industry, the longer it took to get the next increment of performance improvement.

From the viewpoint of the institutional leaders of the time, this was not particularly worrisome. In fact, it had a calming effect. The more mature an industry became—the more it accumulated experience producing and marketing the products that defined the market—the more difficult it became for new entrants to enter. Experience effects led to stability. Institutional leaders could keep their leadership positions safe by continually getting bigger, and reducing costs further, thereby staying at the edge of performance improvement.

There was no need to worry about smaller competitors out on the fringe—fringes were largely destined to become even more marginalized than they were already; operational scale trumped everything else. Fringe players seeking to challenge core players faced a nearly insurmountable obstacle in their efforts to compete with the core—their best hope was to carve out a sustainable but much smaller niche, where they could harness their own experience-curve advantage. The experience curve was the ultimate vindication of push institutions in a push economy.

As for individuals, they had to fit into institutions and adapt to the demands of push-production systems if they wanted to be successful. Individual success came with institutional success, but only if the individual played a carefully scripted role as one (usually tiny) gear in the overall machine. The man in the grey flannel suit and the unionized worker dreaming of early retirement became role models. Retirement, when it finally arrived, was celebrated with the gift of a gold watch, a suitable symbol for the decades ticked away in dreary labor.

This chapter explores the third level of pull—achieving our full potential as individuals and institutions by pulling out of each of us the potential that resides within (see the diagram on the next page). This third level of pull builds upon the first two levels of pull—we can use access and attraction to achieve the potential within ourselves. But it goes one step further, focusing on the techniques required to reach new levels of performance faster and therefore to learn faster by working with others. We make the case that for the first time in history we may have the opportunity to transform diminishing-returns performance curves into increasing-returns performance curves.

We begin by discussing the famous experience curve that describes how firms in the twentieth century improved their performance and the stress that these traditional approaches generated in a world of increasing performance pressure. In such a world, following a different model—and making our passion our profession—can significantly reduce stress. But, as we begin to pursue our passions, we find ourselves participating in platforms that can help us to improve our performance more rapidly than ever before. In particular, we focus on how to develop "creation spaces" that attract performance-driven teams and how to help those teams improve their performance rapidly by fostering rich interactions both within and across teams. These creation spaces are carefully crafted to integrate three elements: participants, interactions, and environments. Although the concept of creation spaces is still quite new, and is still in fact in an early stage of

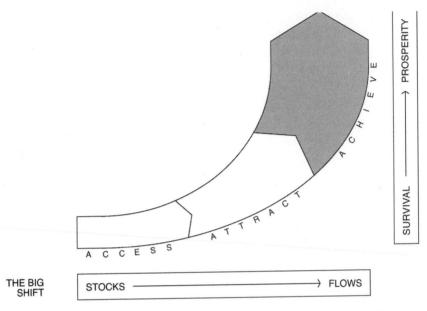

Havilland Studio, Palo Alto, California, and Lahaina, Hawaii

development, early evidence suggests that they drive increasing-returns performance curves so that learning accelerates as more people participate.

So, why does this matter? Performance improvement has always been desirable and, since we first emerged from the forests, we have been on a quest to achieve the potential that each of us believes is within us. What's different now? Once again, we must return to the Big Shift to provide context for why this third level of pull is acquiring new urgency and value.

You'll recall that the first two waves of the Big Shift are creating intensifying competition and growing pressure. As we noted in Chapter 1, the first wave, driven by the deployment of digital infrastructure and public policy shifts toward economic liberalization, reduce barriers to entry and barriers to movement, thereby leading to intensifying competition. The second wave is shaped by the proliferation of knowledge flows, especially within emerging edges and across edge and core boundaries. These richer knowledge flows again help to intensify competition by making it easier to access new ideas on a global scale. In the third wave of the shift, we as individuals and as part of broader institutions begin to find new ways to participate in these knowledge flows to drive performance improvement. Without this third wave, the growing pressure, amplified by proliferating knowledge flows, would rapidly overwhelm us. With this third wave of institutional innovation, we can transform the growing challenges that we all experience into compelling opportunities that can help us to create and capture more and more value.

A NEW IMPERATIVE

In the world of experience curves and diminishing returns, office politics were about as lively as things ever got, for most people at least. But the lack of excitement seemed an acceptable, maybe even a desirable tradeoff for stability.

In the era of the Big Shift, diminishing returns to performance improvement are cause for real concern. As the world speeds up around us and becomes ever less predictable, all of us must run faster and faster just to maintain the same level of performance improvement. We have to work harder and smarter just to hold onto the value created by the labor and capital productivity gains we make; as our Shift Index found, we are still not even staying in the same place in terms of return on assets.[1] This isn't easy or fun: The stress is palpable. "Everybody's nervous, from the highest-level CEOs on down," an executive-search-firm partner told *Portfolio* magazine in 2008.[2] Prozac prescriptions, widely on the rise,[3] back up the impression. Surveys show stress levels going up[4]—for everyone from blue-collar workers buffeted by recessionary cutbacks, "rightsizing," and offshoring to corporate executives facing ever more extreme performance pressures and the prospect of losing their jobs, on average, in four years or less.[5]

Line workers feel it on the shop floor, too, where a study at an automotive plant found, over time, increasing "elevations in all psychological and physiological measurements" of stress.[6] Middle management is also suffering—as millions of clipped *Dilbert* cartoon strips can attest.

Even fast-food workers stress out over low pay and lack of direct control over their working environment.[7]

No small part of the stress comes from the realization that somewhere in the global market for talent there might be someone who can do our job better (and maybe for less pay) than we can. This means that no matter how much education or how many credentials we have, we are continually challenged to improve our performance as the world changes around us. Learning is no longer confined to those early stages of our lives, after which we can harvest its fruits. Learning instead becomes a lifelong journey to help us stay competitive. Said differently, we must be on a permanent quest to achieve the potential that we have within us to respond successfully to unanticipated challenges.

What each of us faces individually, and collectively in institutions, is an unsettling choice: Figure out how to keep learning, at least up to the limits of our potential, or risk becoming increasingly marginalized in a nasty and brutish struggle for survival. That prospect, as it becomes more and more probable and apparent, has a remarkable way of focusing the mind.

Will we react fearfully and cling to our old models for learning and performance improvement? Or will we work together in the creation spaces at the edge to continually learn, grow, develop, and thrive?

The challenge—and the opportunity—is to find a way to turn stress into excitement. How so? By pursuing our passions as our professions, harnessing the power not just of extrinsic rewards, such as a paycheck, but of intrinsic rewards, such as personal growth and satisfaction, as well. In the process, we find we're deeply motivated to get better faster at something that we love.

We become like big wave surfer Steve Pezman, who says, "The ride itself is such a bitchin' feeling. It's so rewarding. It becomes so important to you that it becomes the object around which you plan the rest of your life."[8]

Because they love what they do, surfers like Pezman actually choose to seek out bigger waves and more treacherous breaks, the better to test their abilities. They embrace rather than fear or resent the pressure to improve their performance. They are unstoppable in their quest to achieve their potential. And it isn't for the money, or at least not just for the money. In the words of big-wave pioneer Greg Noll, "Guys say, 'Screw the money, I'm having all the fun I could possibly have spending 8–10 hours a day in the water, doing nothing but surfing my guts out.'"[9]

Not all jobs are as romantically glamorous as surfing. (Maybe not even surfing: Big wave surfers spend their days in cold, shark-infested waters that are among the most dangerous working conditions on the planet.) The point isn't that we should all drop out and be ski or surf bums. The point is that individuals who continue to separate their passions from their professions will find it harder and harder to compete in their professional lives against others who view their work as a passion.

Institutions that fail to motivate their employees to improve performance will also suffer a loss of competitiveness, while those with more passionate employees will generate superior returns to shareholders.[10] As these institutional changes occur, more and more workers will find that, regardless of their job, they can become truly passionate about their work as they are provided with more opportunities to achieve their potential and contribute to the creation of new value.

Now, some might find this an elitist view of work. Of course, creative marketing people or talented software programmers or highly trained chemists can be passionate about their work. But what about janitors, truck drivers, or the assembly-line workers? How will they ever feel passion for the work that they do? As we will explore in a later chapter, these individuals, too, will have an increasing opportunity to become passionate about their work. Most jobs in Western corporations have been engineered (and we use this word advisedly) to become highly routinized, especially if they are not performed by "knowledge workers." As we begin to realize that scalable efficiency cannot see us through a shift to near-constant disruption, we will begin to see that performance improvement by everyone counts, not just performance improvement for "knowledge workers."

We will begin to redefine all jobs, especially those performed at the "bottom of the institutional pyramid," in ways that facilitate problem solving, experimentation, and tinkering. This will foster more widespread performance improvement. Everyone, even the most unskilled worker, will be viewed as a critical problem-solver and knowledge-worker contributing to performance improvement. One need only walk through the assembly lines of a Toyota plant to see highly motivated workers who are passionate about their jobs because they can tangibly see how they are making a difference by tackling challenging work problems and contributing to greater value.

Others will rightly point out that in recessionary times many people may lose their jobs no matter how passionate they might be. This is certainly true. Yet a notable number of people, when the economy nosedives, summon their entrepreneurialism to establish their own businesses—businesses based on what they love to do.[11]

BUILDING UPON PULL PLATFORMS

Contrasting push and pull makes it fairly easy to see which one of them is more effective in helping people to achieve their potential. The role of individuals in these two environments is starkly different. Push programs treat all individuals as consumers—consumers who are supposed to consume resources according to forecast. Push programs actually try to limit consumer choice as much as possible so as to avoid surprises. This applies whether the individual is actually a consumer in the marketplace or an employee working in the firm. Pull platforms, in contrast, treat individuals as creators, providing them with the tools and resources necessary to create new things in response to unanticipated demand. This, too, applies whether the individual is a consumer or an employee. In a pull environment, the consumer has opportunities to tailor the products or services to meet his or her needs.

Rather than prescribing what an individual needs, pull platforms respect the diversity and distinctive needs of each individual and seek to help individuals access and attract the most useful and relevant resources. This approach provides every individual with the degrees of freedom they need to engage in the problem solving, tinkering, and experimentation that drives innovation in all dimensions of activity. In the institutional world, maybe it's finding new ways to collaborate with a key supply partner, or new approaches to providing customer service. For individuals, the tinkering might lead to improvising a new respirator to be used in the basement workshop, as one "steampunk"[12] innovator did when he took a respirator cartridge and hot glued it to the mouthpiece of a diving snorkel.[13] It could be any sort of experimentation that leads to innovation. As individuals innovate, they learn faster, not simply by acquiring previously created knowledge from others, as occurs in push, but by actually creating *new* knowledge from which others can benefit. This dynamic transforms learning from a passive, consumer-style activity to an active endeavor in which the individual is the creator, thus setting in motion a flywheel of beneficial effects. As people innovate and learn faster, they help to generate new waves of performance improvement for everybody while progressing toward their own higher goals.

As we saw in our first few chapters, these pull platforms provide participants with much greater opportunity to engage in the first two levels of pull—access and attraction. One need only look at Google to see a great example of a pull platform that lets people access the information they need when they need it—no matter where it resides on the Internet. One might look at Facebook and other social-network platforms as environments that enhance attraction. Active Facebook users are often approached by people whom they do not know well, or even at all, who turn out to have common interests and complementary capabilities and who prove to be very relevant to the original user. These social networks enhance the potential for serendipity by attracting people to us whom we didn't even know existed and therefore did not know to seek out.

But not all pull platforms effectively support the third level of pull. Many of them have the potential to evolve in this direction, but few are yet the creation spaces that best help participants achieve their potential. Creation spaces help participants engage with each other around collaborative creation activities and, in the process, to build long-term, trust-based relationships. These creation spaces encourage individuals to come together in teams, not only to engage in challenging problem-solving activities within the team but also to create ways for individuals to connect with each other across teams to explore innovative approaches to particularly vexing problems. In the process, they provide robust places for participants to learn rapidly through the creation of new knowledge. Everybody who takes part can achieve their potential by pulling out higher and higher levels of performance.

This kind of dynamic has always been possible in smaller teams and groups. The challenge in designing and managing creation spaces is to provide scalable environments that can accommodate a large and growing number of participants and create the conditions for them to learn faster from each other as the number of participants grows. As we will see, the more participants you add to such a space, the more performance improvement rises. Creation spaces provide the conditions necessary for increasing returns to performance improvement rather than the diminishing returns of the experience curve.

THE NEW CREATION SPACES

Most of the creation spaces that exist today emerged and evolved on the edges of culture and society—even though several of them have millions of participants. Some were started by corporations, such as Blizzard Entertainment, which created World of Warcraft. Not all started out with the intention of making money; however, most—if not all—of the people and institutions in creation spaces do end up deriving commercial value from their participation. Most exist only because some person or group of people with vision and persistence were willing to work outside conventional institutional boundaries. These early instances of creation spaces provide important clues and insights for alert leaders of institutions. And they represent alluring environments for the rest of us as we look to make our passions our professions. We'll discuss three of them here: big wave surfing, online gaming, and commercial software development.

Big Wave Surfing

Although big wave surfing is a global sport, central groups of big wave surfers have migrated over the past sixty years from Southern California to Hawaii. At first blush, this extreme sport appears to be driven by obsessed individuals with a passion for learning how to master ever bigger waves. Looking more closely, though, we see something quite different beginning to emerge.

The performance envelope for big wave surfing is now being pushed by teams of surfers who work closely together over years, rather than by individuals. In large part, this is the result of innovations in tow-in surfing, which requires one or more individuals to operate and maneuver jet skis that tow surfers to locations where they can catch bigger waves. Behind these teams are even broader gatherings of surfers working in tandem with surfboard shapers to push their performance; the improvements come through a complex interplay of elements, including new designs for surfboards and new practices on the waves. Segments of these networks usually begin to form around specific surf breaks. A group of surfers will collectively take on the challenge of riding the particular wave formations that a particular surf break generates. These surfers watch each other experiment and tinker; they offer feedback to one another and learn from their shared experiences. Learning occurs across even broader networks through discussion forums, remote video cams, and surf competitions that bring world-class big wave surfers from around the world to challenge each other at a particular surf break. As surfers bring their practices from their home surf breaks and seek to modify them to address the particular challenge of the competition surf break, new knowledge and practices are generated and shared among a broader set of participants.

One place where this occurred is less than thirty minutes from where we live in California, at a surf break called Mavericks. The waves at Mavericks often reach 50 feet or more, and the rocks underneath are treacherous. When surfers wipe out, the waves crashing down push them 20 to 50 feet under the surface, where the pressure can be strong enough to rupture their eardrums. Once under water, they must quickly figure out which way is up or risk being pinned below the surface for two or even three consecutive waves. World-class big wave surfer Mark Foo drowned here in 1994. Others have lost their lives at Ghost Trees, a powerful surf break just to the south.

In the surfing world, Mavericks is now legendary. The big wave contest held there each winter makes headlines across the globe. But thirty-five years ago, when a local high-school kid by the name of Jeff Clark skipped class to paddle out and brave the menacing swell, Mavericks was pretty much unknown. For fifteen years, Jeff Clark surfed this break alone, unable to convince anyone else to join him. During that period, he began creating the equipment needed to ride these giants and became adept at mastering the powerful waves that surged forward on this break. But he was learning alone. Over time, without a community of fellow big wave surfers with whom to develop his skills, he began to improve more and more slowly, in smaller and smaller increments.

At the same time, a community of enthusiastic big wave surfers had come together in Hawaii. This community was migrating from surf break to surf break, challenging themselves on a variety of increasingly bigger waves—first at Makaha Beach in Oahu; then on the North Shore of that same island, where the swells were more consistent; and next at Waimea Bay, where for weeks they watched the thunderous waves from the shore before finally working up the courage to enter the water. At every step of the way, they learned by watching each other and spurring one another on. They interacted with surfboard makers to come up with creative new designs for surfboards to increase their performance. From time to time, they would gather with big wave surfing enthusiasts from other parts of the world—places as far away as South Africa, Australia, and South America—to challenge each other in surfing competitions. The collective learning effort helped this community get better faster. A certain dynamic took place when they were learning from each other. Rather than experiencing the diminishing returns that Jeff Clark encountered while surfing alone, they kept pushing the performance envelope and mastering ever more challenging waves.

These surfing enthusiasts were gathering at the edge—a place where new knowledge was being created in real time about how to surf ever-bigger waves. While Clark struggled on his own, the surfers in Hawaii were using the surf breaks and their own experiences there as a creation space—even if they didn't call it that—in which they could rapidly improve their performance and stretch the limits of what had previously been thought possible. Creation spaces, as we have seen, often emerge at the edges of existing institutions, cultures, and even geographies: in this case on the then-remote North Shore of Oahu, where there was nothing but pineapple plantations, taro farms—and surfers.

During the past sixty years, big wave surfers have rapidly progressed from riding relatively modest 10-foot waves to ones exceeding 60 feet under a very broad range of conditions—"cleaner" waves on one day, waves that break at faster intervals on another, high winds or calm conditions, foggy or sunny visibility, and so on. As more and more participants join this extreme sport in many different parts of the world, they learn faster by working closely with each other and driving the sport to performance levels never imagined by the early pioneers in Southern California.

Massively Multiplayer Online Role-Playing Games

Around the world, a growing number of people are joining a massively multiplayer online role-playing game known as World of Warcraft (WoW). Introduced in 2001 by Blizzard Entertainment, the game now counts nearly 12 million members. Contrary to popular stereotype, the bulk of the players are not pimply teenage boys—the largest demographic segment in World of Warcraft consists of males between the ages of twenty-four and thirty-nine. The average player finds the game so engrossing that he spends more than eleven hours a week playing it.[14]

The players are drawn to the game and stay in the game because they are presented with a series of progressively more difficult challenges with continual feedback regarding their performance levels.

The game now encompasses eighty levels of play, with the degree of complexity and challenge increasing dramatically as a player advances through them. Furthermore, the game as a whole is fluid: It continues to evolve and change not only through the actions of the game developers at Blizzard, but through the direct actions of the players themselves. In this way, WoW mimics the physical world, which evolves in part through the actions we take individually and collectively.

As this takes place, according to Doug Thomas, a researcher who both plays and studies the game, players discover or create new uses for items, uncover synergies among skills or player talents, and continually test new styles of play and new techniques to be more successful in overcoming the challenges of the game. As a result, nothing about the world remains static and knowledge is being produced constantly. That new knowledge literally remakes the world, rendering some things vital and other things obsolete. Accordingly, players are faced with a serious set of problems. How does one know what information is useful and relevant in a constantly changing world?[15]

There are in fact two primary ways to keep abreast of the changes, both involving social networks. The early levels of the game are simple enough that individuals can address the difficulties they encounter on their own. As players advance along the levels and the difficulty of the game increases, however, they find it necessary to come together into larger teams, known as guilds. Participants in these guilds come from many different parts of the world and from all walks of life, with university professors such as Doug Thomas joining supermarket bag boys in the same guild. In the course of addressing progressively harder challenges together, these participants form deep bonds with their fellow guild members—and even begin getting together offline, in the physical world, for guild meetings, which are held in sunny spots such as Las Vegas.

Beyond the guild, however, is a second, broader social network in which participants from all the guilds come together in a vast and diverse complex of discussion forums, wikis, databases, and instructional videos. Here they share experiences, tell stories, celebrate (and analyze) prodigious achievements within the game, and explore innovative approaches to addressing the challenges at hand. Although a few of these forums are officially sponsored by the game designer, most of them have emerged spontaneously, organized by participants seeking access to more advice and insight regarding the challenges they face in the game.

This "knowledge economy" is impressively large: In the United States alone, the official forums hosted by Blizzard Entertainment contain tens of millions of postings in hundreds of forums. There are an equal number in China and Europe.[16] By providing the most up-to-date in-game information, this knowledge economy gives players a hedge against the ways in which World of Warcraft is constantly changing, allowing them to keep pace with their unpredictable in-game surroundings.

As they do so, most advanced players make use of customized performance "dashboards" created either by themselves or other players. Most gamers monitor their dashboards continually as they embark on quests to raid dungeons, kill monsters, and collect "loot." The dashboards give players rich, real-time feedback on their performance along a range of dimensions. Though some elements of these dashboards were introduced by the game designer, an entire cottage industry has emerged among participants who specialize in modifying them to suit the needs of different players. The detailed information they capture becomes invaluable during after-action reviews, when guild members gather to reflect on their individual and collective performance and brainstorm about ways to improve.

As the creation space within and around World of Warcraft has taken shape, participants have found that they learn faster by collaborating with each other and taking advantage of the tools and resources available to be pulled as needed.

For instance, when Blizzard introduced an additional ten levels of extremely difficult challenges in early 2007—in a release called *The Burning Crusade*—it took a French player by the name of Gullerbone twenty-eight hours to advance through them. Gullerbone's remarkable accomplishment stunned even experienced gamers, most of whom had assumed it would take months at the least to attain that goal. The feat made headlines in the gamer world.[17] It would have been impossible without the resources available in the WoW creation space.

Commercial Software

Germany's SAP AG is one of the world's largest and most successful software companies. Founded in 1972, it had, by 1996, more than 9,000 of its enterprise software systems installed at companies around the world.[18] These big systems had one application each to keep track of financial, accounting, customer, materials, and other information and to help with reporting, planning, and forecasting in areas such as finance, marketing, supply-chain management, and other important functions. Unfortunately, as the applications flourished and multiplied, each came to have its own database, making it difficult to search across applications to find, for example, all the information that might be needed pertaining to a particular customer.

The rise of the Internet—and the advent of new ways of organizing software, called service-oriented architectures (SOAs)—posed an opportunity for SAP. This difficulty could be overcome if the isolated applications (and their databases) could "talk" with one another more freely and easily. SAP began developing an application called NetWeaver to fit on top of (and around) all its existing enterprise applications so that they could work together more seamlessly.

When they were done, the members of SAP's product development team knew they had a terrific product. In selling NetWeaver, however, they faced something of a dilemma. The product's full potential wouldn't become apparent until customers began using it and discovering what it could do. Yet they might not buy NetWeaver until they could grasp its potential.

To address this dilemma the company launched a creation space consisting of forums, wikis, videos, and blogs targeting a diverse set of relevant participants. The SAP Developer Network (SDN) provided a forum in which software developers could create and share knowledge about platforms and products sourced from SAP and its partners. The Business Process Expert (BPX) Community welcomed people specializing in business procedures and protocols. And Industry Value Networks (IVNs) brought together customers to address issues specific to particular industries—for instance, bank managers looking to develop software interfaces to help them collaborate more effectively.

SAP realized that collaboration among participants was essential, and it designed these creation spaces to encourage peer-to-peer interactions. The creation space replaced the hub-and-spoke model that technology companies had traditionally used in their sponsored communities and networks. To further demonstrate NetWeaver's capabilities, SAP built each of its new networks on the NetWeaver platform.

The results have been impressive, not only in the scale of the creation space but in the learning and performance improvements it has produced. More than 9,000 companies participate in SAP's various partner networks globally and 1.2 million people participate in SAP's online communities. The creation space continues to grow at a healthy pace—more than 25,000 new participants sign up each month in SAP's online communities and the number of page views doubled between 2006 and 2007, reaching 150 million. Strong network effects appear to be in play as participants find that the value of the creation space as a whole increases with the number of participants.

Interactions are also increasing with the number of participants. For example, participants contribute more than 6,000 posts per day in SAP's online communities. More than 60,000 wikis have been created to handle specific FAQs, and more than 1,200 bloggers comment regularly on community topics. So far, more than 3.5 million posts have accumulated in these forums—and the pace of activity is accelerating. It took three years to reach the first million forum posts, nine months to reach the second million, and only six months to reach the third million. In total, 100,000 members have contributed posts to the online forums.

Most of the participation is in the form of individuals seeking help from others to solve difficult technical problems. Customers find that they can leverage the various forums in SAP's ecosystems to get answers to questions quickly. In the SDN, it takes, on average, seventeen minutes from the time a developer posts a question until the developer receives a response, and two to three additional responses typically come in over the following twenty-four hours to refine and amplify on the initial response. About 85 percent of all discussion threads are closed as complete.

But troubleshooting is not the only subject of postings. Over time, these individuals are increasingly coming together to form teams engaged in shared creation activities. Sometimes these efforts are organized by SAP. For example, twelve hospitals came together in an Enterprise Services Community Definition Group and worked together to define the key service interfaces for several business processes. They achieved their objective in less than six months.

But in a growing number of cases, these collaborative creation efforts are driven by teams of individuals who connect on their own initiative around interesting technology opportunities and challenges. ESME, the Enterprise Social Media Experiment, provides one interesting example of this emergent collaboration. Initially this effort started as an online conversation among a group of individual software programmers from around the world who became intrigued with the possibility of taking the concepts behind Twitter and applying them to business process problems that occur inside the enterprise. Twitter had emerged as a messaging platform in the consumer space, but it was not very stable; it needed higher levels of security and more functionality to support further development of ideas generated in messages if it was going to be useful in a corporate context.

In the early stages the team had a tangible action point to focus its efforts: SAP would soon hold its Tech Ed conference with a highly visible DemoJam competition that would give out awards for innovative new products. The six founding team members were from various countries in Europe and India, but they soon gathered together a broader cohort representing a diverse set of technical and business skills from even more distributed geographies, including the United States, Australia, the Middle East, and Peru. All of the team members in one form or another had a history of interaction with other individuals on the team, so they came into the project with trust-based relationships already formed.

The team developed the application in time for DemoJam. As one of the team members commented, "We could have put together the same kind of team, though not the same quality of team, and completed the product in three months if we'd been working full time. Instead, because of the quality of the team, we were able to complete the project in the same period of time but working only part-time while still pursuing our day jobs."[19] In interviews after the fact, several team members said the community-based nature of the project increased the fun factor while helping them acquire new skills. For SAP, meanwhile, the project was evidence that its creation space could deliver rapid innovation on the NetWeaver platform.

SECRETS OF SUCCESS IN CREATION SPACES

Creation spaces do not somehow come into being on their own or thrive through self-organization. But the myth that they do leads many observers—particularly institutional leaders—to assume that forming a creation space requires completely surrendering control to participants. It's true that creation spaces, in order to grow, require no small amount of self-organizing and emergent behavior from participants. Self-organizing behaviors are in fact a good sign when they occur: They demonstrate that participants have begun to see the opportunities available in the creation space and have begun shaping the space to more effectively meet their needs. But in every case, the success of creation spaces can be traced back to careful design at the outset by a small group of people who were very thoughtful about the conditions required to foster or "scaffold" scalable collaboration, learning, and performance improvement.

These conditions must not only encourage people to create new tacit knowledge within teams but also encourage the teams themselves to collaborate, one with the other, so that tacit knowledge can be created at scale as the entire endeavor grows larger. The people who designed the creation spaces we've discussed in this chapter all figured out one way or another to create an environment in which cross-team collaboration could take place.

No one can determine right at the start how a creation space will ultimately evolve. Their best uses unfold over time as participants experiment and improvise. Nevertheless, the direction and form of a creation space can be significantly influenced by its organizers. Early efforts and decisions often make the difference between success and failure, particularly when the difficult transition time arrives when a creation space approaches the critical mass of participants needed to unleash increasing-returns dynamics.

Designing Creation Spaces

Our research into emerging creation spaces has identified three elements that combine to set in motion the increasing-returns dynamics that make these spaces successful: participants, interactions, and environments. One size does not fit all—the nuances vary from situation to situation—but in various forms these elements have been carefully nurtured and monitored in every successful creation space we've studied.

Participants

The more people join a creation space and the more contributions they make once they're there, the more successful the space becomes—particularly once the number of participants has reached critical mass. To help the process along, start by keeping barriers to entry low. Next, give participants the real-time feedback and clear performance measures they need to advance quickly within the community.

Both of these factors are at work in the three creation spaces we've been discussing. In World of Warcraft, the early game-play is fairly simple and requires relatively limited investments of time. For most creation spaces, initial participation is even simpler—it consists of observing others. Many big wave surfers began by visiting surf breaks and watching from a bluff above the beach as surfers tackled the waves offshore. In the case of SAP, the vast majority of participants register and log on to a wide variety of discussion forums where they observe and learn from the discussions taking place there—without initially contributing anything themselves.

Participants can advance beyond the "lurker" stage with only small investments on their part—usually by starting to post questions and comments themselves. Although these contributions are still relatively modest in terms of the time invested by the individual poster, they enhance the diversity of the discussion, introducing valuable questions and ideas as well as feedback on existing ideas.

Over time, some participants begin to develop a reputation as the number of their contributions increases. Indeed, the desire for a high reputation is an important motivator for increasing one's participation, leading some contributors to evolve into discussion leaders or even to help design enhancements to the creation space.

To reduce barriers to entry, few of these creation spaces require participants to join teams at the outset, but it is a natural evolution for those who become more actively engaged to seek out people with complementary skills and shared interests and to eventually coalesce into teams with sustained membership. These teams often call out even more active participation in shared creation. The Enterprise Social Media Experiment team at SAP offers one example of the kinds of teams emerging spontaneously within a broader creation space. Even in World of Warcraft, where guilds tend to stay together for a longer period of time, advanced-level players sometimes gather in a pickup group of random players.

Even if the designers of the creation space had not anticipated the emergence of teams, this appears to be a natural evolution within open innovation environments. The executives running the InnoCentive open innovation platform were surprised to discover that the most productive individual contributors of solutions to problems posed on that platform were actually forming teams offline to research potential solutions. Having discovered this, the organizers of InnoCentive began developing enhancements to their platforms to encourage teams to form and to support them when they do form.

Interactions

Unleashing increasing returns in a creation space requires two forms of interactions to evolve simultaneously—team interactions and looser interactions across a broader range of participants. Either of these in isolation is helpful, but combining the two is essential to driving increasing returns.

As we have seen, team interactions are those exchanges that occur when participants share and develop new tacit knowledge relating to difficult performance needs. Whether they are in the raiding team of a World of Warcraft guild or part of the ESME team seeking to develop a Twitter-like service for corporate users, these team members build a deep, shared understanding and mutual trust that enables them to make the most of each other's knowledge and experiences in the process of innovating new approaches and generating new tacit knowledge. In the case of big wave surfing, it was a member of Laird Hamilton's team who first noticed the importance of an innovation Laird had used while surfing the treacherous waves of Teahupoo in Tahiti in 2000. Contrary to conventional practice, Laird put out his right hand into a left-breaking killer wave to improve his board control. He did this instinctively, and it was a team member who saw the significance of the innovation and helped to make it explicit. "I'm only riding at this level because I'm being driven by these guys to this level," Laird said later in an interview about his team.[20] And Gullerbone, the French gamer who tore through *The Burning Crusade* in twenty-eight hours, later credited the forty members of his guild who had helped him conduct the necessary raids and make the killings needed to succeed. The team-and-leader dynamic will be familiar to fans of the Tour de France, where the team keeps its leader out of the wind for the first 100 miles of a mountain stage only to fall away as the leader rides the final 10 miles, up the steepest grade, battling *mano a mano* with the leaders from other teams.

But teams can only get so big. One way to address this limitation is to design a space where large numbers of teams can operate in parallel. Creation spaces go one step further by introducing the opportunity to participate in peer-to-peer networks that cut across teams, leveraging their individual experiences and providing access to a much more diverse body of expertise than would otherwise exist. These learning networks organize around shared resources such as discussion boards, video repositories, and archives of previous contributions. In some cases, they may also benefit from physical gatherings, such as conferences or competitions. Although much of the interaction at this level involves the transfer of knowledge, new knowledge is often generated as participants hold sustained discussions about their performance challenges. New knowledge also emerges as peer-to-peer networks like these apply innovations and new knowledge in diverse environments where they can be tested and improved.

Environments

Creation spaces need careful planning and design at their inception, but the organizers' initial design often evolves rapidly thereafter as participants begin to make their own contributions. Each release of World of Warcraft, for example, starts out as the sole creation of its designers, but as soon as players begin playing, the game actually changes, evolving as a result of the actions of its participants. To work successfully, the creation space must be designed to work at three levels, with the second level building on the first and the third building on the first two. First, the creation space must be designed to foster the formation of teams and interactions within each of the teams. Second, it must be designed to encourage the formation of robust and diverse peer-to-peer networks that expand knowledge-sharing and knowledge-creation activities across teams. Third, it must be designed to reach beyond the creation space and engage a broader set of participants in the products of the creation space, as when nightclub DJs play music created online at ccMixter, or when employees of other corporations participate in SAP's Developer Network.

Getting the balance right between design and emergence is critical to the sustainability and scaling of these environments. Often the participants themselves contribute enhancements to the early platforms, define additional governance protocols, and strengthen incentive structures through shared and evolving norms. When these environments perform well, they offer rich and rapid performance feedback to participants and provide scalability consistent with the performance advances achieved by participants.

Achieving this balance requires careful design of environments along three dimensions: platforms, governance protocols, and incentive structures.

Creation Platforms. Creation platforms are either technological or physical or a combination of the two. For participants, platforms reduce interaction costs. The basic game environment of World of Warcraft is an example of a technological platform. Big wave surfing competitions, by contrast, provide an example of a physical platform, one in which surfers gather from all over the world. In recent years, this physical platform has been augmented by webcasts that allow anyone anywhere to watch the competitors ride the waves. These spectators may gain significant insight from observing the evolving practices of the competitors. Of course, the interactions of the webcast watchers are not as rich as the conversations that occur among participants on the beach watching the event. Perhaps live chats will soon be incorporated into the webcasts to extend the richness of these online interactions.

Creation platforms are to be distinguished from the shaping platforms we'll discuss in Chapter 7, and, indeed, from pull platforms more broadly, by their use of "dashboards" and other analytic tools that provide nuanced feedback to participants, often in real time, the better to accelerate performance improvement.

Creation platforms might also consist of shared instruments or analytic tools. For example, amateur astronomers are able to contribute to, and in a growing number of cases, even help to shape, the work of professional astronomers. Using old telescopes augmented by CCD (charged-coupled device) sensors and DSP (digital-signal processing) algorithms on a home computer—which can turn a cheap, old backyard telescope into something more powerful than the famed 200-inch scope on Mount Palomar—and by connecting with each other on the Internet, amateurs are constantly monitoring the skies for interesting cosmic events. In so doing they're amplifying the abilities of professional astronomers and even getting their names added to the occasional peer-reviewed scientific paper.

One of the most interesting elements of World of Warcraft's platform is the ability of players to craft their own dashboards to monitor their performance along many dimensions in real time. WoW supports this activity with a powerful set of application programming interfaces (APIs) enabling players to write their own reflection and analysis tools. How many people are in your raid? What time is it inside the game? How many "arena points" does a given player have available to spend? Players have written scripts for each of these functions using the WoW API.

World of Warcraft introduced the dashboard concept and provided some basic functionality right from the start—illustrating the importance of careful planning and design at the inception of such a project. Very quickly, however, the game designers opened this feature up to third parties, allowing the players themselves to develop additional features for other players to adopt and incorporate into their personalized dashboards. This flexibility was a successful element of the game, showing that creation platforms may operate at different levels in the creation space—learning networks, teams, and individuals may all require creation platforms tailored to their specific needs. On the other hand, these platforms need to be interoperable, allowing participants to move seamlessly from one level of the environment to another.

Governance protocols. Given the diversity of backgrounds and perspectives that participants bring to these creation spaces, not to mention the passion they feel for the subject, friction will occur. This friction is not always a bad thing; on the contrary, it can become a catalyst for major new insights and innovations. If not appropriately managed, however, it can poison the interactions and relationships within the creation space. This is where governance protocols come in. Organizers must define procedures that enhance the opportunity for resolution of disputes when and where they arise while still providing clearly defined pathways for escalation of disputes where necessary. The goal is to quickly and effectively resolve disagreements and quarrels in ways that support all participants.

More generally, governance protocols also must cover approaches to decisionmaking. Who makes which types of decisions, and in which contexts? In many cases, the decisionmaking protocols are quite diverse at the team level but become more consistent and generally looser as one moves into the learning network more broadly. In World of Warcraft, for example, one finds both highly militaristic guilds with command-and-control governance structures and more egalitarian guilds that take a consensus-driven approach.

Another key governance protocol involves admission and expulsion. In general, admission to creation spaces is loosely governed, if at all, to reduce barriers to participation. But many creation spaces have much more detailed protocols for advancement into more experienced ranks as well as protocols regarding the potential expulsion of participants who prove to be too disruptive to the innovation and learning process. In the case of big wave surfing, while many of the surf breaks are public beaches with open access, surfers can shun disruptive participants—those who endanger others by dropping into a wave out of turn, for instance—and have effective ways of making these folks feel unwelcome. Step out of line at the famous Banzai Pipeline on the North Shore of Oahu—one of the locations for the Vans Triple Crown of Surfing—and you'll have to deal with the Wolf-pak, a group of local surfers who sometimes enforce the rules with their fists.[21] Expulsion methods also exist in online communities such as World of Warcraft, where underperforming or misbehaving guild members are asked to leave by the guild leader.

Incentive structures. The third level of pull motivates and mobilizes participants within creation spaces by using incentive structures. These structures define how performance will be measured and rewarded—even though they leave wide open the means to achieving those ends, thus preserving the spontaneity of creation. As we have seen, many of the most active participants in these creation spaces are driven by intrinsic motivations—the passion they have for the domain, the satisfaction they feel when solving difficult problems and helping others, or a desire to build their skills and experience base.

Extrinsic incentives often serve to amplify and focus these intrinsic motivations. For example, by creating a point system to recognize contributions, organizers of creation spaces can draw attention to the valuable role that participants play when they support other users. Points might be awarded to participants for providing answers to questions on discussion boards, for instance, and then other modest rewards (such as T-shirts that acknowledge status) might be given to those who accumulate a certain number of points.

More generally, defining ambitious performance goals is a powerful way to tap into intrinsic motivation. World of Warcraft creates an explicit and elaborate series of eighty performance levels, each requiring successful handling of progressively more difficult challenges. These levels focus players on achieving shared goals while participating in the sheer enjoyment of solving difficult problems. Similarly, when an early group of big wave surfers migrated from the relatively modest waves of Southern California to the much more challenging waves of Makaha Beach on Oahu, they helped to drive another stage of innovation in this sport, both in terms of the design of the surfboards and the practices required to ride the bigger waves.

Creation space designers must be careful to maintain a delicate balance to avoid both frustration and boredom. On one hand, if the challenges are too great and perceived as unattainable, they can lead to frustration and disengagement from the space. If, on the other hand, the challenges are not difficult enough, they can lead to boredom and disengagement. The challenges must be designed and staged in such a way that they require real effort to address and yet provide participants with frequent and positive recognition for successfully overcoming them. This is a key factor in motivating participants to take on new challenges and to invest time and effort into achieving new goals.

The general truism that what gets measured and rewarded gets done certainly applies here. It is one of the most significant ways that creation-space organizers influence and focus the behavior of participants.

THE POTENTIAL FOR COLLABORATION CURVES

Earlier in this chapter we highlighted how the experience curve came to symbolize twentieth-century thinking about performance improvement. The bigger your business operation became, according to this thinking, the more cost-efficient you became because you could follow increasingly bigger push approaches to managing and moving raw materials and other resources. Yet companies can only squeeze costs so much until they finally reach a point of diminishing returns.

We now have the chance to transcend the limitations of the experience curve. The more participants one adds to carefully designed creation spaces—and the more the interactions that occur between and among them—the greater the chances are that everybody participating will get better quicker at whatever it is they're doing. Rather than each new increment of experience contributing less and less—as in the experience curve—each new participant in a creation space makes all the previous participants—and interactions between them—incrementally *more* valuable. A virtuous cycle begins to emerge as more and more people connect with each other. This is what we call the "collaboration curve"—a curve that points upward when more participants join and when the interactions between the participants increase. Collaboration curves are a reversal of the diminishing-returns dynamics of the experience curve, delivering increasing returns to performance instead.

What do we mean by increasing returns? The idea of network effects provides a useful starting point. The fax machine (which is fast becoming extinct) provides the classic example of network effects in action. One fax machine is useless. It even has negative value, since it costs money to purchase and operate and generates no value. But as more and more people purchase fax machines, the value of that fax machine increases at an exponential rate. If everyone has a fax machine, it generates enormous value, because the number of fax machines it can communicate with is very high. And yet the performance of each fax machine is static—its increasing value is only a function of the ability to add more nodes, each of which has static performance capability.

What would happen if, at the same time that more and more fax machines joined the network, the performance of each fax machine was also rapidly improving? We would get an amplifying effect on the first level of exponential performance. That is precisely what we see happening in emerging creation spaces: Performance is amplified not only as more participants join, but as each of them gets better faster by working effectively with other participants.

Right now, we don't have a lot of hard quantitative evidence supporting the existence of collaboration curves. That's perhaps understandable, given the fact that many of these creation spaces are very new—and how difficult it is to establish uniform quantitative measures of performance once one moves beyond cost reduction to value creation. Perhaps the most quantified creation space to date is World of Warcraft, where evidence solidly points to the existence of collaboration curves.

Performance in World of Warcraft is measured by experience points (XPs), which are awarded to players as they successfully address progressively more difficult challenges. As Figure 4.1 indicates, it takes roughly 150 hours of accumulated game-play to earn the first 2 million experience points, but players, on average, are able to earn another 8 million experience points in the next 150 hours of accumulated game-play. In other words, players are improving their performance four times over as they master the resources and practices that are available in this creation space.

Although more qualitative, there is early evidence from SAP's Developer Network suggesting scalable growth of participation and contributions in this creation space. The SDN was already quite large in 2004 with 100,000 participants, but by 2008 there were almost 1 million participants. During the same time, total accumulated points for contributions were rising ten times faster than the number of participants.

To the extent that these collaboration curves begin to gain force, we would expect to see performance results creating even more virtuous cycles. Creation spaces offer the potential to shift the dynamics of collaboration in a profound way. Rather than focusing on short-term, zero-sum transactions in which your gain is my loss, creation spaces foster long-term, trust-based relationships on multiple levels with the prospect of significantly higher performance by everyone, creating a win-win situation. As participants get to know each other and find that they share similar ways of looking at their endeavors, they start to trust one another, which prompts even deeper levels of collaboration (and tacit knowledge creation) around the difficult challenges they share.

||||||||

IT IS NO ACCIDENT that the creation spaces described in this chapter are emerging first on the edge. The surf breaks of Oahu's North Shore. The dungeons of the online gaming world, which emerged to

Figure 4.1. Exponential Learning Curve in World of Warcraft

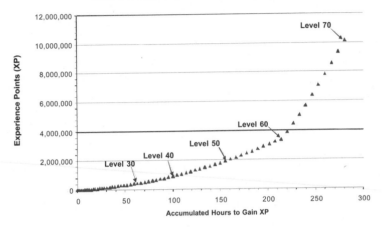

Hours to Gain Experience Points (XP) in WoW

Source: Palo Alto Research Center (PARC). Deloitte analysis.

compete with traditional video games and provide a new set of challenges for collaborative risk takers. These edge players—the first to be drawn into creation spaces—go on to form the kernel that then attracts larger numbers of participants.

Nor is it an accident that these creation spaces are initially organized by, and engage, people operating outside of traditional institutional boundaries. As we suggested earlier in this chapter (and will develop more fully in the next chapter), individuals are fast becoming the essential catalysts for institutional change as we move from a push to a pull economy. The early participants in these creation spaces are individuals with the questing dispositions often exhibited by edge participants. These dispositions lead them to discover and bring to the surface new practices and ultimately new institutional arrangements to support these dispositions. A key attribute that all of these individuals share, whether they are extreme sports enthusiasts, avid gamers, or software geeks, is an enormous passion that drives them to push the performance envelope and that draws them together to help each other get there.

Up to this point, we have described the three levels of pull—access, attraction, and achievement—that are becoming increasingly important to individual and institutional success in a world of near-constant disruption. In the next three chapters we will describe ways to implement these three levels of pull in three ever-expanding domains—at the level of the individual, at the level of the institution, and in broader markets and geographies. Although the individual is the starting point for the massive changes ahead of us, with time they are changes that will transform every major environment in modern life.

BRINGING IT HOME

- What are the most promising emerging creation spaces related to your passions or interests?
- In how many of these creation spaces are you active?
- Are you as active as you could be in these creation spaces? Are you mostly an observer? A contributor? At what level do you participate? Why or why not?
- If there are no creation spaces related to your passions or interests (are you really sure?), what would it take to help catalyze one?
- To what extent do the institutions you work for or with encourage participation in relevant creation spaces?
- How have you engaged your network of acquaintances during the past year to help each of you improve your performance more rapidly? Was it really a mutually beneficial interaction where all parties learned faster as a result? How do you know? How do you measure success?

Chapter 5

The Individual's Path to Pull

| | | | | | | | | | | | | | | | | | |

Ellen Levy loved gadgets as a child. This is a common thread in the stories of many successful entrepreneurs and venture capitalists like Ellen. But there is something more to Ellen's story because her interest evolved in unexpected directions, helping her to carve out a distinctive role in Silicon Valley.

Ellen remembers very well her early days as a child taking apart watches, driven by a quest to find out what made them tick. By the time she reached high school, she had graduated to robots and was an active member of the local robotics club, fascinated by the intricacy and power of these devices. But she also became deeply immersed in photography—she loved cameras as another type of gadget, but she also loved the infinite range of possibilities in terms of the images that could be created with this gadget.

In college at the University of Michigan, Ellen's passion had evolved in two related directions. She discovered computers and, thanks to some early exposure to programming in computer science class, became entranced with the challenge of making code as efficient as possible: What were the fewest lines possible to cover the broadest range of potential outcomes?

But she also discovered something else in college—the human brain. That most complex contraption of all was an irresistible lure for Ellen—and her quest to understand it led her ultimately to major in psychology, following brief stints in pre-med programs and mechanical engineering. From the outside looking in, it might have seemed that Ellen was making random movements across a broad range of disciplines and fields of interest, but in fact she was pursuing her passion.

This passion did take her into a broad array of fields, but it was shaped by a couple of overarching themes. Ellen did not just want to understand how devices worked; she wanted to understand how they could be used to expand options for the people using them. She loved edge cases—those unexpected situations that tested the agility and robustness of the device design—and wanted to see how devices could be designed more efficiently to handle a broader array of edge cases.

After college, Ellen worked briefly for a technology consulting firm, but she soon became disillusioned with the rigid career path the firm kept trying to push her into. Fearful that this focus on specialization and push-driven career paths was the inherent nature of business, Ellen returned to academia to pursue a Ph.D. in cognitive psychology at Stanford. She had to choose between MIT and Stanford for her graduate studies, and one of the reasons she chose Stanford was that she had lived in Cambridge but had never lived in California. The unknown exerted a far greater pull than the known.

It turned out to be a fortuitous choice. Ellen discovered Silicon Valley and a totally different way of doing business. She loved the way Silicon Valley entrepreneurs engaged in exploring interesting ideas with each other regardless of name, rank, or serial number. Ellen learned that these restless entrepreneurs were eagerly seeking out new connections in an effort to gain new perspectives on challenging business problems.

It was not long before Ellen was building her own personal network in Silicon Valley. She had a passion for golf and ended up meeting some amazing people on the Stanford golf course during her hours of practice every day. One day at a golf tournament, she met a professor at Stanford Law School who became one of her many mentors. That chance encounter and the mentoring relationship that developed led to an invitation to a dinner where Ellen met George Scalise, who ended up making her an offer to join Apple Computer in 1996. Ellen never looked back.

She had discovered something even more powerful than gadgets—networks of personal relationships that helped her to more effectively surface powerful new ideas and tackle challenging performance issues. Ellen thrives by making valuable links between people and ideas that nobody had previously thought to connect. She makes these links precisely because she loves the world of ideas and discovering unexpected patterns and questions that connect seemingly different concepts and arenas.

One day she's talking to the whiz kids at Tesla Motors. The next day to the retailing mavens at Best Buy. Suddenly she puts two ideas together. Tesla was taking advance orders for its Roadsters. Why couldn't Best Buy get customers to commit in August for what they wanted to purchase at Christmas? Best Buy would guarantee as low a price in August as would be available come December—or adjust it retroactively, if need be. Customers could lock in the best deals now instead of having to scramble at the last minute. And Best Buy would get an early window into one of the thorniest challenges that retailers (and their suppliers) face: how to anticipate demand.

It's only one small example of what Ellen does all the time: taking ideas from one place and cross-pollinating them in another. She finds that she can fit easily into virtually any discussion and hold her own, even if she has had little exposure to the topic. She has found that the key is to listen carefully, probe beneath the idea by trying to discover its root, and then finding ways to make connections with arenas with which she's more familiar. Ellen doesn't know that much about the technologies underlying clean tech, for example. But she sits on a number of clean-tech advisory boards. Why? Because her colleagues value her ability to recognize patterns and connect the dots. Who knew what the big-box retailer could learn from electric car making?

In the process, Ellen has discovered that framing the right question is often the best way to add value. Often, diverse groups have a hard time engaging with each other because they all have a different question in mind or simply are not clear about the question at hand. By framing a question in a way that is actionable and draws upon diverse perspectives, Ellen can take a group that has hit a bottleneck and provide a foundation for them to make progress again.

"I love idea generation and coming up with something that other people haven't thought of," Ellen says. "And the best way to do that is to be in the middle of lots of different people and ideas."[1]

Even apparent detours can often turn out to be extremely productive and connect back to her passion. Several years ago, Ellen became involved with Media X, a high-profile initiative at her alma mater, Stanford University. She initially joined this effort because she was passionate about Stanford and wanted to help the university in a way that would make the most of her skills, even though she initially thought it would distract her from the network and the work she had been pursuing in Silicon Valley. In fact, the opposite occurred. Media X became a platform to deepen and broaden Ellen's personal network while at the same time enhancing Stanford's ability to connect more effectively with the Silicon Valley community and the broader business world.

Now, as head of strategy at LinkedIn—and in her Silicon Valley Connect advisory business—Ellen is using pull to create value in and across networks of relationships. She's practicing a form of brokerage, yes, but it's not the old Machiavellian brokerage in which what you know and I don't gives you the strategic advantage. Instead, it's a new form of brokerage joining seemingly disparate people in a structured (but usually informal) process of idea generation and cross-pollination; it involves waiting for those magical moments when a group of people, often from diverse backgrounds and with dissimilar modes of problem solving and prediction, comes up with something nobody had thought of before. Interweaving herself among them, Ellen helps them take a piece of this, and mix it with a bit of that, to see if something new emerges. What would happen if she introduced the broadcast executive to the woman running the charity? How about connecting the Stanford professor with the lobbyist? And so on. Ellen Levy is practicing pull, using the approaches we described in Chapter 3: deep listening, beacon sending, pattern recognition, surface exposure, and, above all, a passion for new ideas and gifted people.

What makes all of this work, and makes it very different from traditional forms of networking, is Ellen's focus. In the old days, networking was all about meeting people who could help you advance in your own career. Ellen takes a very different approach. From the outset, she has used deep listening to develop a deep understanding of the other person's needs and interests. Then she creatively thinks about ways she can connect that person with others in her network who might be able to help that person better tackle those needs and interests. She observes, "When people realize that you genuinely want to help them become better at what they are doing, trust can be built in ways that pay off many times over in the years after. What could have become a short-term transaction in fact becomes a sustained relationship, yielding value to all sides over many years."[2]

She was doing it back in Ann Arbor, too—albeit in nascent form. But Ellen didn't fully make explicit what she was up to until years later, and then she realized it almost by accident. She had begun creating a daily journal of her own life in 1999 as a way to chronicle all the fascinating and newly emerging events happening during the Internet boom—as filtered through her own experiences in the tech world. The journal revealed an intricate network of relationships.

"I didn't structure the journal this way in the first place," Ellen recalls, "but it became a mapping of six degrees of separation. So if I were writing about you, I'd say, 'Okay, you know, we may be sitting in this room, but it's not the first time I've written about you,' so I'd write how we knew each other and then work back through all the connections to how we'd met." No matter what happened, she wrote down everything, every day, creating a kind of real-time autobiography from the flow of her experiences. "I'd write down the conversation with the taxicab driver," she explains, "and I'd write down the conversation with Francis Ford Coppola and Bill Gates when we were at COMDEX together, or I'd write down whatever was happening. I ended up documenting a wide array of interactions with a very diverse group of people."[3]

Ellen's "year in the life" became a visible map of the ecosystem of disparate relationships within which Ellen, like Yossi Vardi, was becoming a super-node: someone who bridges groups of people who might not otherwise be aware of each other. She realized she was not only mapping the connections between herself and other people but overlaying that "network" information with rich knowledge about what the people in that network cared about and were pursuing professionally. She realized how much she loved being deeply involved with passionate people and their great ideas. Silicon Valley was full of them. She has been in Silicon Valley ever since.

Ellen's journal exercise revealed something else as well. She was spending a lot of time with people who really were not high quality. As her network was growing, she was getting distracted by a lot of people who consumed time and attention but did not provide much insight or learning in return. Ellen began to prune and filter her network. She identified the people with the greatest quality in her network—insight, judgment, caring, and great values—and began to use these people as filters, looking to them for recommendations regarding both people and ideas that she should seek out. Multitasking also became a key practice, when appropriate, to help her get more value from the time invested. Ellen finds that she can often invite a business acquaintance on the walks she takes with her child, for example.

Ellen also learned from her journal exercise how little she remembered from her encounters and the rich discussions that had actually occurred. By writing down the substance of her interactions shortly after they took place, she found that she could reflect on the discussions and make connections that she otherwise would have missed. To this day, she still keeps a written record of where and when she meets people and what their interests are. This becomes a trigger for generating a lot more value from the encounters and remembering them so that she can make new connections in the future.

Ellen Levy's journey from Ann Arbor to Silicon Valley is emblematic of the journey we must all take from where we are now to where we want to be. We need no longer remain passive cogs in a deterministic machinery. We need no longer remain slaves to a set of rigid and controlling organizational routines overseen by mandarins and bureaucrats. The time has come to cast off our shackles. If we don't each of us do it, nobody will do it for us. And our institutions will have nobody to follow, nobody to lead them out of the push world that is failing us so badly.

We *can* do it. Why? Because big institutions need us more than ever. Making money from intangible assets—from knowledge, brand, and other nonphysical sources of value—is the primary way corporations make profit these days.[4] Many analysts have noted the increasing importance of intangible assets in business, but people often think about these assets in static form—for example, stocks of knowledge, established brands, and existing relationships. It is the growing pressure in the Big Shift to refresh these assets more frequently that makes institutions increasingly dependent on the individuals who create new intangible assets by interacting and collaborating with others.

Innovation is an inherently *human* activity, one pursued and achieved by individuals. Despite many efforts to try to standardize or routinize the way innovations occur, they cannot in fact be programmed or predicted. There is no process from which innovation springs out the other end. The best an institution can do is to increase the rate at which it learns: If you want to innovate faster, you have to learn faster. And institutions don't really learn: We do.

In Chapter 4, we made the case that institutions will need to shift their focus from scalable efficiency to scalable learning. Defining the carefully scripted push programs required for scalable efficiency is perfectly feasible for a few well-placed institutional leaders. But scalable learning cannot be mandated from above, it must be shaped and pursued by many individuals distributed within and across a large number of institutions.

That's why each of us, individually and together, are now, for the first time in history, in a position to collaborate in a complete reimagination of our biggest private- and public-sector institutions that will eventually remake society as a whole. In sharp contrast to the rise of twentieth-century institutions, in which a few visionary institutional leaders drove institutional innovation by focusing on scalable efficiency, in the rise of the pull dynamic many of us, distributed across a large number of institutions and residing at many levels of the institutions, will become the catalysts for massive institutional change as we find and connect with others who share our passions.

As customers, we have more choices, and more information with which to make those choices, than ever before. We can vote with our wallets. As talented employees we have greater power too than before—since we create the lion's share of today's corporate profitability. Furthermore, because individuals feel the pressure first, since we have fewer resources to draw upon, we've got the incentive to speak up. We've also got less inertia, which means that we are able to change course and move in different directions more quickly than large and unwieldy institutions can. Despite the growing performance pressures portrayed by the 2009 Shift Index, companies do not generally feel the same pressures as quickly as individuals do: They can persist for quite a while before they actually are in danger of disappearing.[5] They also are very tightly grooved into a particular way of doing things, a natural consequence of their relentless focus on scalable efficiency, and this makes it much more difficult for them to change course. But the consequences will become increasingly clear: As each of us votes with our feet and allies ourselves with new generations of institutions, we'll abandon the old ones, leaving them to drift into obsolescence and setting in motion a reshaping of broad arenas of economic and civic life. What gets born on the edge comes to the core with astonishing speed.

Going forward, individuals will increasingly reshape institutions rather than vice versa. For this reason, we start here by focusing on the journeys all of us will have to make as individuals. If we do not sustain these journeys as individuals, institutional leaders will have a rough time connecting to enough passionate individuals to drive institutional transformations. The more passionate people become, the more they will put pressure on their institutional homes to remake themselves so that they can truly develop talent faster than competitors. They will become the catalysts for much broader changes playing out across the business and social landscape.

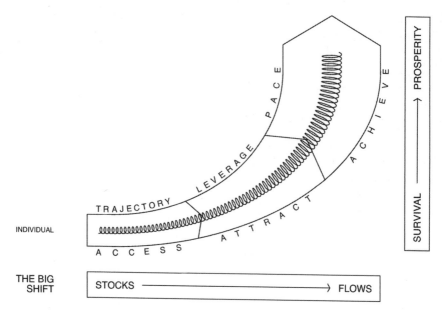

Havilland Studio, Palo Alto, California, and Lahaina, Hawaii

EMERGING ELEMENTS OF TRANSFORMATION

As we look across these three levels of change—individuals, institutions, and the broader social and economic arenas—certain elements become apparent as they promote the transformation from a push-driven to a pull-driven world: trajectory, leverage, and pace. These factors guide direction and action on the path that individuals and institutions—indeed, our society as a whole—must take in the journey from push to pull (see the diagram above).

You have to know where you're going or you risk running around in circles. That's *trajectory*—the path toward a meaningful destination, one that helps shape choices and action in the near term. Defining a destination helps to focus effort and initiative. At a time of rapid change, when it's all too easy to spread resources too thinly across too many fronts, trajectory is essential lest we find ourselves going either nowhere or to the wrong location. One of the greatest risks in these times is that we will fall into a reactive mode, responding to the latest development in our environment, but being completely unable to differentiate or prioritize in terms of which developments matter the most. By defining a meaningful destination for ourselves, we also create a powerful signal to others indicating where we are headed, strengthening our ability to attract others headed for similar destinations. For this element of the journey, our passion is our constant guide, starting out with the question, "What are you really passionate about?" and then continuing to correct course thereafter to make sure we're still on the right heading.

Leverage is the opportunity to connect with others through the mechanisms of pull. These interactions make it easier for us to get the knowledge that we need and then to do something with it. Leverage means we don't have to do everything ourselves. We can make the most of the abilities of others, and we can do so in a relatively low-cost way. Leverage initially takes the form of access and attraction, but over time it evolves into relationships that help all participants more effectively achieve their potential. In times of increasing competitive pressure, this can increase flexibility and enable us to do more with less.

Pace helps us to move quickly at a time when everything around us is changing at an accelerating speed. Certainly, capability and learning leverage contribute to pace. Rather than having to invest in building new resources, with the inevitable lead times that requires, leverage helps us connect with and mobilize resources that already exist. More importantly, learning leverage increases the pace of new knowledge creation, which can become a key source of strategic advantage for those who are particularly adept at this.

There are other ways to influence pace. Tools of various types— such as personalized dashboards in World of Warcraft, personalization and serendipity services that improve return on attention, Web 2.0 information-technology platforms for the enterprise—all of these and others can help take the acceleration already available through capability and learning leverage and increase it to new levels. Depending on the level of change in question, these tools can become a critical element in both creating and capturing value from the richer knowledge flows unfolding around us.

These three elements can be pursued in parallel rather than sequentially, although the focus of attention and effort will evolve naturally from trajectory to leverage and then to pace as the journey unfolds. The journey necessarily begins with trajectory, so that our sense of direction can help us determine where to get leverage. Trajectory can also help us to define the networks and ecosystems that we will choose to participate in as individuals. But once the journey is underway, proceeding in parallel can build in useful feedback loops: The trajectory may need to be adjusted as a result of what we discover as we try to gain leverage, efforts to accelerate pace will lead to new insights about the ecosystem required for leverage, and so on. The elements are mutually reinforcing and amplifying.

We'll spend the rest of this chapter exploring how these three elements come together to enable each of us to navigate more effectively through the gales of change unfolding around us. Applied well, they can help us to set change in motion and "steer" it rather than merely reacting to it as it happens. In this way, we have the opportunity to turn deep stress into sustained calmness—and boredom into passion.

Before we do, however, it must also be said that we recognize that this journey, for many of us, will present challenges. It will take us out of our comfort zones and require taking what may seem like significant risks. We will almost certainly make some big mistakes along the way as we try to master new techniques, and perhaps we will risk alienating friends and business associates. Furthermore, some of us will feel a sense of loss at the passing of the old certainties. We have a friend in the dance world who laments the passing of traditional voices—the critics who used to write reviews of dance performances in newspapers. Now these newspapers are disappearing, or cutting back staff (such as dance reviewers), and less traditional voices (for example, bloggers) are gaining more airtime. One author expanded this lament to book length, equating the rise of digital culture with the decline of Western civilization.[6] A U.S. Supreme Court justice pines for the "utopian" days of the Hoover administration.[7] These emotions are understandable.

Of course, most of us also recognize that there is no going back to an earlier era. The genie can't be put back into the bottle. As Clay Shirky pointed out in a widely circulated piece, "there is no general model for newspapers to replace the one the Internet just broke."[8] Knowing that, however, doesn't seem to resolve the certain reactionary peevishness with which some people dismiss social media and digital culture. "Ah, blogging," one academic we know commented to us. "That's just a way to waste time and postpone serious work." But what if blogs are a way to connect to vital flows of what other people are thinking and doing and feeling? What if social media is a way to turbocharge your brain? What if the digital infrastructure in fact enables exponential learning to take place among all of us as more of us begin to participate and interact? Perhaps the more we all participate, the faster we will all learn and grow. And what if it turns out that it's really a lot of fun, too?

Part of this dynamic emerges from fearfulness. We were talking to the VP for online strategy at a big Silicon Valley company recently who, among other tasks, helps the company's senior executives create a presence on Facebook and Twitter. "Some of them are terrified," she told us. What's so scary? Many executives fear that posting something personal might prove damaging. It needn't be a lampshade on the head, either. Perhaps it's vacation photos from a second home that looks too opulent at a time when employees are losing jobs. Or maybe their support for a controversial ballot proposition proves a bit too vocal. That's why you see some executives, if they're on Facebook at all, posed in their profile picture as if it's for the annual report, and with nothing personal posted to their "information" tab. Such reticence will soon be scarce as all of us recognize the powerful and important reasons for sharing our personal selves online.

DRIVING INDIVIDUAL TRANSFORMATION

What can we do as individuals to harness the power of pull? It begins by finding our passions, growing our social networks, and increasing our return on attention. Passion guides and focuses our choices—it defines our trajectory. Social networks give us leverage. And increasing our return on attention becomes ever more critical, enabling us to participate in the knowledge flows that really matter and helping us pick up the pace.

Trajectory: Pursuing Passion

We all have passions. Some of us have been fortunate enough to pursue our passions as our professions. Most of us have not. We learned that passions were something we pursued after hours—whether they were athletic, artistic, or intellectual; related to social or political causes; or were craft based. We compartmentalized our lives—work was something we did so that we could pursue our passions outside of work. In extreme cases, we suppressed our passions in order to be responsible employees and family members. There just wasn't enough time—and passions tend to consume a lot of time.

For Ellen Levy, it wasn't so easy to separate her passion from her profession. The very fact of having an identical twin forced her to learn to be a "super-node" very early in life and to develop the social skills and the empathy that goes along with such a role, including learning how to handle the new situations and encounters with strangers that came from being a twin. For one thing, people often mistake one twin for the other, which forces twins to learn how to talk to people they don't know who think they know them. "I had to get used to talking to people I didn't know," says Ellen, "because they often thought I was my sister." She soon realized she had an aptitude for it—and she developed a real passion for cultivating connections. Our 2009 Shift Index revealed that only one out of every five workers in the United States is really passionate about his or her work. A Gallup poll recently indicated that, at the other extreme, another one out of five employees is so disengaged that he or she actively seeks to undermine colleagues at work.

Of course, most of us are somewhere in the middle of those two extremes. But we should emphasize that we see a clear distinction between passion and satisfaction. The latter is often the focus of employee surveys, but it measures something quite different from what we are talking about. Satisfaction is a measure of how content people are with their jobs. Are they feeling secure and reasonably rewarded? Do they feel they are making an impact?

Satisfaction need not be correlated with passion, and in fact often it is not. Often the most passionate workers are quite frustrated with their employers and bosses. They can see so much more that can be done, and they are acutely aware of the many ways that institutional environments hold them back. They are not satisfied. Far from it. They want to do more, but they feel held back by the institution.

Our Shift Index survey in 2009 indicated that passionate workers are least often found in large companies. Workers are 60 percent more likely to be passionate in smaller companies than they are in the largest companies. Passion is increasingly hard to find as companies get bigger. Perhaps even more revealing, workers are twice as likely to be passionate about their work if they are self-employed than if they work for someone else.

Yet, if we don't have passion in our work, we will have a very hard time enduring the growing pressures that we encounter. An interesting thing happens when we pursue our passions: We actually seek out more challenges. Rather than viewing them as sources of stress, we view them as opportunities to get better faster. We want to push ourselves to the next level, and we get restless if we remain at the same level too long. No matter what the area of work, there are some people who actually are quite passionate about what they do. They can't wait to get to work and test themselves. They love to drive their performance to new levels.

Increasingly, these are the people we will be competing with as we move into the future. If we are not equally passionate about the work we do, we will undoubtedly get marginalized. The pressures will just be too overwhelming if we are not motivated in the same way that passionate workers are.

So what can we do? We can find or develop our passion. One way or another, we will need to pursue our passion as our profession. Until and unless we do that, we will remain vulnerable to focused competition from those who are pursuing theirs. And even if we can prevail without passion, we will lead lives filled with stress and pressure that sooner or later will become intolerable.

Some critics will push back and say this goal is unrealistic. It sounds very elitist—it may be feasible for the research scientist or the software engineer, but what about the manual laborers—the legions of workers supporting our factories, distribution centers, and fast-food restaurants? Is it really realistic for them to become passionate about their work?

The truth is that virtually any type of work can become the focus for passion. Many auto-repair mechanics are passionate about cars and knowing what makes them run. Carpenters can take great delight in building things that are beautiful and enduring. As Matt Crawford, the author of *Shop Class as Soulcraft*, so eloquently points out, working with one's hands can have deeply philosophical, even spiritual, overtones.[9] One of the great lessons that Toyota taught us is that assembly-line workers in a car factory can become enormously passionate about their work if they are treated as problem-solvers who can innovate rather than automatons who are simply carrying out detailed instructions defined by someone else. It is actually very elitist to suggest that one could not be passionate about work in certain job categories—it reveals the low opinion we have of the work.

Most of us have one or more passions that we have developed in the course of our lives. Even if we worked hard to suppress those passions for most of our lives—because we just could not see a way to find the time to pursue them—they still lurk close to the surface waiting to be called out. We would be well advised now to step back, reflect on those passions, and see if we can find some creative way to pursue them, either through a full-fledged career change by redefining the work we are doing, or by edging into it through a reduced workload arrangement.

Another option is to find the parts of our current work that are truly satisfying and engage our interest. In even the most pedestrian work, there are usually elements that we find to be tremendously interesting and rewarding, even though other parts of the job weigh heavily on our spirits and deplete our energy as we cope with boredom or bureaucratic obstacles. We can choose to focus on and develop these elements of our work, thereby uncovering the passion latent in our current work environment. These efforts will be more successful if we can reach out to others in our work environments who might share similar passions and find ways to connect with these people.

However we do it, we must find a way to pursue our passion as our profession. This leads to the emergence of new dispositions that are extremely powerful in helping us to fully leverage the opportunities created by richer knowledge flows. Our 2009 Shift Index survey revealed that workers who were passionate about their jobs were more than twice as likely to engage in inter-firm knowledge flows than less passionate employees were. These passionate workers have a significant advantage over their colleagues in terms of refreshing their knowledge stocks.

Connecting with our passions inevitably leads to a questing disposition: Once we engage our passion, we also engage our curiosity, and we'll start to connect with what we find most meaningful. As our trajectory becomes clear we become consumed with a desire to seek out and connect with others who share these passions and to develop these connections, and in the process we become better faster and drive our performance to new levels. And it is not just a one-way street. As we develop our passion, we find that we want to reach out and help others with the same passion to get better as well. We are more willing to take risks because the perceived rewards in terms of advancing our passion are so compelling. We will stop at nothing to find opportunities to feed our passion. We seek out and embrace challenges, rather than trying to avoid them, because they provide us with a way to test ourselves and explore new dimensions of our passions. What is deeply stressful for other, less passionate workers becomes profoundly exhilarating and satisfying for the passionate. As soon as we overcome one challenge, we begin scanning the horizon to find the next challenge. When engaged with these challenges, we naturally and instinctively seek out others who share our passion and can help us to develop approaches that can enable us to be successful. Because we share passions with these people, we are more likely to develop deep, long-term relationships with them rather than resorting to opportunistic, short-term transactions with less potential for sustained knowledge flows.

Something else interesting happens when we connect with our passion. We cannot remain silent. We become more visible to others as we talk to and engage with others around our passion. Word spreads, and we begin to attract others who share our passions and who experience a similar need to connect with others around these passions. We shape serendipity by pursuing our passion, because reaching out in this way enhances our findability and draws people to us from the most unexpected quarters.

As we pursue our passions, we are also drawn into creation spaces where we can engage with others around particularly challenging issues related to our passions. Although there are many motivations for participating in creation spaces, a significant portion of the participants cite the opportunity to challenge themselves in collaboration with others as their reason for joining the discussions. These passionate participants form the core of these creation spaces—they tend to be the most active contributors and become attraction points for much broader groups of participants. These creation spaces not only provide outlets for our passions but also tend to reinforce our passions. The knowledge that there are others who share these passions, and the opportunity to engage with these people, not just in the abstract, but around very tangible and exciting problems, feeds our passions and spurs us on to greater learning and achievement.

Earlier on, we said that the first element in the transformation process would be trajectory, which would provide focus and motivation for the journey ahead. Passion may not define a destination—it is a constantly shifting horizon that we head toward. But it does provide a compelling direction that shapes our efforts and provides a tight focus. It also certainly provides powerful motivation to address any challenges in front of us and to harness the power of pull to achieve our full potential.

Leverage: Harnessing Ecosystems

We live in personal "ecosystems"—our local communities, our extended networks of friends and associates, and, increasingly, virtual networks and communities that dramatically amplify our reach. As individuals, we can do a lot to shape those ecosystems to make them better able to help us develop professionally and enrich our social lives. These ecosystems, as they evolve, provide us with an opportunity to make use of the second principle involved in adopting pull approaches: leverage.

In the past, our personal ecosystems were largely given to us as a by-product of our other experiences. We were born into a specific geography, and most people lived in the same place throughout their lives. Our networks of friends and associates was primarily driven by this initial accident of birth and key life experiences—where we went to school, where we worked, and where we worshipped. Our networks of relationships tended to be heavily concentrated in our local geographies, they were not very large, and they did not change very much over long periods of time.

Geography still matters, but we have more and more flexibility in shaping our social networks to enhance our ability to connect to the most relevant edges in our areas of passion and in our professions. We can craft a social network that pulls in people who share our interests, and we can reach out to more and more people with those interests to enlarge the network. As we discussed earlier, our social networks encompass both strong ties and weak ties. The strong ties—the deepest and richest relationships we have—provide us with the most day-to-day support. But it is the weak ties in our network—the relationships that are much less well developed, and that seem peripheral in our daily lives—that most often provide us with opportunities to connect with people who are active in the emerging arenas that are most relevant to our passions and professions.

Although most of us have a tendency to focus on the strong ties, in times of growing pressure we all have a natural tendency to focus even more on the strong ties, seeking support and reinforcement from those whom we know and trust the most. We should resist this temptation. It is very comforting for us, and certainly, we should make sure that our strong ties remain strong. But times of growing pressure are a sign that our strong ties are no longer sufficient to support us. In this context, pursuing our passion can help us to overcome this temptation. If we are truly passionate, we will be driven to reach out beyond our current relationships to find others who can provide us with new perspectives and experiences. Without this passion, we will be much more likely to succumb to the stress that mounts on a daily basis.

For the same reason that we need to shift our focus from knowledge stocks to knowledge flows, we need to shift our focus in our social networks from our strong to our weak ties. It can take significant time to inventory those weak ties and identify the people who have the greatest potential to introduce us to emerging challenges and opportunities on edges that are relevant to our passions. We need to take the initiative and reach out to these people, communicate our areas of interest, and then invite them to help us meet others who share these interests on relevant edges. Wherever possible, we should define interesting and promising initiatives that could be pursued jointly, both to motivate people to build deeper relationships with us and to provide a context for building shared understanding, trust, and insight.

This is one place where attraction can come into play. Through the principles of attraction, we can expand those weak ties and gain unexpected opportunities to build out our social networks on relevant edges. In this way, we can get more insight into emerging opportunities on the edge. Attraction can also help us find environments where people on relevant edges spend their time, either in virtual space or in physical space. This could take the form of discussion forums online, conferences, associations with a variety of professional organizations, or geographic talent spikes that attract people sharing our passions and interests. We have to make many efforts to become visible in those spaces, communicating our passions, making contributions, and starting to build a reputation that can draw others toward us over time.

As we make efforts to reach out to, and expand, the relevant weak ties, we should seek not just to meet these people and engage in discussions but to engage them in problem solving and the joint pursuit of opportunities. As we pursue these collaborative efforts, we will find that our weak ties evolve into strong ties, helping to refresh our core social network in ways that strengthen our ability to respond to the challenges and opportunities continuously arising during the Big

Shift. In fact, the complex interplay between the strong ties in our core network and the weak ties at the edge of our networks will allow us to pull more value out of both types of relationships. In the process, we will need to master new genres of communication, ranging from blogs and twittering to visual presentation and mobile presence.

The bottom line is that we all should take a much more active role in shaping the personal ecosystems in which we operate. It starts with choices about where to live, which are becoming increasingly important rather than less important. But then it quickly extends into the social and professional networks that provide the context for our daily interactions. Although we certainly do not have control over these networks, we have more ability than we might think to shape them in ways that position us to pursue our passions more effectively and drive our individual performance to new levels. We can find enormous leverage by connecting with others who share our passions and by together exploring the edges that will challenge us both to deepen and expand our skills. But to participate in the most relevant knowledge flows, we need to use the power of pull to reshape these networks.

Pace: Maximizing Return on Attention

As the Big Shift unfolds, we are beginning to realize that individual attention is becoming more and more valuable to others and to ourselves. As other forms of scarcity, such as shelf space, continue to dissolve, how we allocate our attention will increasingly determine who creates and who destroys economic value. The pace of life in the Big Shift requires that we manage the scarce resource of attention if we are to avoid becoming overwhelmed with knowledge flows and interactions with people.

Deciding how to allocate our attention becomes both a challenge and an opportunity. We are inundated with a growing array of options to explore in terms of information, products, and people all promising to offer value. Most of these options end up being a distraction, while a few turn out to make the difference between success and failure in our endeavors. But how to determine in advance which is which? The most successful people will be the ones who can figure this out, and they will earn a large and growing return on attention while many of us find ourselves struggling to keep up, forever distracted by promising leads that turn out to be disappointing dead ends, and losing sight of the people and information that matter the most. Maximizing return on attention becomes a key way to accelerate our movement along our chosen trajectory and to amplify the impact that we want to have as we pursue our passions.

One temptation might be to shut down the proliferating sources of information, narrowing the channels of information that come to us and reverting to the tried and true sources of information that we have relied on in the past to bring us insight. Don't take this path. Like the natural instinct to fall back on the strong ties in our social networks, this instinct is driven by a desire to seek reinforcement and stability as a source of comfort. But in a world where edges are more rapidly rising up to transform the cores that many of us live in, this instinct is a dangerous one. It blocks access to the flows that matter the most and gives us a false sense of security, making us think that the cores will hold firm when in reality the cracks are already becoming visible on the periphery.

We all talk loosely about information overload and assume that this is the real problem. In fact, we live in a world of increasing knowledge scarcity. The most valuable knowledge is in very short supply and extremely hard to access. Information overload is a distraction. As we discussed in earlier chapters, in a world of accelerating change, the most valuable knowledge is highly distributed and may be embedded in the heads of people who are not well known and who are difficult to identify. Even if we could find these people, we would discover that they have enormous difficulty articulating their most valuable knowledge, not because they are reluctant to do so but because their experience with it is so fragmentary and new. (This is where the deep listening practiced by Yossi Vardi and Ellen Levy is such an asset.)

It's not so much about finding which information is most valuable, as many of those who fret about information overload would have it. Improving return on attention is more about finding and connecting with people who have the *knowledge* you need, particularly the tacit knowledge about how to do new things. The danger is that we all get so busy assimilating explicit knowledge that we have no time to connect with people and build the relationships through which tacit knowledge flows. We get so busy reading about steampunk, or brewing, or building networks, that we don't actually find and connect with and learn from the people who are doing it. It's not so much information that we need as knowledge. And knowledge means people.

In this context, the three levels of pull can be particularly helpful, especially when we focus them on pulling people—in other words, finding, attracting, influencing, and ultimately creating relationships with people in the process of addressing performance challenges. By connecting with more people on relevant edges and investing the time to build sustaining, trust-based relationships with them, we can begin to position ourselves as a concentration point for flows of tacit knowledge that are extremely valuable, yet very difficult to access in any other manner.

These people and the knowledge flows they generate can then become effective filters for information more broadly. By harnessing social media such as blogs, social-network platforms, and wikis, we can begin to rely on these mechanisms to expose ourselves to information that has been curated and passed on by these people. Since we deeply understand their contexts and passions, we can begin to determine when their recommendations are most reliable and increase our return on attention for both the tacit knowledge they offer and the information they recommend to us. Our personal social and professional networks will be far more effective in filtering relevant knowledge and information than any broader social-technology tools we might access. Beyond our immediate social networks, we will also become more adept at tapping into broader social networks and online communities to increase our return on attention through a broader field of vision, but one filtered by people we trust—not because we know them individually, but because they share interests and experiences similar to ours. Identity and reputation mechanisms will help to determine how much to trust specific contributions from these participants.

Having established our primary focus on our expanding networks of relationships, though, we must add that there is still room for other filters that can further strengthen our peripheral vision. By shaping serendipity in the ways described in Chapter 3, we can increase the probability of being exposed through unexpected encounters at appropriate times to relevant people and ideas on emerging edges.

We also can be on the lookout for "editors" who have a talent for searching out new edges and providing early perspectives on why these edges might be gaining importance. In his book *Chief Culture Officer*, Massachusetts Institute of Technology professor Grant McCracken discusses a whole range of these "editors"—such as Mary Minnick, head of marketing at Coca-Cola, and the late Gerry Frost, who brought Motorola's Razr phone to market—people who, by "mastering culture," know how to extract value from culture for a wide range of participants: companies, consumers, and employees.[10] When it comes to the written word, this new generation of editors won't just edit content developed by their own publications, they'll focus on curating a much broader range of third-party content available throughout the Internet. Some of these editors will likely focus on tracking the emergence of promising new edges, searching out the most promising content from the edges to help their audience sort out the signal from the noise. In this case, our serendipitous encounters will be with content that provides early visibility into the innovation opportunities arising on emerging edges. One role of this new generation of editors will be to help us to see relationships between new stories from the edge and our own passions and interests.

Before leaving this topic, we should also mention that return on attention works in two directions. Pull in fact only works when a given action or interaction is in the interest of all parties concerned. Reciprocity is key. So far, we have been discussing ways to increase the return on our attention. At the same time, we need to engage the attention of a broad range of people who share our passions and who might be able to help us drive our performance to new levels. In this context, we will need to carefully monitor whether we are delivering sufficient value to our networks of relationships to ensure that the people in them continue to follow us and pay attention to our contributions as they are made.

For Ellen Levy, it is this reciprocity that has made her successful. "The crux of what I do is in the mapping back to what the other person cares about," Ellen says. "What I found during that year chronicling my life was that people are amazed, a year later, when I can remember what's most important to them. And this thing that's important to them becomes the most natural hook into when and how and why we might reengage with each other. It also gives me a bunch of ideas. It's almost like I'm setting flags everywhere all the time. Each time I meet some-body I'm setting markers that may yield benefit to that person or other people later." Ultimately, Ellen knows, that will in turn create benefit for her, too.

Ellen found that a focus on the needs of others also helps her to build institutional platforms that can achieve even greater impact. In the process, she highlights her role in addressing "the integrator's dilemma"—a term she coined a few years back. In organizations that are deeply siloed internally and that have a hard time connecting ef-fectively with those outside the organization, there is a strong need for someone who can help cut across all the silos and bring people together to engage in difficult performance challenges. Yet, at the same time, the people who engage in this activity, such as Ellen, find themselves in an awkward position in the organization. Their roles are often poorly understood, their performance difficult to measure using conventional metrics, and their rewards often do not match the contributions they have made to the organization.

Despite these obstacles, Ellen persists, describing herself as a "re-spectful disruptor." She sees a need to cross boundaries in ways that are often viewed as disruptive by the rest of the organization. But she invests the time to understand the needs and interests of all parties in-volved and to structure interactions that will benefit all concerned. In this way, she respects the needs and interests of the people involved while disrupting the established procedures and boundaries where necessary to resolve difficult issues.

||||||||

Pursuing our passions as our professions will inevitably lead us to ex-plore the weak ties at the edges of our social and professional net-works in a quest for new challenges. Participants in our social and professional networks will in turn help us to maximize our return on attention as we seek out scarce tacit knowledge that can give us the ability to achieve new performance levels and, in the process, to build new tacit knowledge.

These are the elements that need to come together in order for the transformation of our individual mindsets and practices to take place. From individuals, we now turn to institutions. With institutions, the effort will be highly dependent on finding and nurturing a critical mass of participants both inside and outside of the organization in question. These individuals will collectively deploy the mechanisms of pull to transform the institution overall, enabling the institution to make a greater impact than ever through its products or services and in its other endeavors.

BRINGING IT HOME

- If given a choice, where would you invest the bulk of your time? Of these areas, where would achieving peak performance be the most important? Would you be willing to make significant sacrifices in other parts of your life to achieve this peak performance?
- Does this area define your profession today? If not, what would it take to make it your profession? If that is not feasible, are there dimensions of your profession where you would be willing to make significant sacrifices in order to achieve peak performance in other dimensions?
- Do you live in a city where a large number of people share your passion?
- How actively have you sought to develop your social network by deepening relationships with those who share your passion or who could help you to pursue your passion? How many of your acquaintances who share your passion live in your local area? How many of them live in other countries? How many of them do you mostly interact with online rather than in person? Do you extend your online relationships into the physical world, and vice versa?

- How many people in your network are aware of your passion? What prevents you from making your passion more visible in your social network?
- Who are the five people you can identify who would have the best visibility into the knowledge flows most relevant to your passion? Are you connected with them yet? How could you more effectively interact with these people to enhance both your awareness of relevant knowledge flows and their awareness of your efforts to pursue your passion?
- How often do you deliberately move outside of your comfort zone to acquire new experiences or develop new relationships that might help you to advance your passion? How much discomfort do you experience in so doing? At what point does discomfort give way to familiarity and ease?

Chapter 6

Pulling from the Top of Institutions

||||||||||||||||||

When Shai Agassi joined the seven-member SAP executive board in 2003 at the tender age of thirty-five, he made some startling pronouncements. SAP, he declared, should simply give away its software and only charge for IT support. The company should go open-source with its database business. It should put a partnering gene into its corporate DNA.

"At a company that had grown dominant by moving slowly and conservatively," *Wired* magazine later pointed out, "these were heretical ideas."[1] It wasn't long, however, before at least some of Shai's heresies became orthodox, leading to the creation and launch of the SAP Developer Network.

The changes Shai Agassi wrought at SAP, at one level, tell the story of how ideas come from the edge to the core. Web 2.0 technologies and practices, in this case, came from the outside of the enterprise to its center. And Shai himself, despite his increasingly senior positions within SAP (he was the heir apparent to the CEO role before leaving the company in 2007), was a relative outsider at the company. He had only joined the company in 2001, when SAP bought his independent software company for $400 million. More importantly, Shai himself had an outsider's perspective—in this case the point of view of an independent software vendor. These vendors develop and sell software on the margin of bigger vendors such as SAP. This outsider's perspective helped Shai think outside the box of SAP's prevailing management culture. It led him to want to experiment and tinker—something SAP itself wasn't designed for.

Much like the surfers who asked themselves, "What if you dipped your trailing hand in the water on the face of the wave?"[2] Shai Agassi challenged SAP to rethink crucial aspects of how it did things in general, and innovation in particular. What if, he asked, SAP tried to unleash a swarm of innovators independent of its own group of paid engineers? What if SAP harnessed the power of the many independent vendors the company worked with?

And that's why Shai's story isn't just about institutional innovation or creative thinking. Shai's is the story of an institutional leader "pulling from the top" by mobilizing talented people and valuable resources across institutional boundaries. Even though he might not have called it that, Shai believed in the power of the collaboration curve to mobilize vastly distributed resources in the right environment so that everybody gets better faster by working with others. Shai was practicing pull—even if he didn't know it. "True innovation does not happen when we control creativity," Shai wrote in 2005, "but when we challenge, create shared vision, and passionately pursue excellence."[3]

Not all institutional leaders will be endowed with Shai Agassi's vision, passion, and skills. Yet his philosophy and approach could be applied widely. Institutional leaders who understand the potential of pull may be able to drive organizational change in ways that differ dramatically from the change-management efforts of the past. Rather than pushing down, institutional leaders will need to learn how to pull out from the center to the edge—just as Shai did when he took SAP into the world of open innovation and Web 2.0. Significant inertia and resistance will stand in the way, but pull, appropriately applied, can prove up to the challenge.

In this chapter, we explore the journey that institutions will take from the industrial-era rationale for the firm, in which push held sway, toward an entirely different reason for being, one centered on pull.

Any of us working for big institutions today know that, with a few pioneering exceptions, most companies are deeply wedded to push—not just in their mindsets and in the assumptions underlying their dispositions, but in the ways they organize themselves (mostly hierarchical), share information (from the top down through layers of authority), set budgets (the proposed numbers roll up the hierarchy, and the approved numbers cascade back down), and even monitor social media usage (often restrictively). To a considerable degree these organizational structures represent the "anatomy" of the firm. "Anatomy is destiny," argued Sigmund Freud (albeit in a slightly different context). And companies with push anatomies are going to have a tough time reshaping themselves for pull.

Can they do it? Certainly the impetus is there in the form of performance pressures that farsighted institutional leaders can use to build a case for change and to motivate key parts of the organization to develop pull structures and the set of practices that go with them. As with individuals, certain "elements of the journey" can help institutional leaders conceptualize and carry out this transition: trajectory, leverage, and pace (see the diagram on the following page).

Although we are focusing primarily on commercial enterprises, a broad range of institutions experience the same performance pressures. Educational institutions have been under growing pressure for decades. More and more nonprofit institutions are competing for scarce funding and contributions. Government institutions face their own pressures as companies make choices about where to locate operations on a global scale. All of these institutions evolved in the twentieth century to take advantage of new infrastructures and, like corporations, began to grasp the promise of scalable efficiency that these infrastructures offered. These institutions have a challenging journey ahead of them, but they, too, can use trajectory, leverage, and pace to harness the power of pull and deliver more value to their constituents using fewer resources.

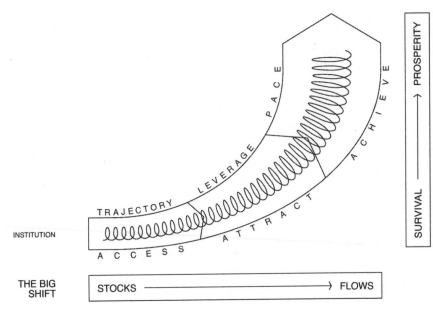

Havilland Studio, Palo Alto, California, and Lahaina, Hawaii

PRESSURE IS MOUNTING

As we have indicated, normal may be a thing of the past. The rules of the game are changing. And yet many institutional leaders are still playing by the old rules even though traditional management approaches are quickly becoming outmoded and less effective than they were in a push world.

Why don't these institutional leaders see that the rules are changing and adapt accordingly? Here's the problem: The changes playing out over the past couple of decades have been so fundamental that they have challenged even our most basic assumptions, the assumptions that enabled CEOs and other executives to build their institutions in the first place. At times the question has seemed to be not how to change specific practices or institutional arrangements, but whether the "institution" is still a viable form of organization at all. We find that we must reassess the rationale for the institution itself.

That challenge was so profound that, paradoxically, it faded into invisibility. We felt the growing pressure, but we assumed that it simply meant we had to work harder, faster, and more efficiently. So we squeezed more and more efficiency out of our operations—but the pressure kept mounting.

It's time to stop putting off what needs to be done: The only way out of this stressful situation is to step back and reassess the very rationale for the firm. Applying the techniques of pull will enable institutional leaders to navigate a challenging transition for their institutions as they wrestle with the arrangements required to be successful in the Big Shift. The changes that institutional leaders will need to set into motion in their organizations are very similar to the changes that all of us as individuals are making as we seek to turn challenges into opportunities. Once again, effective change requires trajectory, leverage, and pace.

DRIVING SUCCESSFUL INSTITUTIONAL CHANGE

Any student of management knows that efforts to make massive organizational changes have a very poor track record, with at best one-quarter of these programs yielding fundamental and sustained change. The quarter that do succeed tend to occur in large, hierarchically organized firms where the leadership team has considerable resources to push its programs out to all corners of the firm.

Perhaps that is exactly the problem. Push is seductive. It creates the illusion of great power in an era when power is shifting. It can delude organizational leaders into thinking they need only roll out the new plan and massively detailed organizational blueprints will become the new scripts that everyone will surely follow. But this view assumes that individuals are still the passive consumers and employees of yesteryear, who are simply awaiting their instructions from above. As we have seen, fewer and fewer of us match that description. In fact, that assumption may never have been valid, although a whole panoply of institutions, beginning with our educational system and proceeding all the way to the nursing homes that cared for us in our final years, did their best to socialize individuals into their scripted roles as part of massive push programs. Even the most ambitious push programs, those designed and deployed in Communist bloc countries, began to fray and unravel in the face of a basic reality: Individuals have aspirations and needs that extend far beyond the roles that any centrally scripted program can define.

But, as we have mentioned, the rationale for the firm, propelled and enabled by the new digital infrastructure, has changed to scalable learning, and new approaches to organizational change are now necessary as companies reorient around helping individuals achieve their true potential.

Younger generations of workers, who have grown up with the tools for individual and collective expression available to them all their lives, are now entering the workforce and the marketplace. They're joining older workers who are ready for change. Any effort to seek institutional transformation must begin with that reality. It must find ways to connect with, and build upon, the initiatives of individuals in ways that can gather force and overcome the powerful resistance that will inevitably come from entrenched interests in the existing institutional order. Push is not only seductive, it concentrates power. Those holding this power will not relinquish it easily or willingly. Power must be pulled from their hands.

For many institutional leaders, going to the edge will involve facing down their own fears. Embracing the new always creates perceptions of risk. Just as Joi Ito went to Dubai, just as Jack Hidary wandered into a conference where he didn't know the acronyms or the topics—all of us as individuals need to move out of our comfort zones in order to continue to grow, learn, and thrive. All of us have a role to play, no matter what "rank" or tenure we hold in the institution where we work. Without us, the journey won't take place. For institutional leaders the challenge is even bigger. Not only must they engage in their own quest toward the new, but they must find ways to motivate their followers to do the same.

Let's look at three broad approaches they can take to do so.

Defining a Trajectory for Change

Individuals, as we've seen, are increasingly discovering and pursuing the activities, endeavors, and jobs for which they have the most passion. Not surprisingly, this tends to make them less happy in the institutional environments they occupy—the ones that are built around and fixated on massive push programs designed to deliver scalable efficiency. Passion has little place in push programs. Passion is by definition hard to predict or channel. People with passion tend to want to pursue uncharted paths in their quest to achieve new levels of performance. Everywhere they turn, individuals find that the institutional environment tends to put up roadblocks to these unanticipated forays. All they can see are the possibilities that are blocked by institutional policies and processes.

It is not a surprise then that many of the most passionate and talented individuals are leaving their institutional homes and striking out on their own. Our 2009 Shift Index revealed that self-employed individuals are twice as likely to be passionate about their work than their peers who work for institutions.[4] Many observers interpret this as a long-term sign that more and more individuals will strike out on their own and that our large institutions will gradually yet inexorably shrink as we move into a "free agent nation."[5]

We suspect that the truth is quite different. Passionate individuals are fleeing the institutional environs that constrain, rather than amplify, individual passion and creativity. They can no longer abide being a passive cog in a highly scripted and often stultifying corporate machine. But the flight from big institutions will be a temporary, transitional phenomenon if those institutions figure out how to pull rather than push and commensurately reimagine how they can organize themselves and conduct their operations. Once they do, they'll become a natural home for passionate individuals who are themselves pulling with all their might.

Individuals seem desperate to find platforms and environments that can amplify their passion and are even now willingly seeking out emerging institutions that offer this potential. As institutions begin to realign themselves around different rationales, the exodus of passionate individuals will actually reverse. As word spreads, individuals will seek out the leverage that these new generations of institutions can provide. It's up to institutional leaders to compellingly evangelize the new direction in which their firm is headed. The new direction will act as a beacon for talented, passionate individuals. That's our goal.

Evangelizing the trajectory. The challenge for institutional leaders in the near term is to find and motivate talented individuals to engage in the task of transforming institutions rather than fleeing them. Unfortunately, these individuals are scattered throughout large institutions and often seek refuge on the periphery, where they find greater freedom by maintaining distance from the push-driven center. Still others of them have yet to be hired, or are employed at other firms, or are working as free agents and individual contractors. How can leaders pull these passionate individuals into the fray?

First they have to identify them. Not every questing individual is going to wear a tag saying how passionate they are. If they're a potential new hire, their resume might not make it clear either. Nor can institutional leaders necessarily know who the passionate people are among current employees. Sometimes the tendency that passionate individuals have to go to the edge can make them appear like less-than-stellar performers in an evaluation system geared toward submission to routines within core activities.

The Silicon Valley entrepreneur Tara Lemmey (who founded six companies before her current LENS Ventures, which brings business leaders, doctors, scientists, technologists, economists, writers, psychologists, and designers together to spur innovation) has a couple of useful ways to help identify questing, passionate individuals. In general, she's looking for people who can move and interact and thrive in different kinds of cultural environments and domains and for indications that they can "cross-pollinate" ideas and practices between and among them. She's also looking for a certain level of curiosity about the world.

To try to establish whether these qualities are present in an individual, the first thing Tara does is to take the person in question out to lunch, and then, once the food arrives, to offer to share a bite of hers. Some people will, in effect, say, "No thanks, I ordered what I want and I'm sticking to it." Others will gladly accept the bite Tara offers and proffer one from their plate in return. Guess which one is the cross-pollinator? Tara in fact finds a high correlation.

"People who won't share food don't do well with us," says Tara. "It's a brutal indicator."[6] (Though she's learned that this test doesn't always extend across cultures and nationalities. The British, in her experience, simply don't like to share food.) "People who share food tend to be less territorial. They're less likely to say, 'I ordered that. That's what I wanted. I got exactly what I wanted,' and more likely to say, enthusiastically, 'Hey, what's the table ordering? I want to try a little of everything.' Those folks tend to have a lot more ease in our working process."

Tara also likes to ask people if they were popular in high school. "High school is a time when people tend to be in a lot of emotional pain," she explains, "and they're either going to conform, or they're not going to conform. And, you know, how they made their choices about what they were going to do is what I find very revealing."

Tara's looking for two types of people: the "explorers" who create the innovations and the "diggers" who help "backfill" how you got there, make it look linear, and explain it to the diggers in the rest of the institution and in other institutions. The important thing is to be clear which disposition best characterizes a given candidate and to select people accordingly. It's easy to think that "passion" translates only into wild abandon, but you can be passionate and systematic. You need passionate diggers, too.

To attract these individuals, the institutional leader should strive to articulate a new rationale for the firm, one that can appeal directly to passionate individuals and offer them the promise of more rapid development of their talents. Even if it takes years to fully transform our big institutions from push to pull, clearly articulating a new rationale for the firm also will serve to focus initiatives. The efforts of individuals throughout the organization must begin to reinforce and build upon one another rather than bursting forth as isolated, fragmented forays but then quickly fading away.

This new rationale of scalable learning can immediately give rise to a certain degree of skepticism. Isn't scalable learning really about talent development? Isn't talent development something that every institutional leader embraces in words and largely ignores in practice? Institutional leaders seeking to champion this new rationale for the firm will have to be prepared to deal with this mindbug, which we call the Dilbert Paradox: How can we explain the continuing popularity of the *Dilbert* comic strip—and other media such as the television series *The Office*—which shows in graphic detail the stultifying effect of our work environments, when virtually every institutional leader today maintains with great conviction that talent is one of his or her highest priorities? How do we explain this wide gap between rhetoric and reality? Are institutional leaders simply being insincere, or is there another explanation for the wide gap?

Perhaps the answer is that institutional leaders are quite sincere, but they are generally trapped in traditional mindsets within institutional settings that undermine any efforts to genuinely develop talent. Let's start with how most executives interpret their commitment to talent. Press most executives for the next level of detail, and they will instinctively begin to discuss their efforts to attract and retain talent.[7] In a world of scalable efficiency, this is completely understandable. The major challenge in scaling operations is to find enough talent to fill the organization and then to retain that talent once it has been effectively integrated into the operations of the firm.

This way of framing the "talent challenge" diverts attention from the real challenge and opportunity. If executives invested more time on efforts to develop talent more rapidly throughout the organization, they might find that they began to attract all the talent they could possibly handle; word would spread that the firm was committed to developing its talent more effectively than other firms. And such a firm would have little issue with retaining talent: Why would anyone leave an institution that was helping them to develop faster than they could anywhere else?

Once executives hear about talent development, they immediately want to know what kinds of training programs we have in mind. This is a second misunderstanding driven by an outmoded push-based mindset. From a push perspective, talent development is all about training programs—anticipating what employees will need and designing training programs in advance that can then be pushed out to employees at the right time. In fact, training programs are only a very small part of the talent development equation. Most learning occurs on the job as employees tackle challenging performance requirements and find new ways to deliver that performance. The real opportunity is to rethink all aspects of the institution through the talent lens—what would the strategy, operations, and organization of the firm be like if talent development were the top priority of the firm?

We've already talked about how institutional leaders have to focus on *everyone* in their organization—and not just the so-called knowledge workers. But let's take it one step further, because there are yet more misunderstandings that arise on the topic of talent development, revealing some of the key assumptions that most executives bring to this topic. We have already noted in earlier chapters that Western executives tend to draw a firm line between "knowledge workers" and the rest of the workforce. If we are going to mobilize our entire workforce, we need to abandon this artificial distinction and recognize that everyone brings talent to the job that must be developed.

With few exceptions, executives immediately narrow the scope of discussion around talent development to their own employees. Yet, if we take talent development seriously, we begin to realize that, in the words of Silicon Valley icon Bill Joy, "There are always more smart people outside your company than within it."[8] If we are serious about developing our own talent, we must find more ways to connect with and collaborate with all of those smart people outside our organization. Even more important, we should aggressively create opportunities for people within our organization to work with leading-edge talent outside our organization. They may be talented already, but in this way, they can develop their talent more rapidly. In driving scalable learning, we must expand our horizons far beyond the boundaries of our own firm.[9]

This may sound a bit like open innovation, but it takes the idea of open innovation several steps further. Open-innovation efforts reach out to talent beyond the firm, but most of these efforts involve narrowly defined, short-term transactions—for example, posting a problem and offering a reward to individuals proposing an effective solution. These transactions miss the opportunity to build much longer-term, trust-based relationships that can be used to engage diverse teams in tackling much more diffuse and broadly framed challenges. Engaging in broader forms of collaboration has the potential to drive cumulative waves of performance improvement and talent development for all participants.

What does this redefinition of the rationale for the firm accomplish? It begins to define a compelling pull-based trajectory for the firm. By refocusing the firm on helping every individual achieve his or her full potential, institutional leaders can begin to find promising new ways to enable the firm itself to achieve its full potential. By communicating this new rationale aggressively throughout and beyond the firm, a leader can also begin to attract passionate individuals from all areas who are inspired by the opportunity to get better faster. The institutional leaders will thus be able to identify and connect with individuals who are motivated not only to change themselves but also to change their firm in profound ways.

The role of growth strategies. Institutional leaders can encourage the transition to pull-based models by defining aggressive growth objectives for the firm. They must resist the instinctive tendency that all of us have when under pressure to batten down the hatches and assume a defensive posture, the better to protect the core that generates the cash. In the Big Shift, such a posture is in no way protective. In fact, it puts the core at risk. Defense is no longer sufficient. Scalable efficiency is no longer sufficient. Margins will continue to deteriorate and economic value will continue to be destroyed until the leaders of today's big corporate institutions begin to pursue major new sources of growth.

A defensive posture is deadly for talent development. Why would questing individuals, who are currently running away from their institutional homes, want to work for companies that, in the face of a radically changing world, choose to cling to the outmoded approaches of yesteryear? Talent thrives when there are new challenges and opportunities to pursue. Institutions that are on the defensive with low-growth strategies simply cannot offer the same level of talent development to their participants. When such institutions are at their worst, we begin to see a vicious cycle take hold—as the firm goes on the defensive, the most creative talent becomes more vulnerable to offers from higher-growth firms, then performance deteriorates further as talent flees, and finally, the institution settles even further into its defensive posture and another wave of the talent exodus begins.

This is where leadership is desperately needed. Without clear and compelling long-term growth aspirations—and the short-term initiatives necessary to give them credibility—the defensive posture reigns supreme. Sure, it would be helpful to have a company's entire leadership team behind these aspirations and initiatives, but a single leader can achieve real impact—even if it's not the CEO. You might be a business unit leader or even a mid-level manager who is sufficiently autonomous from the rest of organization that you can initiate pull-based models even if the rest of the institution is not yet willing to take that step. As your unit begins to generate meaningful impact, other parts of the company may begin to see the benefits.

An institutional leader must provide compelling motivation for participants in the core to venture out to relevant edges in search of major new growth opportunities. This means putting a premium on strategies that move beyond straight-line growth within the core and that motivate investment in new growth options. This shift in strategic focus will inexorably pull the organization toward promising edges where growth potential is the highest—indeed, that's virtually the only place where major new growth options can be found. Recall that we defined edges in very specific terms involving geographic, demographic, and technological edges where unmet needs and unexpected capabilities tend to arise and intersect in ways that create rich seedbeds for innovation.

The 80/20 lens can be an effective tool for figuring out how to redeploy the resources that every company has stored in its core. This is an analytic tool that asks management teams to identify the 20 percent of customers, products, and geographies that generate 80 percent of the profitability. It then shifts the burden of proof on the owners of the 80 percent of the resources (which are only marginally profitable) to justify why these resources should continue to be supported. Those who control the marginally profitable sides of the business might have a number of valid ways to justify continued support; the key is to focus attention on different rates of profitability and to be prepared to eliminate activities that cannot be justified in terms of actual or potential economic contribution. In many cases, these efforts to restructure the economics of the core will lead management teams to raise the most fundamental question of all: What business are we really in?[10]

These parallel initiatives—reimagining the firm through the talent lens and identifying tangible and significant growth objectives for the firm—define a compelling trajectory for change. In practice, they are deeply related and mutually reinforcing. The talent development imperative helps attract and mobilize participants from the edge of the firm at the same time that compelling growth objectives motivate those in the core to connect with and support these edge participants. The two initiatives together help motivate people who are from the different cultures, skill sets, and economics of the edge and core to work together in driving change.

The key, however, is to make sure that these twin goals are clearly framed in terms of the role of the edge in driving the process of change. Participants in the core have a significant role to play—but it is to support initiatives that are designed to target opportunities on the edge.

Creating Leverage

Redefining the rationale of the firm will begin to attract a critical mass of passionate individuals from all parts of the firm, but especially from the periphery, where many of the people with the greatest passion tend to congregate. Why are we more likely to find passionate individuals on the edge of the firm? Because it is on the edge, in functions and remote branch offices that interact with people outside the firm, that people typically first encounter new challenges and opportunities. Customers unexpectedly appear with new needs. Suppliers introduce new capabilities that we had not anticipated. Business partners discover new approaches to challenging business problems. As a result, these areas tend to attract risk-takers, people who seek out new challenges and opportunities to drive their own performance to new levels, people who are not only more passionate than those at the core but who tend to have different approaches, practices, and dispositions than core participants. They don't sit home by the fire but set out for the Golden Fleece. Institutional leaders must find these people in their own organization while also striving to hire more of them and connecting with them across institutional boundaries.

Pulling people out of the core. Even then, however, these questing explorers are likely to be in short supply. That's why institutional leaders must also find ways to motivate the more risk-averse employees in the core of the business—who are likely to be the vast majority of their employees—to venture out and connect with their more passionate, questioning colleagues on the edge. Without this motivation, employees in the core are likely to dismiss those on the edge as a distraction to the real business of the firm—and to continue to marginalize them politically. These questing explorers need access to ample resources in the core of the firm and the ability to mobilize them so that they can scale the emerging growth opportunities that they tend to see and embrace first.

Rather than trying to pull the edges into the core, as many management pundits recommend, the key institutional challenge will be to develop mechanisms to pull the core out to the most promising edges. That's what Shai Agassi did when he took SAP to the edges represented by open innovation and Web 2.0 with the SAP Developer Network. In supporting these efforts, institutional leaders need to actively seek out "reverse mentors" from the edge who can work closely with them to help them understand and master some of the many edge practices.

Unfortunately, most senior executives sit in their offices at headquarters and invite younger people in occasionally to give them advice, thus bringing the edge to the core rather than vice versa. Imagine how much more powerful it would be for a senior executive to commit to spending one or two days each month on-site with reverse mentors so that he or she can develop a better understanding of the emerging practices situated in that context. As one example of this, one CEO of a retailing company regularly goes out to visit one of his stores without any entourage. He simply drives up in his own car, often unannounced, and spends the day with the store staff discussing the problems and opportunities they see. He finds the insights invaluable.

In some cases, these reverse mentors will have intriguing inter-generational overtones. Many of today's institutional leaders are part of the baby boom. They grew up in an era of push. Many (but by no means all) of today's edgier employees, by contrast, belong to "Generation Y"—the generation born into the digital world, often called "digital natives." Along with many members of Gen X (the cohort born between the Baby Boom and Gen Y), and even many baby boomers, Gen Y employees have themselves pioneered the uses of digital technology. For instance, they have realized how social media such as wikis, blogs, and discussion forums can be used to turbo-charge performance improvement—as it has both in World of Warcraft and software development. If you're an institutional leader with less familiarity and dexterity with new digital technology, it only makes sense for you to ally yourself with those who are ahead of you in this area and learn from them, even if they prove to be younger than you. Not everyone on the edge will be a young person, however. The point is to find reverse mentors at whatever age or on whichever edge you happen to find them.

Providing leverage through focused initiatives. As groups of questing individuals coalesce both within and across the boundaries of the firm, they can begin to set pull in motion through low-risk, high-reward initiatives. Rather than seeking the journey's end in one massive bound, it's best for these groups to recognize that a journey of a thousand miles begins with a single step, followed by another, and another. Starting slowly, below the radar, gives the champions of change opportunities to have small successes and gain strength while gradually neutralizing the inevitable resistance of entrenched interests.

Institutional leaders should be aware, however, that it's not enough for passionate people to simply be able to identify and connect with other passionate people. All of them must also begin interacting around some difficult problem within the institution. Say, for example, that a company has an aging group of loyal customers but has yet to reach younger consumers with its product or service. Perhaps there's a set of passionate people in the company who are frustrated by this. In such a case, these passionate individuals could be rounded up and given the assignment of designing new products or services for the company to introduce to meet some unmet need of these younger consumers.

It may help to provide leverage for these individuals by setting things up in short, consecutive waves of effort, iterations that foster deep, trust-based relationships among the participants. Once these relationships are established, individuals will begin to feel more comfortable with constructive conflict and productive friction—the hallmarks of a healthy group effort. Knowledge begins to flow and the team begins to learn, innovate, and perform better and faster. Having some significant problem or challenge to tackle causes these individuals to work together closely as they learn how to build on each other's diverse experiences, perspectives, and skill sets, discovering new practices that boost everybody's performance.

These tangible yet challenging operational initiatives, once established, draw out other passionate individuals in different parts of the organization who are inspired by the opportunity to achieve their own potential by joining into the pull-oriented efforts.

As these individuals begin to tackle the growth initiatives, they will start to identify opportunities to drive organizational changes that will help to accelerate talent development. Rather than focusing on talent development as an end in itself, the institutional leader can build support for talent development as a means to drive more rapid growth. The talent-driven firm emerges organically in response to the exigencies of substantial, profitable growth.

Providing leverage through pull platforms. One of the most powerful ways to drive leveraged growth is to begin to design and deploy scalable pull platforms that reach well beyond the boundaries of the firm to access and attract relevant talent wherever it resides. (We've discussed these as "creation spaces" in Chapter 4. Here we'll add just a few more comments.)

Pull platforms work in part because they use modularity to reduce the complexity that occurs when one tries to coordinate large numbers of diverse participants. Rather than trying to specify the activities *in* the processes in great detail (which is what the push approach would do), the orchestrators of the pull platform specify what they want to come out of the process, providing more space for individual participants to experiment, improvise, and innovate. This kind of modularity—in which the outputs are specified but not the inputs—is powerfully motivating for passionate individuals. Nobody stands over their shoulders telling them exactly which order to do things in or how exactly to plug together or integrate various elements of the project or design. Nobody insists that they achieve their output in the first 10 percent of the available time, or that they wait until the final 10 percent, or that they spread it evenly across the entire 100 percent of the time they have—just as long as they get the job done. As the legendary coach and general manager Al Davis, of the Oakland Football Raiders, used to say: "Just win, baby."

That's not to say the ends always justify the means, but rather that if you treat adults as grown-ups and give them sufficient leeway to accomplish what you ask them to—without trying to control all the ways they do it—then you'll end up with a much better outcome than if you treat them as children for whom every step must be specified. This is particularly true when it comes to using knowledge to create economic value.

In any case, as Tom Davenport pointed out in his book *Thinking for a Living*, it's both less valuable and more difficult to enumerate the specific activities required to create value from knowledge.[11] And your employees may well resent you for trying. Try it for long enough and you'll find them leaving your company altogether.

Amplifying the Pace of Change and Impact

Now that we've covered trajectory and leverage, we'll highlight the third element of the journey—pace—and discuss two key ways to amplify the pace and impact of efforts to make institutional changes: embracing new information technology platforms, and fostering new dispositions among the individuals who work both within and outside of the enterprise.

Amplifying impact through IT investment. No one who's made it this far into our book should be surprised to hear that, up until now, most of the IT investments that big companies have made have been related to scalable push ideas. Generalizing broadly, we might say that the largest component of IT spending in the enterprise over the past several decades has been to standardize and automate the core operating processes of the business in a quest for greater efficiency. Significant operating cost reductions have come out of the business as a result of these IT investment programs, to be sure, but ultimately all in the service of a diminishing returns game: Each increment of operating-cost improvement becomes harder and harder to achieve. Moreover, these improvements in efficiency have come at a significant price—they have tended to support the very same highly specified, tightly integrated activities that stultify workers while making it far more difficult for them to tinker, experiment, and achieve the rapid incremental innovation that is the essence of effective growth strategies. By making operational routines even more rigid than they were previously in a code that is difficult to modify, many IT investments also hinder the ability of firms to operate flexibly and fluidly with large numbers of specialized business partners in the process and practice networks that increasingly drive value creation.

Pull requires a very different set of technologies from those used in push. As with other dimensions of institutional change, leaders would be well advised to start at the edge as they craft a path to this new information technology. The challenge for institutional leaders is how to embrace and broaden the application of these edge technologies without, at least initially, directly challenging the core technology platforms of the firm. One of the most promising opportunities for applying these new social-media technologies in the near term lies in the area of exception handling. It turns out that a substantial portion of employee time in supply-chain management, sales, and customer service is devoted to handling exceptions that the automated enterprise

IT platforms cannot process. We're not talking about, for example, entering an address with the numbers transposed in a ZIP code. We're talking about a broad range of situations where the needs of the participants fall outside of currently defined policies and protocols even if no "error" has occurred. In these cases, it takes an inventive individual way too much time and requires too many resources (including other employees' time) to solve the problem.

These exceptions can take many different forms. They might be customer requests for certain financing terms for their purchases that were not anticipated by existing policies. They could be an unexpected disruption in the supply of a critical component in the manufacturing process. These exceptions are identified by the automated system and typically handed off to an employee. Generally, the exceptions cannot be resolved by a single employee, so appropriate individuals need to be identified, often across very different parts of the organization, and convened, along with appropriate data and analytical tools to support effective resolution.

Exception-handling activities tend to be highly inefficient and poorly supported by IT departments in today's push environments. It can be difficult, for example, to quickly find the people with the right experience and authority needed to resolve the exception, and it can be difficult to equip the exception handlers with the data they need to get the job done. As a result, considerable operating expense is consumed in pursuing exception-handling activities. It turns out that social-media technologies and web services are ideally suited for these tasks because they can flexibly connect people with necessary resources on a highly tailored basis to address unanticipated needs. Many employees are already cobbling together such technologies on their own to support longer-term initiatives—often in the context of a team that has been assembled to address key business initiatives.

The problem is that exception handling and most of the rest of the business usually operate according to radically different time frames. Instead of having the six to twelve months that might be available in an operating-team context for a project, for example, exceptions generally must be handled in a twenty-four- to forty-eight-hour window. Take, for example, that troublesome customer who is asking for special finance terms on his purchase—terms that go beyond the bounds of established policy. Typically, someone in sales support would be handed the exception as the enterprise applications discover a violation of policy. That person in sales support might have to bring together the salesperson responsible for the account, possibly a regional sales manager, certainly at least one person from finance, and probably one or two other people from the corporate sales group. It might be easy to specify the right people in the abstract, but finding the specific individuals who are prepared to resolve the exception and determining when they will be available to discuss it is a different story, especially in a large organization.

To complete the task, these people would need quite a bit of data, including information on the profit potential of the transaction in question both with and without the special terms, estimates of the long-term profitability of the customer, assessments of the likelihood of the company losing the order if the special-term request was rejected, projections concerning the long-term profit impact of the exception if a precedent is established with this particular order, perspectives on the relative importance of revenue versus profit goals in the current quarter, and so on. Assembling all of this data is time consuming, and it is typically done very inefficiently.

Institutional leaders can support exception handling of this type by creating operating environments in which social-media tools and web services can be used to pull data and people together quickly.

The business case for IT investment in such contexts is compelling—it can help to significantly increase near-term operating efficiency while at the same time creating more visibility regarding the extent and scope of exception handling. Since most exception handling today is a manual process, it tends to have limited visibility. Executives currently have a hard time identifying patterns in exception handling. Which exceptions are truly one-off, and which ones are beginning to surface with increasing frequency? The latter can be powerful leading indicators of emerging needs and capabilities that can help to focus innovation and growth initiatives in the firm. Thus, IT investment in exception handling can deliver near-term cost savings and provide a platform for identifying and targeting new innovation and growth opportunities.

These IT platforms are particularly powerful in supporting growth initiatives on the edge of the firm. Since these growth opportunities are still in an early stage of development, it is much harder to support them with the standardized, automated enterprise platforms used to support activities in the core of the business. Properly focused to support near-term growth initiatives, existing social-media tools and web services can significantly amplify the performance of edge participants, especially because they can connect edge participants across enterprise boundaries.

But existing tools and services are only the beginning. Institutional leaders can further amplify the pace and impact of their growth and talent-development initiatives by championing entirely new generations of IT architectures. Today's IT architectures evolved from the inside out, starting in the centralized glass house of the management information system (MIS) function, gradually extending out to operating departments, eventually reaching the desktop, and then only tentatively connecting beyond the enterprise to key business partners. As institutional leaders begin to pursue more aggressive leveraged growth and talent-development initiatives, they will increasingly run into the limitations of these inside-out architectures.

What's needed in a world of pull is the opposite: an information technology set-up that supports and organizes the crucial activities occurring on the edge of the firm. Such "outside-in architectures" would begin with the challenge of organizing IT resources across a large ecosystem of individual and institutional participants—most of them unrelated to each other by ownership. Since there won't be any single control point from which the designers of such an architecture could mandate adoption of specific applications or hardware platforms, this kind of technology design would need to acknowledge and embrace a degree of heterogeneity far greater than exists in even the most decentralized organizations today and find ways to connect these diverse technology platforms so that they can interact effectively.

Moreover, the very purpose of these large IT set-ups would shift. Instead of focusing on supporting short-lived transactions—such as a purchase order or a credit check—as most "inside-out architectures" do today, they would support knowledge flows and real-time interactions across a whole range of diverse participants, some of whom may be large or small corporations, some of whom might be free-agent contractors, some of whom might be small research firms, and so on. As a result, the purpose and function of corporate information-technology systems would gradually evolve from transaction to relationship architectures, supporting the development of long-term, trust-based relationships across large networks of participants who generated rich knowledge flows as they tackled more and more challenging performance objectives. In short, they would support and help to organize both the individual and the institution's ability to pull.

It might sound as if what we're calling for here has much in common with the so-called Enterprise 2.0 technologies, which use social media to help people within enterprises find and connect with each other. But we're calling for something that would extend beyond institutional boundaries to connect talent wherever it resides, even outside the firm. These outside-in architectures would get their start working across enterprises, but ultimately they would penetrate back into the enterprise, where their advantages would quickly become apparent.

Already we may be seeing the beginnings of this transition in the movement to cloud computing. As companies access more and more of their IT resources from cloud service-providers, these providers will learn to facilitate coordination of activities across large numbers of business partners, each of whom may have different ways of doing business as well as different terminology, policies, and procedures. This will set the stage for further evolution of IT architectures to support more complex, long-lived interactions across networks of diverse participants.[12]

Pull-based IT platforms represent a very tangible way to amplify the efforts of institutional leaders to move their firms from scalable push to scalable pull. An additional element to amplify these efforts is far less tangible, but no less powerful. It involves the evolution of new dispositions within the firm.

Amplifying impact through mindset. Institutional leaders cannot force people to go to the edge. It's not a matter of incentives, or other kinds of sticks and carrots. But leaders can create environments that attract and reward those with questing attitudes and mindsets, and they can indirectly foster the broader emergence of these mindsets.

They can also lead by example. This may mean taking a hard look at their own mindsets and attitudes as well as at their own assumptions about the sources of business success. Executives are often unaware of the unstated and unexamined assumptions underlying their approaches. It may not oversimplify things to characterize today's prevailing management mindset as follows: "We live in a largely static, zero-sum world where change is episodic and unpredictable. Change is threatening because it inevitably creates winners and losers. The best way to capture value in this world is to tightly control intellectual property and all the resources required to generate value from that intellectual property. Collaboration, to the extent it is necessary, works best with a few carefully selected partners with similar mindsets."

Contrast this statement with one representing an alternative management mindset: "We live in a dynamic world where the patterns of change are discernible and understandable, even if specific events are less predictable. Continuing innovations create the potential for much greater resource abundance and positive-sum outcomes where all participants can gain from collaborating with each other. Collaboration is essential to tapping into this potential, and the most powerful forms of collaboration are highly scalable, mobilizing large numbers of participants with diverse and very deep specializations."

The first management mindset—let's call it the control mindset— offers limited room for pull approaches and organizing the firm around the talent lens. If the world is largely static and control is the name of the game, talent certainly counts, but there is little need for it to be continually refreshed. In this worldview, talent development on the job actually undermines the higher goal of control.

The second management mindset—let's call it the collaboration mindset—provides a much stronger foundation for the pull-based firm. If the world is continually changing in discernible patterns and continuing innovation is the source of significant new value, talent development becomes a much higher priority. Executives with this mindset will recognize that existing talent rapidly obsolesces and that success depends upon continually renewing the skills and orientation of their employees. These executives are also more inclined to recognize the importance of accessing talent wherever it resides.

As we indicated at the outset of this chapter, in this process the institutional leader acts as a facilitator, promoting individual initiatives and pulling resources from the core to the edge. By defining compelling trajectories for change, providing leverage to the passionate individuals who are attracted to these trajectories, and helping to amplify the impact of these individuals, institutional leaders can play a meaningful role in increasing the likelihood of success in the institutional transformation from scalable push to scalable pull. But it is important to emphasize that this process of transformation will ultimately be driven by passionate individuals throughout the organization, and even from outside the organization, rather than by a few people at the top of the organization. Institutions that can evolve to support the needs of these passionate individuals and accelerate the development of their talent by providing platforms for scalable pull will thrive. Those remaining wedded to the principles and practices of scalable push will be increasingly marginalized as talent seeks the most hospitable organizational homes.

The power of pull does not end here, though. As we will explore in Chapter 7, the techniques of pull can be used to shape entire markets, industries, and social arenas. Properly harnessed, these techniques can, indeed, change the world.

BRINGING IT HOME

- How aligned is the leadership of your institution regarding the importance of accessing and developing talent, both inside and outside the institution? If not very aligned, are there at least one or two senior leaders who have this commitment? In what ways could you ally yourself with them?
- In what ways does your institution fall short when it comes to accessing talent—wherever it resides—and helping talent develop?

- What specific, short-term initiatives could act as a beacon to help your institution attract and engage passionate individuals both within and outside your institution?
- What growth initiatives have the greatest potential to help your institution rise to new levels of performance and be most effective in developing talent more rapidly?
- How effectively is your institution mobilizing technology to help people engage in on-the-job problem solving in order to develop their talent more rapidly? Is social media embedded into the daily work performed by the employees in your organization?
- Regardless of your tenure and position within the organization, what can you do to become a more effective catalyst for efforts to develop talent more effectively?

Chapter 7

Using Pull to Change the World

T ara Lemmey was watching the FBI agents closely, waiting for the
bulb to light up—the split second when the audience suddenly
understands what she's trying to tell them. The ah-ha moment
occurs at different times for each audience. For senior officials—such
as those to whom she'd presented at the CIA, the Department of Homeland Security, and the National Counterterrorism Center—the bulb
tends to light up as it becomes clear how all the pieces fit together into
a seamless whole. For ground-level agents, the ah-ha moment more
likely arises from how the details work.

Tara is an expert on how big institutions innovate—and why they
often don't. In 2001, she was asked to join the Markle Task Force on National Security in the Information Age, a group formed after the 9/11
attacks to help the intelligence community conduct counterterrorism
in a digital age. The task force faced a daunting task, to say the least.
Not only were all the different federal, state, and local agencies unused
(and often resistant) to sharing information among themselves, many
of them faced fundamental barriers to doing so. For instance, many
FBI agents lacked the typing skills they needed to enter information
into computers.

To stymie would-be terrorist attacks in a digital age, the task force was picturing a "share network" in which an alphabet soup of local, state, and federal government agencies in the United States—from the Centers for Disease Control and Prevention (CDC) to the National Security Agency (NSA)—would form ad-hoc teams to quickly share, analyze, and collaborate around flows of information and knowledge so as to learn faster about terror threats and shut them down when potential threats arose. The task force was hoping to create institutional innovations and harness the power of digital technology to improve performance.

In this regard task force members faced a set of challenges similar to those we've seen in the corporate sector. Like many of today's corporations, the majority of the U.S. intelligence and law-enforcement agencies, and the people within them, had been created for a bygone era, the Cold War—when security agencies tightly controlled access to intelligence information with the assumption that "the risk of inadvertent or malicious disclosure was greater than the benefit of wider information-sharing."[1] And they had developed skills suited to that era. But this mindset and approach was ill-suited to the digital age, and the 9/11 attacks galvanized the impetus for change.

The intelligence community, as we've all heard by now, had the information it needed to thwart the 9/11 attacks. But it had failed to get that information into the right hands. Too many of the agencies, with all good intentions, were busier protecting *stocks* of information (in the name of security) than they were engaging with *flows* of information that could have been analyzed and turned into the knowledge that might well have enabled them to identify and stop the terrorists involved in the attack.[2] Much like corporate-sector institutions engaged in industrial-age models of protecting knowledge stocks, intelligence agencies were fighting the last war.

The Markle Task Force aimed to change all that. First its members created a vision of what a newly collaborative environment might look like. Next they conceived of a platform for the interactions and collaborations. And then they set about convincing all the various stakeholders that it was in their best interest to participate. These are the same steps, more generally, that many institutional leaders have followed as they have looked to create massive change.

Consider Shai Agassi, who when we last left him was "pulling from the top" of SAP. Shai announced he was leaving SAP in March 2007 in a move that took many people by surprise. After all, Shai was heir apparent to SAP CEO Henning Kagermann when he resigned.[3] And his considerable passion for software was evident to everybody who encountered the SAP executive. So why, then, would he choose to leave?

Well, it turned out that Shai had an even bigger passion than software. He himself hadn't been aware of it until he was asked in 2005 to become one of the World Economic Forum's Young Global Leaders, an invitation-only group of people under forty from business, government, academia, media, nonprofits, and the arts, chosen from around the world. During their first meeting in Zermatt, where these young leaders were challenged to "make the world a better place" in the following ten years, Shai began to think big. How could he help to wean the world from its addiction to hydrocarbons? Soon he was spending all his spare time talking to energy policy wonks, reading books, going to conferences, and learning everything he could about energy. Not long after, convinced that he had a vision for speeding up the world's transition from CO_2-emitting internal combustion engines to electric vehicles, Shai Agassi began evangelizing, at conferences and in speeches and presentations, a new view of the transportation system.

Was anybody listening? The answer came in the form of a middle-of-the-night phone call from Shimon Peres, the head of the Israeli labor party, who had recently heard Agassi present his new view of the transportation system and wanted, there on the phone in the middle of the night, to know what Shai was going to do to "make this a reality."[4]

What Shai did was to leave SAP in order to bring into being Better Place, a company mobilizing diverse and distributed resources to build an infrastructure supporting electric vehicles running on batteries charged with renewable energy. With Better Place, Shai was tackling what he saw as the primary stumbling block to widespread use of electric vehicles: "range anxiety"—the possibility that your car's battery will run down before you make it home, with nowhere to recharge it.

By proposing a huge network of switching locations—where a robotic arm, in a less than a minute, would remove a rented battery from your car and put another one in its place—Shai was targeting the second big drawback of electric cars: They take a long time to recharge. (It takes nearly four hours to completely recharge a Tesla Roadster using Tesla's 70-ampere wall boxes.) Better Place's first battery-switching network is already under construction in Israel, soon to be followed by similar ones in Denmark, Hawaii, Australia, and northern California. Thus Better Place provides a crucial platform on which a diverse and distributed set of resources—start-up carmakers like Tesla Motors,[5] big auto companies like Renault-Nissan, and, eventually, perhaps tens of millions of car drivers—could come together to make electric cars (and lower emissions) a reality.

"After a career spent thinking exclusively about business software," *Wired* wrote in a 2008 cover story, "Agassi now thrills to the idea that he's changing the world. 'I get to shift multiple markets,'" he told *Wired*. "'I get to shift economies. It's extremely liberating. I breathe differently.'"[6]

Others began breathing differently, too, including a host of former SAP colleagues, who flocked to the new company, and a young man from Boston Consulting Group (*Wired* called him Shai's first "groupie") who followed Shai from conference to conference, handing him his resume. In fact, one or two talented people come up to Shai every day asking to join Better Place. Few of them had even looked at the Better Place business plan before joining. As *Wired* put it, "They were joining the cause, not just the company."[7]

Most will have trouble going back. "Once you have a mission," Agassi told *Wired*, "you can't go back to having a job."[8]

Having a mission. It's what Tara Lemmey calls "going big or going home." If you're going to do something, choose something that really makes a difference—a project, an endeavor, or an organization that addresses what people find meaningful and valuable. Something that stimulates their passionate desire to make the world a better place. It may be the drive to produce some social good, but it can be as simple as the profit motive—improving standards of living through increased business productivity. The key is for it to have shared meaning among a group of participants. Meaning is the opposite of boredom. It's present in many of the institutions that have changed the world. The point is not to find one vision, one meaning, one mission that fits every purpose, but simply to find one big enough to help mobilize a great number of people behind it.

Not that shared meaning, in and of itself, is enough to mobilize the masses. To set people and institutions in motion toward a common goal—to create the *leverage* that generates disproportionate impact—big visions like Shai's also need to vividly and explicitly describe what the world will look like and be like once it has been reshaped, refashioned, and reimagined—and they need to make clear what is required from nearly everybody who participates as well as what the rewards will be for those who participate.

We call such a vision a *shaping view*, a galvanizing statement about the future of a market, an industry, or a broad social arena that says how tomorrow will be different from today and how everybody will be better off thereby. A shaping view becomes the catalyst for a flow of participation by people and resources toward a common goal. When combined with the right platform and certain acts and assets, shaping views, now more than ever, hold the power to change the world. Given the challenges and difficulties facing the human race—from climate change to armed conflict to poverty—we need this power as never before.

Fortunately, today's digital infrastructure gives us new ways to make the most of what all of us can achieve together. We need new practices and approaches that can help us move beyond nice ideals and pious statements to actually behaving in ways that create disproportionate impact. It's not just theory or concept. Enabled by the Big Shift, small moves, smartly made, really *can* set big things in motion. It's happening right now. And it's being set in motion by people who've mastered the potential of pull at an individual level and have now turned their attention to making pull work in the biggest way they can to have the most impact—whether they're CEOs of big companies, founders of small entrepreneurial ones, or simply daring individuals with the foresight and moxie to make a shaping strategy work from outside the boundaries of institutions.

In this chapter we explore the concept of shaping strategies and how they represent pull at its broadest scope and biggest scale. We examine why shaping strategies are becoming increasingly powerful and relevant, and the specific techniques required to put them into play. As we shall see, appropriately applied, these strategies can help us to more effectively achieve our potential in the broadest economic and social environments (see the diagram on the following page).

SHAPING THROUGH PULL

If you saw an opportunity to radically reshape the world, would you pursue it? And if you understood that your success in doing this could be enhanced by persuading many other individuals and institutions to follow your lead, how confident would you be that you could prevail?

In the business world, it has been exceptional individuals who have managed to reshape the terms of competition in markets, industries, and even entire economic sectors. In Salesforce.com's early years, for example, founder and CEO Marc Benioff painted a compelling view of how to reshape the software industry around a new form of delivery: software as a service. The Fung brothers revolutionized supply-chain practice in the apparel industry. Malcom McLean led Sea-Land to a preeminent position in the containerized shipping business by driving standardization around his innovative container designs. And Dee Hock helped Visa make an exemplary shaping move in the 1970s at a time when banks had gotten into difficulty by aggressively sending out preapproved credit cards (even to newborns and family pets) without the infrastructure needed to support such large-scale transactions, or to sufficiently guard against fraud. The notion of "shaping" the world isn't new. Throughout history, in commercial, religious, and civic arenas, other people have shaped and reshaped their local areas or their regions, and even the world, as they pursued their visions.

But today's digital infrastructure can strengthen the hand of shapers while reducing their exposure to risk. The digital infrastructure enhances the ability of aspiring shapers to reach out to, connect with, and coordinate the actions of very large numbers of participants,

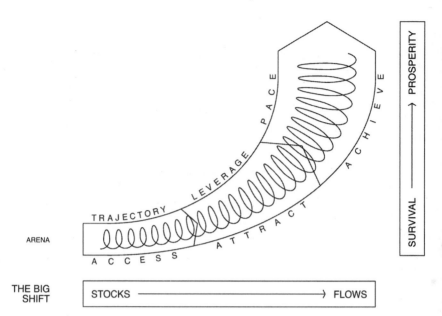

Havilland Studio, Palo Alto, California, and Lahaina, Hawaii

increasing the potential for leverage and for rapid and sustained distributed innovation. These relatively recent developments take the prospects for shaping success from the realms of the improbable and rare into the zone of the merely difficult. We've already seen Shai Agassi trying to reshape the world's transportation system around more renewable resources. Could such a shaping strategy help settle today's troubled financial markets? Or provide a way to resolve U.S. health-care challenges? Both health care and financial services, after all, have lots of potential participants and widespread uncertainty about the future—two conditions that make them ripe for shaping. But we get ahead of ourselves.

This chapter will define what we mean by shaping strategies and explore the key elements that our research suggests are essential for these ambitious strategies to exceed. We will explore in some detail who might aspire to play a shaping role, discuss other roles that might be appropriate in a shaping strategy, and suggest where these shaping

strategies are likely to be most appropriate. We also seek to differentiate this pull-driven shaping strategy from other forms of shaping strategies, while suggesting that this particular form has specific advantages.

Shaping Strategies Defined

As the name suggests, shaping strategies focus on reshaping broader
markets, industries, or social arenas rather than just an individual
company. These strategies explicitly seek to alter relationships across
large numbers of independent entities to create more value for all
concerned (though the shaper benefits disproportionately). How do
they do that? By creating and communicating positive incentives that
will mobilize very large numbers of participants. Various forms of
ecosystems can emerge and evolve around a shaping strategy. Aspiring
shapers would do well to make explicit decisions about the form of
ecosystem most appropriate for their particular business goal. Whatever the form, the goal is to engage these participants in distributed
innovation that accelerates movement toward the shaping destination.
This notion of positive incentives is essential—although shaping
strategies benefit the shaper in meaningful ways, to be effective they
must also create meaningful benefits for a broad array of participants.
The positive incentives can take many forms, but the key is that the
shaper is able to flip conventional perceptions of risk and reward that
tend to arise in times of high uncertainty. While rewards may take the
form of profitable growth in commercial arenas, different forms of
rewards will likely be the primary drivers of shaping strategies in nonprofit, social, and political arenas. The key is that the participants perceive a meaningful upside in terms of achieving their individual goals
by participating in a broader shaping ecosystem.

Shaping strategies draw people together even when they may not
know each other or have worked together before, even when they may
not live near each other, and even though they're in different lines of
work and may have different political beliefs, different ways of problem
solving and looking at things, and different terminology or languages.
Shaping strategies both embody and express the principle that all of us

together are stronger than any of us alone. They hand the lever to Archimedes and give him a place to stand in order to change the world.

With shaping strategies, the broad scope of the aspiration finds its match in the sheer scale of people and institutions participating. We are not talking here about a few key strategic partners, but thousands and in some cases even millions of participants collectively moving together to realize a shared view of the future. They may be motivated by economic considerations, but they may also be motivated by deeply held feelings of fear and hope, risk and reward. All of us, confronted with rapid change and uncertainty, tend to instinctively perceive risks as being bigger than they actually are while discounting potential rewards. This calculus often freezes us in place. Shapers use their powerful view of the future, as well as their robust shaping platforms—and, indeed, their own acts and actions—to diminish perceived risk and maximize perceived rewards, thus motivating investment and action.

Shaping strategies stand in sharp contrast with much of the conventional wisdom that has emerged about strategies in times of high uncertainty. Conventional wisdom suggests that in uncertain times, the winning strategy is one of adaptation—sensing and responding quickly to events as they unfold. Although we would certainly support the notion that all companies must become more adaptive—indeed, that is the entire thrust behind our emphasis on pull approaches—we are also concerned that this perspective misses one of the biggest opportunities arising in times of rapid change and high uncertainty, in which we have far more degrees of freedom to shape broader markets, industries, and social arenas than we do in more stable times. Our focus here is on how to address that opportunity in the most powerful and effective way possible using the techniques of pull.

Shaping strategies make the most of all three levels of pull. Through shared platforms, they make it possible to *find* and *access* highly specialized resources among the participants in the ecosystem—the first level of pull. Positive incentives also help *attract* and *influence* very large ecosystems of people and institutions—the second level of pull. By focusing attention on a particular long-term direction and highlighting both the opportunity and challenges involved in getting there, these strategies motivate people and institutions to more fully *achieve their potential*—the third level of pull.

In the end, shaping strategies are where pull can achieve its biggest and widest impact. They are a natural outgrowth of our efforts to master the power of pull at the individual and institutional level. As we become more comfortable with our ability to achieve our potential at these levels, we will begin to see more and more opportunities to amplify our potential even further by reshaping broader and broader arenas. We will also have more insight into, and experience with, the pull techniques required to pursue shaping strategies.

How Shaping Strategies Are Different from Other Strategies

Shaping strategies differ significantly from other well-known strategies. Clayton Christensen and Michael Raynor have painted a very compelling picture of the potential to pursue disruptive innovation strategies.[9] These strategies can generate enormous wealth for the innovator but, in general, they are different from the strategies we are discussing on two important dimensions. First, they often involve a single company making significant commitments to a disruptive innovation in technology or business design, rather than an individual or group bringing together very large numbers of companies to make complementary investments. Think of the iconic examples of disruptive innovators such as Nucor or Southwest Airlines. These companies bet big, but they largely bet alone. On one hand, for those who win in pursuing disruptive innovations, the prize is very large because it does not have to be shared with anyone else. On the other hand, there is little opportunity to manage risk by sharing investment across large numbers of players. These shapers often literally bet the company and live or die based on the outcome of the bet.

The second key difference in disruptive innovation strategies is that these strategies motivate others to invest and move based on negative incentives. The basic proposition is that, if others do not invest to adopt the disruptive innovations, they will die. Imminent death does focus the mind. But it is a negative incentive rather than a positive one, and positive incentives are central to the shaping strategies we are discussing.

Another form of shaping strategy depends on mobilizing large ecosystems of players. The iconic example in this domain is Apple, which has fundamentally reshaped the music industry by designing and deploying a new kind of portable digital music player (the iPod) and linking it with an online music service (iTunes). But think carefully about this example. Apple does depend on the cooperation of large numbers of other participants, especially music companies, to contribute their creative products to the Apple music platform. But it does not expect, or seek to motivate, innovation from all of these participants (unlike with the iPhone, where Apple's strategy relied more heavily on distributed innovation by a growing number of independent application developers). All it asks is that the participants on the iTunes platform adopt a certain standard format in the way they present their music products; Apple takes care of the rest. This is a much more static form of shaping strategy than the type we are proposing— it seeks to leverage resources already available but does not seek to become the catalyst for new levels of performance or new capabilities on the part of participants in the ecosystem. The shaping strategies that we are discussing are much more dynamic.

ELEMENTS OF THE SHAPING JOURNEY

Having said what a shaping strategy is, let's look more closely at its key elements. These closely parallel the elements of the journey we've described for individuals and institutions, only this time, the scope of the endeavor is even broader.

Three elements need to come together for a shaping strategy to succeed: a shaping view (which sets the direction, or trajectory); a shaping platform (which creates leverage for participants); and shaping acts and assets (which accelerate pace by building the conviction needed to speed investments and innovation on the part of participants, enabling the shaper and the ecosystem as a whole to make more rapid progress in realizing the shaping view).

Trajectory-Shaping View

The first step is to shape the mindsets of potential participants. By shaping mindsets, shapers can materially influence perceived economic and other incentives, which become the key to shaping action. This goes far beyond the conventional public relations campaign.

Shaping strategies begin with a clear and compelling long-term view (measured in decades, not years) of the future contours of the relevant industry or market. This view establishes the trajectory for all concerned—decreasing the perceived danger of taking the wrong path while clarifying the focus of activities and investments. Building upon the fundamental forces at work, this long-term view helps to make visible the significant rewards that will accrue to those who act accordingly. This shaping view helps to reduce perceived risk while at the same time strengthening perceived rewards. The shaping view is never very detailed. It leaves much room for refinement, but it is clear enough to help participants make difficult choices in the near term. Trajectory, remember, is about the goal, not the process.

The classic example of a shaping view is the one articulated by Bill Gates in the early 1980s, which could be paraphrased as: "Computing power is moving inexorably from centralized mainframes to the desktop. Companies that want to be leaders in the computer industry need to be on the desktop." Many executives in the computer industry made the trek to Redmond in the early 1980s at a time of great turmoil and uncertainty in the computer industry. They returned vastly reassured that someone had a compelling view of the direction of the industry.

Even more importantly, this shaping view helped to focus these executives in terms of investment opportunity. At a time when many options were competing for investment, the ability to focus more clearly on the opportunities with the highest return on investment proved extremely valuable. Microsoft has become such a significant player in the computer industry that it is often difficult to go back in time and imagine the importance of this shaping view in driving the early success of the company.

This example of a shaping view highlights an important distinction relative to more conventional corporate "visions." Corporate visions tend to be both too narrow and too broad. They are too narrow in the sense that they focus on describing the direction of the company. In contrast, shaping views start with a clear view of the direction of the relevant market or industry and then move to implications for all companies in terms of creating value. The shaping view articulated by Bill Gates certainly applied to Microsoft, but, more importantly, it spoke to anyone who wanted to be successful in the computer industry. The creative act in a shaping view is to imagine what an industry or market could look like and to challenge conventional assumptions about what is required for success.

Corporate visions also tend to be too broad in the sense that they describe the future in such vague terms that they can accommodate virtually any choice or action. Although shaping views must acknowledge the uncertainty on the broader business landscape and provide sufficient room for experimentation and innovation, they also must offer a more tangible focus in terms of where to invest.

Salesforce.com provides a more recent example of a shaping view at work. Started by Marc Benioff less than a decade ago, Salesforce.com has emerged as a highly successful maker of software for companies. It started with a focus on salesforce automation and customer-relationship management applications. In less than a decade, Salesforce.com has become a public company with a market capitalization of almost $7 billion. It has nearly tripled its revenue over the past three years, and it mobilized more than 700 independent applications on the application platform that it recently introduced.

From the outset, a clear shaping view drove Salesforce.com's entry into the enterprise application space. In the early days, watching Marc Benioff at an industry conference could be quite instructive. Most entrepreneurs would use the opportunity to give a strong pitch for their own company and its products. Benioff was different. He would spend 80 percent of his time talking about fundamental forces at work within the enterprise application arena.

Two themes dominated his early talks. First, customers were gaining more power and the companies that focused on helping other companies become more responsive to customers and effectively manage relationships with customers would be the big winners in increasingly competitive markets. Second, the applications required to support these business imperatives would be delivered most effectively as online services rather than discrete software packages installed on company premises. At a time when the established competition was focusing on creating big applications to help companies manage their internal operations, this was a startlingly different view of the future. When many were wondering about the future of the enterprise-application software market, this shaping view suggested lots of opportunity for specialized players to enter the market and a new focus for investment by existing players.

Of course, it helped that Salesforce.com just happened to have a new online service supporting salesforce automation. But to anyone who heard Benioff it was clear that this was not just a salespitch, but instead a very different view of where the software business was headed, one with much broader implications than just for his company. He was imagining a very different view of the future, and he was a tireless evangelist for this perspective.

Benioff's talks were so compelling in those early days because he went out of his way to tie his shaping view to the fundamental forces at work in the business world. He discussed at length the competitive dynamics on the broader business landscape and the underlying developments in the digital technology infrastructure that were reshaping the software world. Executives left his talk convinced that this was not just a provocative view of the future, but one that was inevitable. Uncertainty dissolved, the perceived risk diminished, and the rewards for participating became far more tangible. The only question was whether to hop onto the bandwagon right away and share in the rewards or risk joining later when the rewards might be far smaller.

The bottom line is that the shaping view helps to focus the investments and innovation initiatives of participants in a shaping strategy. It tells everyone that the opportunity is over here and not over there. For example, it is on the desktop and not in the glass house of the IT organization. It also provides a compelling view of the tangible rewards that will be available for everyone who chooses to participate.

Here are five questions executives can use to test the potential robustness of a shaping view:

- Does the view express a perspective regarding the long-term direction of a broad industry or market and highlight what is different in that view from the situation today?
- Does the view clearly identify attractive business opportunities that can focus the investment of a broad range of participants?
- Does the view tie these opportunities explicitly to broad economic, cultural, and technological forces at work on the business landscape?
- Is the view broad enough to accommodate unexpected developments yet specific enough to provide focus and direction for executives faced with difficult choices?
- Has the view been aggressively and continuously communicated by senior management to employees and external audiences?

Leverage-Shaping Platform

The second component of a shaping strategy is a shaping platform that supports and organizes the activities and efforts of everybody involved in the ecosystem. Shaping platforms deliver the crucial second element of the journey by enabling participants to do more with less. The leverage they provide is especially valuable in times of high uncertainty because it reduces the investment and effort required to target potential rewards and thereby reduces potential risk.

Shaping platforms typically offer one of two forms of leverage. Some shaping platforms offer development leverage. They reduce the investment required to build and offer products or services. These development leverage platforms are often technology based. Some current examples of shaping platforms providing development leverage include the Force.com platform offered by Salesforce.com for developers seeking to develop application services for the enterprise market, and the Facebook platform that makes it easy for software developers to develop mini-applications, or "widgets."

But shaping platforms are not restricted to technology platforms. A different type of shaping platform provides leverage for interaction— it reduces the cost and effort required to coordinate activities across large numbers of diverse participants. Although this type of platform may have a technology component, the key value is provided by a standardized set of protocols and practices designed to facilitate interactions.

Li & Fung developed an innovative shaping platform to coordinate complex supply-chain activities across a global network of 10,000 business partners serving apparel and other consumer goods companies. Google's AdSense platform uses technology to connect advertisers, content providers, and potential customers, but its real value consists in a set of protocols and practices governing how ads are submitted, presented, and paid for, enabling participants to generate value from the platform with minimal investment of time and effort and minimal oversight from Google.

Malcom McLean, the founder of Sea-Land and a successful shaper of the global shipping industry, employed a very different kind of shaping platform to provide interaction leverage. He developed an innovative design for four corner fittings and twist-lock mechanisms on shipping containers. By making these designs available to the broader shipping industry, he encouraged a broader set of investments by port authorities, crane companies, and shipping companies that accelerated the adoption of containerized shipping.

Visa, in the early days of the credit-card business, created a robust shaping platform that merged both development leverage and interaction leverage. One part of the platform involved the provision of back-office credit-card processing services for participating banks using technology to connect a large number of participants together. This significantly reduced the investment required for banks to enter the credit-card business, since they could focus on product design and marketing while offloading the capital-intensive processing activities to a specialized third party.

Another part of Visa's shaping platform provided interaction leverage by defining a governance structure enabling large numbers of banks to jointly own this new business entity while still preserving the ability of the entity to move rapidly and flexibly. Within a year of its development in 1970, Visa had recruited 3,000 banks to participate in this new venture, and within seven years Visa was generating $20 billion in sales, reshaping the emerging credit-card business in the process.

Platforms provide powerful leverage, both for the shaper and for third-party participants. For a participant, they offer significant functionality with relatively low adoption costs, with a value that increases as the number of participants grows. Robust platforms also help to encourage a rich ecosystem of niches so that participants can specialize in the areas that they know best and avoid competing head-on with everyone else participating on the same platform. For example, the Li & Fung global process network encourages individual participants to pursue deep specializations in various elements of the apparel production process, secure in the knowledge that they will find customers for their specialized capabilities through the process network.

For the owner of the platform, shaping platforms accelerate learning by generating and concentrating knowledge flows as participants engage with the shaper, sharing their plans and perceptions while seeking insight into the future direction of the platform. Owners can see the big picture in a way most other participants cannot. When apparel designers and manufacturers from around the world visited with Li & Fung executives to share their needs and capabilities, the Li & Fung executives gained considerable insight into investments being made across the global apparel industry. In high-uncertainty environments, privileged access to rich flows of knowledge can become a significant advantage.

Shaping platforms provide tangible economic leverage to participants by reducing initial investment requirements, and they accelerate the generation of revenue and profits from the investments made. In this way, they significantly alter the economics of participation. They in effect very tangibly reduce perception of risk and magnify perception of reward.

Here are five questions executives can use to test the potential robustness of a shaping platform:

- Does the shaping platform materially improve the economic position of potential participants, especially in terms of reducing the cost of entry for potential participants and/or accelerating the prospect of revenue generation?

- Does the shaping platform support a very diverse set of participants and offer the potential for many distinct niches of value creation?
- Is the shaping platform scalable—that is, can it accommodate large numbers of participants without incurring unacceptable complexity overheads?
- Does the shaping platform have the potential to generate increasing returns—in other words, will it become more valuable to participants as the number of participants increases?
- Will the shaping platform continually evolve in terms of functionality, providing an incentive for participants to engage regularly with the platform owner and share their own learning and plans?

Pace-Shaping Actions and Assets

The actions and assets of the shaping company itself constitute the third component of a shaping strategy. Even the most compelling shaping view and the most robust shaping platform could be marred by lingering concerns that the shaper may not have the conviction or capability required to achieve success. On the flip side, participants are also likely to be concerned that the shaper may eventually become too powerful and target their own business niches for competition. The shaping company, though, can use its actions and assets to persuade potential participants regarding the likelihood of the success of the shaping strategy and the commitment of the shaper to maintain reasonable boundaries in terms of where it will choose to compete. It would be a shame to have a vision and build a platform and have no one show up to use it.

These actions can often be quite dramatic. Novell provides one of the best examples of a shaping action designed to persuade participants. Novell saw an opportunity in the early 1980s to shape the local area network business—an extremely important technology arena emerging on the heels of client server architectures. It had developed a robust network operating system for local area networks and believed this could provide a powerful shaping platform to influence the evolution of the local area network business. At the time, it was also a significant manufacturer of local area network hardware.

In an effort to accelerate adoption of its network operating system, it made a dramatic announcement that it would divest its hardware business, which at the time represented 80 percent of its revenue. The message to the rest of the emerging industry was clear: Novell was so deeply committed to its network operating system that it was prepared to walk away from a significant portion of its revenue. This bold act communicated to other network hardware manufacturers that they could adopt Novell's network operating system without worrying about the possibility that Novell would compete with them in their core business.

This action effectively positioned Novell as a very successful shaper of an important arena of the technology industry, leading to the adoption of Novell's network operating system as a de facto standard in the local area network arena for more than a decade. Novell ultimately diversified into a number of other business areas, losing focus on its core operating-system business. As a result, Novell lost its leadership in the local area networking business, a cautionary tale to aspiring shapers that successful shaping requires tight focus.

Malcom McLean made a similar bold move in his effort to accelerate adoption of his shaping platform for the containerized shipping industry. He held valuable patents for his innovative design for four corner fittings and twist-lock mechanisms on shipping containers. In the 1960s he issued a royalty-free release of these patents to the Industrial Organization for Standardization, a move that demonstrated his commitment to accelerating the adoption of his shaping platform. McLean could afford to be magnanimous with the intellectual property from his shaping platform because he was the founder and major shareholder of Sea-Land, a shipping company that was a pioneer in the use of containerized shipping and that stood to profit handsomely from broader adoption of containerized shipping standards.

Assets of the shaping company also become a significant factor in persuading potential participants to invest in support of the shaping strategy. In this domain, large, established companies have a potential advantage as shapers. Their massive assets can help to establish credibility for the shaping view and shaping platform. On one hand, few would doubt that these companies have the assets required to support a shaping strategy. On the other hand, smaller new entrants face a significant challenge on this front. Anyone considering investing behind their strategy will understandably wrestle with the concern that the shaping company may not have the assets necessary to support a promising shaping strategy. The risk of stranded investment becomes very real.

A smaller new entrant can often address this concern through strategic relationships designed to access the assets of larger, better-known companies. For example, Microsoft in its early days negotiated an important relationship with Intel, the leading manufacturer of microprocessors, which helped to enhance Microsoft's credibility. Somewhat later, Microsoft's relationship with IBM to provide an operating system for a new line of desktop personal computers communicated to the world that this small company in Redmond, Washington, was a force to be reckoned with.

More recently, Microsoft is playing the reverse role with Facebook, helping to lend credibility to this much smaller aspiring shaper with the announcement of a significant minority investment in Facebook and a broad set of joint initiatives. In another recent example, Google, a well-known company but with minimal experience in the telephone industry, has gained much more credibility for its shaping platform in the mobile phone industry—the Android operating system—by announcing the Open Handset Alliance.

Shaping strategies rely on a number of elements that must be effectively integrated to achieve their full impact. Conflating the strategy into one of its component elements misses much of the power—and makes it less likely that one will take a firm on the journey to pull. For example, platforms are a key element, but harnessing the full potential of platforms to reshape markets and industries requires coupling these platforms with a compelling shaping view and the actions required to give credibility to this view. Moreover, platforms in this context go well beyond the technology platforms that currently occupy much of management attention.

Similarly, shaping strategies accelerate adoption of de facto standards and harness the economic power of increasing returns. Once again, though, the de facto standards discussed here go well beyond more conventional technology standards to include institutional arrangements like those developed by Visa and management practices like those developed by Li & Fung. While increasing returns are a powerful force in mature shaping strategies, these strategies focus on the deep challenges involved in getting to the critical mass required to unleash increasing-returns effects.

Here are three questions that executives can use to test the potential robustness of the actions and assets required to be a successful shaping company:

- For large incumbents, what actions have been taken to persuade potential participants that the firm will remain committed to its shaping view and platform even in the face of inevitable short-term setbacks, given all the other business initiatives the firm is pursuing?
- For new entrants, how will the firm gain access to the assets required to persuade potential participants that the firm has the resources necessary to pursue a successful shaping strategy?
- For all potential shapers, what actions have been taken to assure potential participants that the firm will not compete with them over time?

WHO CAN SHAPE?

Reading how the three shaping elements come together to restructure markets and industries, you might be thinking, "This is not a strategy for me." Maybe you're an institutional leader who figures that shaping is a game for more nimble start-ups. Maybe you figure that you lack the deep pockets such a strategy might require. Maybe you're a mid-level manager at a big firm thinking that you lack the clout and autonomy to inspire your firm to devise such a strategy. Or maybe you don't work for either of these types of companies and are wondering if all of this is just for business institutions, not individuals.

Shaping strategies are in fact feasible for people in any of these roles, though each of them will have particular strengths and weaknesses as they pursue them. Even if you're not cut out to be the shaper yourself, there are other valued, valuable, and profitable roles within a shaper's ecosystem that you might consider playing.

Big Company Shapers

It's not surprising that big company executives sometimes express skepticism about their company's ability to succeed with shaping strategies. They are all too aware that their institutions often carry the "curse of deep pockets": They can afford to go it alone with their own relationships and resources and often have a hard time seeing the benefits of collaborating. There's also the "not-invented-here" syndrome: companies that are successful under the current industry structure in the marketplace can have a difficult time embracing new ways of doing things for that very reason. These companies have difficulty seeing the need for the institutional innovations necessary to making shaping strategies work. Existing market participants may also have "abuse-of-power concerns"—the worry that the incumbent will abuse its power as a shaper, for instance, by beginning to compete with them once it has lured them into a shaping strategy. Big companies can also be hindered by short-term time horizons driven either by capital markets or by internal compensation systems.

Despite these difficulties, big companies have a number of advantages as shapers:

- *Capabilities:* Incumbents have processes and people they can use to decrease the cost of implementing a shaping strategy.
- *Broad relationships:* Incumbents have strong relationships with market participants that can help build conviction and commitment for the shaping view and platform.
- *Track record of success:* Market participants will be more likely to trust and follow a shaper that has a proven track record for innovating.

- *Deep pockets:* Having the financial resources to demonstrate internal support for a shaping view and platform will further
strengthen market participants' perception of a shaper.

Start-ups in many ways have the advantage when it comes to shaping. They don't have years of inertia built into their culture and organizational structure the way so many big companies do. And they're
often playing on the edges of more established markets and industries, which is exactly where a shaping strategy gets its start. But start-
ups also have difficult challenges relating to their credibility as
shapers, including the need to demonstrate the "staying power" necessary to see the strategy through to its conclusion:

- Do you have enough money in the bank to support this
strategy?
- Do you have highly visible investors with deep pockets?
- Do you have blue-chip partners and/or users that legitimize the
potential by bringing in valuable assets (relationships, experience, marketplace trust)?
- Do you have access to the assets needed to build the platform
and to prove your credibility with potential partners and
customers?
- Do you have the skill sets and experience to coordinate hundreds of business partners? If not, can you acquire those skill
sets?

Shaping from Within Large Institutions

What if you are not the leader of a firm or other institution? Is there
anything you can do to shape your environment by mobilizing others
in the ways we have described above? Clearly you can use pull techniques to shape serendipity, as we described in Chapter 3. But here we
are talking about a much more specific type of shaping strategy that
brings together shaping views, platforms, and acts and assets. This is
much less likely to be within the reach of a front-line employee of a

very large firm. And yet, we believe that shaping opportunities are available to a broad range of executives and not limited to those at the very top of large institutions.

Let's take an example. If you lead a relatively autonomous unit within a much larger institution, you have resources and degrees of freedom that could provide a window for you to devise a shaping strategy that might start modestly and expand in scope over time. Let's imagine that you are responsible for managing the supply-chain operations of your company. Like most Western companies, supply-chain operations within companies are currently run in a top-down, tightly integrated, and highly scripted manner with a limited number of large-scale suppliers. As the head of this part of your company, you might decide you want to reshape the supplier industry as a way to generate more distributed innovation. This would clearly benefit your own company, but the aspiration would be to reshape this part of the industry for the benefit of all participants over time.

How might you go about doing this? You might start by defining a shaping view with the objective that over the next ten to twenty years the supplier industry will evolve from a highly concentrated set of diversified suppliers to a much larger number of more specialized providers that are far more innovative in their areas of expertise than suppliers are presently and that are all actively accelerating their performance improvement. The restructuring that would take place to accomplish this objective would be driven ultimately by two forces—far more demanding and powerful end customers who would be seeking to improve their own performance, and creative product engineers and designers who were frustrated by the bureaucracy of the large concentrated players today and who would welcome the necessary changes. Note that this shaping view is articulated from the perspective of the players themselves, rather than from the perspective of the executive or company seeking to play the shaping role.

What might constitute a shaping platform in this scenario? The shaping executive might start by joining a connection platform, such as the one operated by InnoCentive, and establishing a more tightly focused space within that broader platform addressing the challenging performance needs in this particular industry. This platform would be open to everyone, not just the company's existing suppliers but also individuals and representatives of smaller companies who might think they have creative solutions to some of the performance challenges presented. Cash awards could be provided to successful problem solvers, and there could be the additional prospect of perhaps joining the shaping executive's supplier network.

A further enhancement to this shaping platform might be to take it in the direction of the creation spaces described in Chapter 4. At this level, the shaping platform could begin to create incentives and tools for small entrepreneurial companies to collaborate with each other in complementary areas to address even more challenging performance issues defined by the shaping executive. Once again, the prospect would be for the most innovative companies to join the broader supply network of the shaping executive.

To accelerate the expansion of the supplier ecosystem, the shaping executive might also target a set of private equity investors who were particularly focused on the technologies and products of his supplier network. He could communicate the most pressing performance challenges confronting his supplier network and encourage them to seek out investment opportunities in companies developing promising approaches to these needs. A significant incentive for this investment would be his commitment to source solutions from early-stage companies. As these companies get funded, they would have the opportunity to join the creation space and find other complementary participants who might help to leverage their own efforts.

To give credibility to this shaping view and platform, the executive would need to be prepared to act in ways that clearly communicated his commitment to broadening and diversifying his supply chain over time. This would likely require him to make some highly visible decisions early on to shift some of his purchasing activity from established suppliers to new, more innovative and specialized suppliers. The executive might also see if the products from his suppliers were also used in adjacent industries that did not compete directly with his company. If this was the case, the executive would be able to build further credibility by mobilizing potential customers in adjacent industries to join the creation space and begin to engage directly with the most promising innovative suppliers.

Could these shaping opportunities exist at even lower levels within a large institution? Perhaps. Let's imagine a team leader for the development of a new product. We'll posit that previously, the company had developed very innovative but tightly integrated products. The team leader expects that a very different approach to product development is essential for success in the future. She might help to shape this future by the actions she takes in the context of her product-development effort. She might start by defining an alternative view of how product-development efforts might be organized in the next couple of decades. This view might anticipate that products will be increasingly modularized and loosely coupled to encourage more active participation by customers and by component and subsystem providers in the product-development process. She could evangelize this view both within her company and with relevant potential participants in a product-development ecosystem.

To support this view, she might create a leveraged product-development platform consisting of a collaborative workspace and various forms of design and analytical tools that accommodated participants from the outside who could contribute to the development of specific modules of the product. She might then use this platform to recruit promising participants from different areas within her own company as well as from the customer base and the supplier base. This platform would help interested participants connect with each other and collaborate in their development efforts.

To build credibility for the shaping view and the shaping platform, the team leader for the product-development effort would need to be thoughtful regarding the acts or assets she might put to use in support of this shaping strategy. For example, she might explicitly reserve certain modules of the prospective product for development only by third parties. She might also focus on recruiting one or two design partners from the outside that were widely recognized in their fields to assure other prospective participants that this product really had the potential to be world class.

If it was successful, this small-scale shaping effort might be a catalyst for much broader shaping initiatives by the company, moving the industry to a much more ambitious open-innovation model of product development. This broader effort would be significantly helped by the initial, much narrower shaping initiative that demonstrated the feasibility and power of this approach.

Shaping from the Outside In

Finally, you may be an individual who does not currently work for any institution, large or small. The temptation is to think that there's little you can do to change the world. But Malcom McLean, who transformed the way the world ships goods, started off driving a truck for someone else. Bill Gates was a college drop-out. But both Malcom and Bill founded start-ups that became their vehicle to shaping strategies and provided significant leverage for their efforts.

Could you pursue a shaping strategy, as an individual, without creating a new start-up of your own, one that instead made the most of other institutions to support your shaping strategy? Could the techniques of pull be harnessed to make it feasible for a single individual, without any institutional foundation at all, to change the world? What would that look like?

Let's explore what this might look like in the arena of energy, where there's growing concern about the impact of the carbon economy on the environment. How might an individual meaningfully shape the innovation in, and ultimately the structure of, the energy business to help bring about a profound shift in the way we consume energy? If we go back to our three elements of a shaping strategy, we can see that one starting point that is certainly feasible for an individual is to have a clear and compelling view of a long-term future that spells out a very different structure for the industry and highlights the broad opportunities available to those who support the shaping strategy. For example, an individual could take the significant uncertainty prevailing in the alternative energy arena today and distill a provocative view of how the future might unfold.

Perhaps the view might state that the key drivers of change will be energy consumers (especially large, energy-intensive enterprises) and new entrepreneurial start-ups, rather than the large incumbents in the industry. When one effectively integrates the interests of these two constituencies, a new structure for the energy industry will emerge that is far more diversified and fragmented in terms of energy sources. Energy consumers themselves might become significant sources of electrical power as they learned how to produce some of their own energy and began to deliver surplus energy to the electrical grid. Electrical grids might increasingly look like distributed computing networks, with complex two-way flows of electricity that would need to be routed to and from multiple locations in the most efficient way possible.

This shaping view would help the aspiring shaping individual determine who would need to be mobilized to accelerate the evolution of this new industry structure—including both large enterprise energy consumers and small entrepreneurial companies.

What would be a potential shaping platform that this aspiring shaper might use to help mobilize these constituencies? One possible starting point would be to define a systematic way to measure the efficiency of energy production and consumption—a carbon-accounting system, if you will—that would provide a standardized way to assess competing claims regarding energy efficiency. This is one of the biggest challenges in the energy field today—producers of energy-intensive equipment, such as computer servers and factory machinery—all make bold claims regarding energy efficiency, but comparability is often difficult because of different ways of measuring efficiency. The lack of effective standards also makes it difficult for major energy consumers to effectively compare their progress in terms of energy-conservation efforts. This proposed carbon-accounting system could become the foundation of a shaping platform.

To establish a proposed standardized approach to carbon accounting, the aspiring shaper might work to convene an energy-consumer council consisting of some of the largest energy consumers and enlist their support in refining and promulgating the new standards, given that they have the most at stake in terms of achieving greater comparability.

This council might then become a catalyst for the formation of a much broader ecosystem of participants seeking to accelerate the movement toward greater energy efficiency and sustainability. By initially mobilizing large energy consumers, the shaper would be immediately attracting the interest of many entrepreneurs and producers of energy-intensive machinery, who might seek to gain visibility with large potential purchasers of their products and services. The shaping platform of a carbon-accounting system would also attract a large number of service providers seeking to provide audit and consulting services to help large energy consumers apply these standards and achieve energy savings.

With this carbon-accounting system gaining traction, the shaper might then seek to mobilize a council of wealthy individuals who would be interested in funding a connection platform designed to help aspiring entrepreneurs in various areas of energy conservation and renewable energy production connect with investors interested in supporting promising new ventures. This connection platform could use the standards established in the carbon-accounting system to enable investors to analyze and compare claims by entrepreneurs regarding their ability to address carbon energy issues effectively. It would also provide a focusing framework for aspiring entrepreneurs so that they could accurately assess their progress in moving toward more efficient and sustainable energy solutions.

Convening an energy-consumer council and a council of wealthy individuals would be important steps toward building credibility for the shaping view and the shaping platform. Effectively executed, such a plan could help to draw a critical mass of participants into the shaping ecosystem.

Now, of course, this would be very challenging for a single individual to pull off. Significant economic and environmental interests are at stake. It would help if the individual already had a reputation in the energy industry to establish early credibility and a rich network of relationships in that arena to draw upon. It would also help if the individual was independently wealthy so that she could devote her time to this effort without being distracted by the need to earn a living. Nevertheless, an individual attempting to deploy this shaping strategy would have some significant advantages. In particular, it might be easier for someone who is not affiliated with a company having significant economic interests in this field to attract and build trust-based relationships with other major players in this arena. Not having a vested economic interest in outcomes would demonstrate conviction and help to build credibility with major players, who often have conflicting economic agendas, and might enable the shaper to serve as a broker who could bring together participants who were suspicious of one another.

This scenario isn't entirely speculative. Our friend Jack Hidary, whom we introduced in Chapter 3, already has some of these elements in place. Though he hasn't gone the full distance outlined above, he has already become very influential in the alternative-energy arena and at least is creating an option to engage in a broader shaping strategy over time.

Nonshaping Roles in the Shaper's Ecosystem

Not everybody, of course, could be a successful individual shaper. Not all of us have the particular blend of smarts, charisma, humor, diplomacy, connections, and moxie that individual shapers need in order to carve out an effective role in major economic and social arenas. And most of us haven't made enough money to be able to focus on such big-picture things, like weaning the world from petroleum. We have to go to work in the morning. But we might find creative ways to support the efforts of these individual shapers in our spare time, or we might join one of the companies coming together in the new shaping ecosystem and work to improve the participation of the company in the shaping initiative.

At the institutional level, the same concept applies. A company might lack the appetite for risk, the coordination capabilities, the conviction, the deep-industry insight, or the many other key qualities that shapers possess. Shaping strategies require a risk-taking profile and distinctive insights at both the micro and macro levels regarding the changing business landscape. Shaping companies also need the management capabilities to evangelize shaping views, bootstrap robust shaping platforms, and coordinate relationships with large numbers of third-party participants. These can be challenging strategies to design and execute. In fact, among the examples of companies that have designed shaping strategies, only a very few have successfully put together all three elements. Yet executives should not lose sight of the fact that many different roles are available in pursuing shaping strategies. Many companies can play participant roles instead of being the primary shaper, as there are many participant roles available.

For example, "influencers" are participants with assets or capabilities that can significantly influence the success of a shaping platform relative to competing shaping platforms. By committing early and prominently to a particular shaping platform, influencers have the potential to reap significant rewards. T-Mobile and Motorola represent examples of potential influencers within Google's emerging shaping strategy in the telecom arena. In an earlier era, Bank of America played this role in Visa's shaping initiatives.

"Key players," on the other hand, might be viewed as "arms merchants," companies that develop key technology or business services that are essential for multiple shaping platforms, maintaining compatibility across these multiple shaping platforms. Various security-software firms play that role in supporting competing social-networking sites, for example.

All participants need to make a key choice: Will they become disciples or hedgers? Disciples commit exclusively to a single shaping platform. These companies have the benefit of focused investment, but they can run significant risks in making this choice if the shaping platform fails to achieve a critical mass or is ultimately overtaken by a competing shaping platform. Hedgers invest in multiple shaping platforms, potentially reducing their risk in terms of betting on a losing platform, but creating a different form of risk by spreading their investments more thinly. Of course, these choices can vary over time, with hedgers ultimately deciding to become disciples as platform competition plays out.

Whatever role one assumes within a shaping strategy, all participants involved must become adept at four basic qualities required to create and capture value. First, they need to hone their ability to assess the capabilities of aspiring shapers and the changing probabilities of success as the shaping strategy unfolds. By applying the framework discussed earlier, focusing on the three key elements required for success, participants can become more effective in determining the potential for success of aspiring shapers and modify their own initiatives accordingly. For example, one common error that participants make is simply to focus on the number of participants declaring support for a given shaping strategy rather than looking beyond that at the level of investment being made by these participants in the shaping platform relative to the investments being made in other platforms.

Second, participants must be clear about their ability to create viable niches that are truly differentiated and offer the opportunity for significant growth and profitability within the broader shaping ecosystems. As already mentioned, platforms can level a playing field and increase the potential for commoditization, so it is critical to determine how one can play on that level playing field and continue to offer differentiated value.

Third, participants must foster a learning disposition. The power of shaping ecosystems lies in their ability to become fertile ground for extraordinary distributed innovation. There is an opportunity for all participants to learn much more rapidly by participating in these ecosystems. To do this, though, participants must cultivate an ability to identify which other participants are most innovative and understand what kinds of relationships will help to foster knowledge creation, and not just knowledge sharing, with these innovative participants. By targeting and building these relationships, participants will become much more effective in creating greater value as a part of the broader shaping ecosystem.

The key strategic question that all of us will face is, Will we shape or be shaped? If the latter, then the question we must turn to is how to create and capture as much value as possible within a broader shaping ecosystem. If we look at historical examples of successful shaping strategies, we find that one does not need to be a shaper to profit enormously from shaping strategies. Many participants have generated extraordinary wealth within the ecosystems defined by shapers. The key is to be very clear about the role one is playing, to understand the rules of the broader shaping game, and to pursue focused actions consistent with the role one has assumed and with the broader rules of the game.

These dispositions, institutional arrangements, and management practices and disciplines will all become significant assets for a participating or shaping firm—whether or not a particular shaping strategy plays out as expected. In thinking about the different roles available in shaping strategies and the potential fit with these roles for their company, executives might consider the following questions:

- Do the members of the senior management team, the board members, and the key investors have the risk profile and long-term time horizon required to commit assets and take the actions required to be a successful shaper?
- Does the company have the capabilities needed to attract and mobilize the large numbers of participants required to realize the full potential of the shaping platform?
- Do the members of the leadership team, and especially the CEO, have the type of personality required to build conviction around a compelling shaping narrative?
- Does the company have a distinctive set of capabilities that can enable the participant to carve out a sustainable niche within the broader shaping strategy?
- Does the company have particularly valuable assets that could contribute to its overall success as a shaper and position it to become an influencer?

WHERE CAN WE SHAPE?

Shaping strategies are not viable everywhere. They tend to be most relevant in environments that are experiencing significant discontinuities brought about by major technology innovations or sudden public-policy shifts. These generate both the uncertainty and the potential for significant performance improvement that make shaping initiatives powerful. Further, shaping strategies work best where there are a large number of participants already in place to be mobilized. If a market or industry has only two or three highly concentrated players, shaping strategies lose the potential for leverage that is at the core of their power. If there are extremely low barriers to entry and movement, it may be possible for a shaper to mobilize a large number of participants in a short period of time. This is, in essence, what Facebook did when it opened up its platform to third-party developers, just as Apple has with the iPhone. Some established software developers jumped in to take advantage of the opportunity, but a much larger number of start-ups quickly arose to take advantage of it as well, fueled by the realization that only a very modest investment was required to participate.

We've also seen that shaping strategies aren't just for business. Some of the greatest interest in shaping strategies that we have seen has come from outside the commercial arena. Educational institutions, foundations, public policy groups, and government agencies have begun to recognize that shaping strategies may actually be applicable in a very broad range of arenas around the world. Any arena that has a large number of participants, substantial uncertainty, and potential for significant performance improvement could be ripe for some form of shaping strategy.

There is perhaps an even greater opportunity for individuals to apply shaping strategies within their own personal and professional lives than there is in the corporate world. Like Jack Hidary, those of us who have a clear vision of what our future world could look like, and the roles we may be able to play in that world, will tend to attract others who are intrigued by the sense of focus and direction that we communicate. This can be especially powerful if we invest some time into exploring and articulating how we can help make others personally and professionally more successful as we pursue our own personal futures. In the personal context, we might well think of our own social and professional networks as the beginning of a shaping platform that can draw others to us and motivate them to collaborate with us. Once again, though, we will need to begin to view our social and professional networks as assets that can be leveraged not just for our own personal success, but to help amplify the success of others. People like Joi Ito, Yossi Vardi, and Ellen Levy deeply understand this principle and apply it in their personal lives.

||||||||

WE LIVE IN TURBULENT TIMES. Faced with such turbulence, it is easy to get caught up in the ebbs and flows, reacting to each wave that unexpectedly surfaces and becoming ever more stressed and exhausted by our effort to stay afloat. Overwhelmed by the swells rising and falling around us, we begin to lose sight of the broader forces generating the turbulence in the first place.

By pulling back and understanding these broader forces, we can begin to see a different way forward. Rather than simply reacting to short-term events, we can begin to shape our environment in ways that turn turbulence to our advantage. In times of growing stress, calmness can emerge. But one must have a growing awareness of the opportunity to shape broader relationships to accelerate one's own movement, while never losing sight of the long-term destination. Change and uncertainty, deeply threatening to those who are focused on protecting existing assets, become sources of opportunity for those who know how to motivate and mobilize others.

This is the most significant aspect of the potential of pull. And it is a natural outgrowth of our efforts to master the power of pull at the individual and institutional levels. As we become more comfortable with our ability to achieve our potential at these levels, we will begin to see more and more opportunities to amplify our potential even further by reshaping broader and broader arenas. We will also have more insight into, and experience with, the pull techniques required to pursue shaping strategies.

With great power comes great responsibility. As the potential of pull becomes more visible, both at the level of the individual and at the level of institutions, we must all become much clearer about what we really want, what will fulfill us, and what will create opportunities for the generations that follow us.

Here is one of the most significant opportunities emerging from the Big Shift: Small moves, smartly made, can result in far greater accomplishments than anyone might have dreamed of. This is the essence of pull. We no longer have to accept a passive role, buffeted against the rocks by unexpected gales of change. Instead, we truly are developing the ability to change the world.

BRINGING IT HOME

- What are the arenas and issues, beyond your immediate family, that have the greatest impact on your life? The quality of local educational options or the cleanup of a local creek or marsh? The ability of your city or region to attract creative talent? A more global arena, such as the impact of the carbon economy on global warming or the need to find a cure for a particular disease?
- What would you want these arenas to look like ten years from now? Can you articulate such a vision in a few sentences?
- How might you or a group of like-minded people reshape these arenas to enhance everybody's ability to actualize their potential?
- Are there efforts underway by others to reshape these arenas? Would they enhance or diminish your ability to actualize your potential?
- Could you help develop platforms that would better connect people and support innovative ways to reshape these arenas?
- What specific relationships could you build or actions could you take to meaningfully accelerate reshaping these arenas?

The Journey from Passion to Potential

In the world being reshaped by the Big Shift, something quite re-markable is happening. As large institutions hold on to what they have, the locus of power and change is inexorably shifting to in-dividuals. As individuals, we are embracing the foundational changes of the Big Shift to enhance our personal lives. More and more of us are adopting and actively using digital technologies that a few decades ago were a mere gleam in the eyes of a small group of futurists and science fiction writers. And while the young are leading the way, older genera-tions are not far behind in exploring the power of search, social net-works, and creation spaces.

Although this journey will begin with individuals, it will never achieve its potential until and unless we bring our institutions along as well. We cannot afford to jettison our institutions. Properly refocused, they provide us with unparalleled opportunities that we simply could not replicate as isolated individuals.

So far, our moves to harness the new digital infrastructures and pub-lic policy regimes have been mostly confined to our personal lives and existing social networks. Even in these domains, many of us have been somewhat sporadic in the development of the practices required to fully exploit the capabilities of these new foundations. Often, our efforts have been stymied by powerful resistance from the institutional environments in which we live so much of our lives—companies, schools, nonprofits, and governments. The examples of people such as Joi Ito, Yossi Vardi, Ellen Levy, Jack Hidary, and Tara Lemmey stand out as exceptional in part because few of us have yet to fully grasp the implications and practices required to maximize value from these foundational forces.

We now have the opportunity to build on these early efforts. To do so, we will have to venture into arenas where there are few defined road maps, where risks arise at nearly every turn, and where we'll need to learn to trust and rely on people that we do not yet know.

Passion will help to orient us and give us the dispositions we need to fully harness the power of pull. Passion will transform us and give us the motivation to find and deploy whatever pull techniques we can discover to help us more effectively achieve our full potential as individuals. The very same pressure that creates stress in a life without passion becomes a portal into exciting opportunities to develop our potential more fully.

Unlike most journeys, which have clearly defined starting and ending points, this journey invites us to embark on a journey without end. The farther we progress on this path, the less we find we need the traditional comfort of a clearly defined end. As the power of pull takes hold, we find that the world around us begins to exhibit broader and broader changes. We find that the pace of change accelerates, rather than slowing down, leading us to continually uncover new possibilities and potential.

It's an exciting journey. As we make our passion our profession, we begin to see that our potential is far greater than we previously believed. We draw more people and institutions into the journey as we make our way through the uncharted terrain. As more people join us, we discover that we get better faster, which then spurs us to find and attract even more people to help us move more quickly and surely through the more challenging terrain.

Those who stay behind in the world of push may be able to carry on for a period of time, drawing on the resources they have accumulated. Beyond the walls of their homes and workplaces, however, pressures will continue to build, making it harder and harder to carry on as before. If we extrapolate the current trends laid out in the Shift Index, the world around us becomes ever more challenging and unfriendly. Without passion, we will find ourselves increasingly stressed as performance pressures inexorably mount until they become unbearable. As stress mounts, relationships fray, and we become ever more protective of the diminishing resources that we have. There is no sustainability to be found here; at best, we can hope for a grace period. But time will grow increasingly short and the likely scenarios increasingly unpalatable. We will seek refuge in the last remnants of push institutions only to find the walls eroding around us.

We can see real risks ahead on the path towards pull, but the true danger is that we will ignore the growing risks of remaining where we are today. There is no doubt that it will be a very difficult journey, that there will be unanticipated setbacks, and that the risks that lie ahead of us may be hard to measure. It is completely understandable that fear would hold us back. Our hope, though, is that by exploring the power of pull and providing a high-level road map for all of us as we seek to navigate the difficult journey from the world of push to the world of pull, we can enable our readers to overcome that fear by helping them to understand the real opportunities that lie ahead for those of us who master these techniques.

In short, the power of pull is not an option—it is an imperative that we ignore at our peril. The consequences of not making the journey are severe. But this perspective emphasizes only the negative incentives. The positive incentive is that the journey offers enormous rewards, and these rewards only increase the more we begin to master the techniques of pull. Ultimately, we believe that the positive incentives, shaped by the rediscovery and pursuit of passion, will draw most people into the journey.

On a journey like this, when we never know quite what to expect, we want to work with people who can be trusted to stand by us even in challenging times and stretch themselves beyond their areas of expertise to come up with creative solutions. We cannot achieve this level of trust without gaining a much more holistic understanding of the individuals we are dealing with, rather than satisfying ourselves with narrow slices of their persona. To build this level of trust, we must begin the process of reintegrating ourselves, and often, in the process, rediscovering ourselves, so that we can present ourselves more fully and authentically to others around us.

The ultimate promise of pull is the opportunity to reclaim our individuality and pursue our potential in ways that were never feasible in a world of push. Many of us will attempt to approach the world of pull in a very instrumental fashion. We will study the techniques and practice them as if they were the familiar scripts that we learned in the world of push, all the while hiding our individuality and defining our potential in very extrinsic, material terms. We will try this, but we won't get away with it. For, you see, pull requires much, much more from us. It requires us to get in touch with ourselves, to relearn how to be, in order to more effectively become.

Those of us who continue to believe that pull can be pursued in the same instrumental way that push programs are will quickly find that we are only scratching the bare surface of the potential of pull. Pull demands that we pull out of each of us an authentic presentation of who we are today so that we can more effectively work together to pull out of each of us our ultimate potential.

To present ourselves authentically, we must first develop a deep understanding of who we are. For many of us, that will be a novel and somewhat discomforting quest as we strip away the scripts, routines, and facades that we have so carefully cultivated in order to integrate successfully into the push world. We must work to reintegrate the compartmentalized elements of our being that we kept so carefully apart.

But we will find that quest deeply rewarding as we gain a much clearer sense of who we are today and what we need to be successful. We begin to learn that who we are and who others are matter just as much if we are to engage in joint knowledge creation. The individual we tried to suppress from an early age springs forth once again and demands attention. In the process, we learn that that individual has passion and that passion provides us with the key to achieving our full potential.

Pull is truly subversive. It forces us to confront and understand ourselves as individuals in ways that most of us have long forgotten how to do. It motivates us to learn more about the people we work with, and it drives us to seek out others who can be trusted to engage with us in very risky yet satisfying ways to push our performance envelopes and learn faster. In the process, we begin to realize there is no going back—and there is no way to accomplish this in more traditional institutions still driven by the push model.

Embracing our individuality and passions, however, doesn't mean breaking free of all organizations; nor are we suggesting an "end to the firm." Instead, organizations of all stripes have an opportunity to tap into, leverage, and magnify the individuals who work for them. This isn't about the *end* of the organization, but its transformation. We won't be working from mountaintops and coffee shops, although we will be looking in new and unexpected places for like-minded individuals. Institutions will remain absolutely necessary as home bases for people looking to use pull to its fullest potential.

Pull is deeply subversive at the institutional level as well. As we begin to discover our passions as individuals and seek to make them our professions, we will increasingly run into the institutional barriers that surround us on all sides and prevent us from moving forward. Those of us who pursue our passions in the workplace, seeking to adopt and nurture pull mechanisms in our existing institutional homes, will find ourselves increasingly frustrated by the roadblocks we encounter. Here's the paradox: The more we choose to pursue our passions within the confines of existing push-based institutions, the more unhappy and frustrated we will become. Many of us will flee these institutional homes, as others already have, in the quest for freedom to pursue passion.

But some of us will see the potential that resides latent in even the largest institutions and become motivated to connect with others in efforts to reorient these institutions around cultivating passion rather than suppressing it. This quest will encounter powerful resistance, especially from those who do not share our passions and instead seek to protect the status quo in an effort to maintain some degree of safety and stability in an increasingly turbulent world. There will be setbacks and even casualties along the way. But those with passion can rest secure in one basic fact—the forces of the Big Shift are on their side. The pressures on our institutions are mounting on all sides, and they will not go away. Instead, they will intensify. And the only way to overcome them will be to reorient our institutions around collaboration curves and talent development.

Our efforts as individuals to work within larger institutions will be aided by the rise of a new generation of institutions. This new wave will be designed from the bottom up and from the edge in with the goal of providing platforms for passionate individuals to amplify the power of pull. The old guard will face increasing pressure from these new institutions.

This will be a long march. But it is an essential part of our journey. If we just focus on our evolution as individuals on harnessing the power of pull, we will fall far short of our full potential. Institutions can significantly amplify the power of pull, making it far easier to connect with a broader range of people and resources and to learn faster from each other than we ever could in the absence of institutions. We must therefore reclaim our institutions—whether from the inside of existing ones or by creating a new generation of our own.

But it is not just about transforming individual institutions in profound ways, either. It is also about engaging more broadly with the world around us and deeply understanding its potential. As we begin to understand the power of pull, we begin to look at the world in a different way. We begin to use much more imagination, exploring possibilities and potential, not just in ourselves, but in the people and arenas around us. We begin to realize that what is, is only a precursor of what could be, and that we can play a leading role in helping to realize that potential. But we do this with a very different mindset from the engineer or technocrat who thinks in terms of detailed blueprints and a carefully designed path to realization of these blueprints. Rather, we adopt the perspective of a gardener who seeds, feeds, and weeds his garden, carefully shaping the vegetation in ways that will create a more fulfilling experience for us.

This is ultimately the power of pull. For the first time ever, we have the real opportunity to become who we are, and more importantly, who we were meant to be. Pull provides us with the opportunity to achieve our own individual potential while at the same time pursuing the enormous potential embedded in whatever institutional environment surrounds us. We now have the ability to shape a world that encourages and celebrates our efforts to become who we were meant to be.

To do this effectively, though, we must first strive to understand ourselves more fully and learn to discern the potential hiding in plain sight of the world around us. As individuals, we truly now have the potential to remake our world, not in a way that simply serves our needs, but in a way that deeply honors the potential of all of those around us as well as our own potential. While pull helps us to connect with others in richer and more satisfying ways, perhaps the real opportunity lies within each of us. To harness the potential of pull, we must begin with ourselves as individuals, join together in the long march required to transform our institutions, and return inevitably to ourselves in a process of discovery that knows no end. On the way, we will continually surprise ourselves as we discover that small moves, smartly made, can set really big things in motion.

Acknowledgments

As much as anything else, *The Power of Pull* is about ever more participants from diverse backgrounds coming together around a challenging undertaking. This book represents such an endeavor, at a small scale at least, and it is appropriate to acknowledge and give thanks to all those who participated in its creation. During the past three years, we have had the good fortune to establish a new research institution called The Deloitte Center for the Edge. (See www.edgeperspectives.com.) The research that underlies this book was conducted there.

The Center for the Edge reflects the unflagging vision and support of a number of senior leaders at Deloitte, including Phil Asmundson, Teresa Briggs, Ed Carey, Bill Freda, Tom Maloney, Karen Mazer, Barry Salzberg, and Jim Quigley. Special thanks go to Deloitte's Eric Openshaw, who has truly been our champion and valuable guide, as well as a friend along the path. We're also grateful for our many colleagues within the firm who've been supportive, including: Mumtaz Ahmed, Jeff Alderton, Sam Balaji, Bill Barrett, Jeff Benesch, Cathy Benko, Bob Boehm, Tom Captain, David Carney, Debarshi Chatterjee, Kim Christfort, Lily Chung, John Ciachella, Dave Couture, Jim Curry, Andy Daecher, Alma Derricks, Tracey Edwards, Bill Eggers, Dan Falkenhagen, Steve Fineberg, Pete Firestone, Lisa Francesca, Brian Fugere, Tom Galizia, Jonathan Gandal, Wally Gregory, Ragu Gurumurthy, Michael Gusek, Jim Guszcza, John Henry, John Houston, Ken Hutt, Arun Inam, Mark Jensen, Ajit Kambil, Mark Klein, Suzanne Kounkel, John Kutz, Steve Lemelin, Dave Lewis, Kevin Lynch, Vikram Mahidihar, Andy Main, Fred Miller, Tomi Miller, Neville Morcom, Ajit Prabhu, Beth Popler, Don Proctor, Michael Raynor, Kevin Reamy, Dave Rosenblum, Jack Russi, Jason Salzetti, Jeff Schwartz, Connie Segreto, Marco Squazzin, Carl Steidtmann, Jennifer Steinmann, Greg Stoskopf, Rav

Suri, Jonathan Warshawsky, Howard Weinberg, Richard Woodward, Jianwei Xie, and Lili Zheng.

One of the real joys of our work at the Center has been our ongoing collaborations with young Deloitte consultants who have come through the Center on six-month rotations as "edge fellows." The edge fellows have helped us build up the concepts and case studies, the methodologies and analyses, the frameworks and narratives that eventually developed into this book. Their tireless energy and bonhomie is proven to last well into the night, many nights in succession. They have included Blythe Aronowitz, Jitin Asnaani, Mark Astrinos, Maryann Baribault, Brendan Brier, Alison Coleman Rezai, Brent Dance, Andrew de Maar, Chetan Desai, Dan Elbert, Indira Gillingham, Neda Jafarnia, Scott Judd, Gautam Kasthurirangan, Catherine Keller, Neal Kohl, Jayant Lakshimikanthan, Adit Mane, Silke Meixner, Jagannath Nemani, Eric Newman, Chris Nixon, Tam Pham, Tamara Samoylova, Siddhi Saraiya, Vijay Sharma, Sumit Sharma, Sekhar Suryanarayanan, and Jason Trichel. To the edge fellows our hearty thanks and appreciation.

The Center for the Edge has also the good fortune to include among its ranks Glen Dong, our resourceful chief of staff; Duleesha Kulasooriya, a man whose insights are matched by his forbearance; Christine Brodeur, who navigates the labyrinths required to bring our work to market; and Regina Davis and Carrie Howell, who keep the trains running on time, and on track.

We have also benefited from the opportunity to test our ideas midstream with senior business leaders, academics, and other thought leaders in small-group workshops in Palo Alto, in various "Dinners on the Edge" held around the United States, and other venues. Their frank and perceptive commentaries have helped sharpen and strengthen the research. These executives have included Steven Aldrich, Brian Arthur, Prith Banerjee, Michel Bechauf, Brian Behlendorf, Ken Berryman, Mike Byron, Elizabeth Churchill, Art Cimento, Bill Coleman, Jay Cross, Chris Curtin, Cathy Eisenhardt, John Garris, Seth Goldstein, Patrick Grady, Spencer Greene, TJ Grewal, Marguerite Hancock, Russell Hancock, Hamilton Helmer, John Horrigan, Scott Johnson, Ritta Katila, Tom Kehler, Justine Lam, Mick Lopez, Martin

Milani, Paul Milgrom, Bill Miller, Simon Mulcahy, Om Nalamasu, Mark Orrtung, Vivek Paul, Roy Pea, Ross Piper, Chris Sacca, Russell Siegelman, Dan Simpson, Sonny Singh, Tom Stewart, Marco ten Vaanholt, Doug Thomas, Denny Weinberg, Kevin Werbach, Jeff Woods, Mark Yolton, and Zia Yusuf.

We'd like also to thank the small group of experts who helps us compile our inaugural 2009 Shift Index, the empirical findings that underpin many of the more conceptual assertions in this book: David Campbell, Mark Cho, Bruce Corner, Misha Edel, Dave Eulitt, David Ford, Steve Graefe, Arian Hassani, Richard Jackowitz, Alan Mauldin, Irene Mia, Ambassador Terry Miller, Scott Morano, Ataman Ozyidirim, Ingo Reinhardt, Robert Roche, and Christopher Walker.

Additionally, the fine group of editors at Harvard Business School Publishing has been of considerable assistance in developing some of the concepts in this book, particularly Eric Hellweg, Adi Ignatius, and Paul Michelman.

Our agent, Jim Levine, provided invaluable assistance. And we are deeply indebted to the whole crew at our publisher, Basic Books, including Sandra Beris, Michele Jacob, and most particularly Tim Sullivan, the book's editor, whose skills, imagination, and sly sense of humor made him truly a pleasure to work with—and made this a far better book than it would have otherwise been.

Finally, we'd like to thank the people profiled in this book who were so generous with their time: Jack Hidary, Joi Ito, Tara Lemmey, Ellen Levy, and Yossi Vardi.

Notes

Introduction

1. The term "soul surfer" is used to "describe a talented surfer who surfs for the sheer pleasure of surfing," Wikipedia, "Soul Surfer," http://en.wikipedia.org/wiki/Soul_Surfer.

2. For more about this billboard, see "What Makes You So Special? With over 1 Million People in the World Able to Do Your Job, Altium Acts to Help More," Reuters, April 20, 2009, http://www.reuters.com/article/pressRelease/idUS180975+20-Apr-2009+MW20090420.

3. Jeff Mull, "Clear to Land: Dusty Payne Wins Kustom Air Strike and $50,000," *Surfer* magazine, April 2009, http://www.surfermag.com/features/onlineexclusives/dusty_payne_wins_kustom_air_strike_and_50000/.

4. Creative talent is increasingly flocking to creative cities. See John Hagel III, John Seely Brown, and Lang Davison, *The 2009 Shift Index: Measuring the Forces of Long-Term Change* (San Jose, Calif.: Deloitte Development, June 2009).

5. See Mark Granovetter, "The Strength of Weak Ties," *American Journal of Sociology* 78, no. 6 (May 1973).

6. See Vanina Leschziner, "Kitchen Stories: Patterns of Recognition in Contemporary High Cuisine," *Sociological Forum* 22, no. 1 (February 14, 2007): 77–101.

7. See John Hagel III and John Seely Brown, "Productive Friction: How Difficult Business Partnerships Can Accelerate Innovation," *Harvard Business Review*, February 1, 2005.

8. For more about the benefits of diversity, see Scott Page, *The Difference: How the Power of Diversity Creates Better Groups, Firms, Schools, and Societies* (Princeton, N.J.: Princeton University Press, 2007).

Chapter 1

1. Timothy Ferris, *The Four-Hour Work Week* (New York: Crown, 2007).

2. A Gallup poll found that 55 percent of all U.S. employees are bored at least part of the time they're at work. See Heath Row, "Yawn and Guarded," Fast Company

Member Blog, February 8, 2008, http://www.fastcompany.com/blog/heath-row/yawn-and-guarded.

3. See for instance, Alfred D. Chandler Jr., *Scale and Scope: The Dynamics of Industrial Capitalism* (Cambridge: Harvard University Press, 1994).

4. Ronald Coase, "The Nature of the Firm," *Economica* 4, no. 16 (November 1937): 386–405.

5. For more about the role of real-time information in the Saffron Revolution, as well as in other political crises, see Nik Gowing, "'Skyful of Lies' and Black Swans: The New Tyranny of Shifting Information Power in Crises," Reuters Institute for the Study of Journalism, May 2009, http://reutersinstitute.politics.ox.ac.uk/fileadmin/documents/Publications/Skyful_of_Lies.pdf.

6. Ibid.

7. See, for instance, "'Neda' Becomes Rallying Cry for Iranian Protests," CNN, June 22, 2009, http://www.cnn.com/2009/WORLD/meast/06/21/iran.woman.twitter/index.html?eref=rss_mostpopular.

8. See John Hagel III, John Seely Brown, and Lang Davison, *The 2009 Shift Index: Measuring the Forces of Long-Term Change* (San Jose, Calif.: Deloitte Development, June 2009).

9. Ibid.

10. Ibid.

11. Ibid.

12. Ibid.

13. Ibid. The index shows that return on assets for U.S. firms had steadily fallen to almost one-quarter of 1965 levels by 2008.

14. Charles H. Fine, *Clockspeed: Winning Industry Control in the Age of Temporary Advantage* (New York: Basic Books, 1998).

15. Conversation with the authors, September 2009.

16. See Hagel et al., *The 2009 Shift Index*.

17. Rick Levine, Christopher Locke, Doc Searls, and David Weinberger, *The Cluetrain Manifesto: The End of Business as Usual* (New York: Basic Books/Perseus Books, 2000).

Chapter 2

1. See Joshua Davis, "Secret Geek A-Team Hacks Back, Defends Worldwide Web," *Wired*, November 24, 2008.

2. This account is drawn from conversations and e-mail exchanges with Joi Ito and other people who were involved in this effort to support the protest movement's freedom of expression.

3. Dunbar fixed his number at approximately 150 people, but field studies performed by anthropologists H. Russell Bernard and Peter Killworth put the number at

290, roughly double Dunbar's estimate. See Wikipedia article at http://en.wiki pedia.org/wiki/Dunbar's_number#Alternative_numbers.

4. This widely cited quote can be found in many places, including Charles G. Sieloff, "'If Only HP Knew What HP Knows': The Roots of Knowledge Management at Hewlett-Packard," *Journal of Knowledge Management* 3, no. 1 (1999): 47–53.

5. "Performance fabrics weave together both business elements (e.g., techniques for building shared meaning and trust) and technology elements (e.g., architectures and technology tools) to simplify, strengthen, and amplify relationships among relevant stakeholders across enterprises, thereby enhancing the potential for productive collaboration across a large number of specialized entities." From John Hagel III and John Seely Brown, *The Only Sustainable Edge: Why Business Strategy Depends on Productive Friction and Dynamic Specialization* (Cambridge: Harvard Business School Publishing, 2005).

6. See David Obstfeld, "Social Networks, the Tertius Iungens Orientation, and Involvement in Innovation," *Administrative Science Quarterly* 50 (2005): 100–130.

Chapter 3

1. David Vise, *The Google Story* (New York: Bantam Dell, 2005).

2. Maayan Cohen, "Revealed: How Israeli Hi-Tech Guru Inspired Google 'Magic Formula,'" Haaretz.com, January 6, 2008, http://www.haaretz.com/hasen/spages/989036.html.

3. Robert K. Merton and Elinor Barber, *The Travels and Adventures of Serendipity: A Study in Sociological Semantics and the Sociology of Science* (Princeton, N.J.: Princeton University Press, 2004).

4. Yossi Vardi, interview with the authors, June 20, 2009.

5. Jennifer L. Schenker, "Yossi Vardi: Israel's 'Mr. Tech,'" *Business Week*, May 19, 2008, http://www.businessweek.com/globalbiz/content/may2008/gb20080519_549076.htm ?chan=globalbiz_europe+index+page_top+stories.

6. Ibid.

7. Glauco Ortolano, "Humaniqueness: The Gift of Your Inner God," LuLu.com, September 2008.

8. Yossi Vardi, interview with the authors, June 20, 2009.

9. There actually is such a conference now, presented by the Alaska Department of Health and Social Services, that focuses on changes to how the state of Alaska awards grant monies. It's called "The Change Agent Conference," and the seventh annual conference was held in June 2009 at Sheraton Anchorage Hotel in Anchorage. For more information, see https://www.signup4.net/public/ap.aspx?EID=CHIL24 E&OID=50.

10. Yossi Vardi, interview with the authors, June 20, 2009.

11. Lucy Kellaway, "Martin Lukes," a long-running column in the *Financial Times*.

12. See John Hagel III, John Seely Brown, and Lang Davison, *The 2009 Shift Index: Measuring the Forces of Long-Term Change* (San Jose, Calif.: Deloitte Development, June 2009).

13. Ibid.

14. For more about the importance of diversity, see Scott Page's superb book *The Difference* (Princeton, N.J.: Princeton University Press, 2007).

15. Yossi Vardi, interview with the authors, June 20, 2009.

16. Ibid.

17. Ibid.

18. Hagel et al., *The 2009 Shift Index*.

19. Doesn't everyone have at least one person in our online social network who seems to post only about himself—how his kid made honor roll, how he's flying to Chicago to give a "major" speech, or how great the products of his sponsor are? Thankfully, most online social networks also give us the ability to "hide" the postings of this kind of online narcissist or even to "unfriend" him entirely.

20. Karim R. Lakhani and Jill A. Panetta, "The Principles of Distributed Innovation," Berkman Center for Internet and Society Research Publication Series: Research Publication No. 2007–7, October 2007, http://ssrn.com/abstract=1021034.

21. Peter Morville, *Ambient Findability: What We Find Changes Who We Become* (Sebastopol, Calif.: O'Reilly Media, 2005).

22. Jack Hidary, interview with the authors, July 8, 2009.

23. Ibid.

24. Ibid.

25. Ibid.

26. Ibid.

27. Ibid.

28. Abbess Zenkei Blanche Hartman, "Beginner's Mind," 2001, http://www.intrex.net/chzg/hartman4.htm.

29. See John Seely Brown and Doug Thomas, "The Gamer Disposition," Conversation Starter, Harvard Business Publishing, http://conversationstarter.hbsp.com/2008/02/the_gamer_disposition.html.

Chapter 4

1. See John Hagel III, John Seely Brown, and Lang Davison, *The 2009 Shift Index: Measuring the Forces of Long-Term Change* (San Jose, Calif.: Deloitte Development, June 2009).

2. David Koeppel, "High Anxiety," *Portfolio*, January 31, 2008, http://www.portfolio.com/careers/features/2008/01/31/Wall-Street-Layoffs/.

3. See Jun Yan, "Antidepressant Use Rises in 10-Year Period," *Psychiatric News*, September 4, 2009, http://pn.psychiatryonline.org/cgi/content/full/44/17/8.

4. In a 2006 global poll, 57 percent of executives surveyed complained of rising stress levels, compared to 39 percent in 2004. See "Asia Worse Hit by Global Stress Epidemic," http://www.management-issues.com/display_page.asp?section=research&id=3019.

5. "Average Executive Tenure Less Than Four Years," press release from ExecuNet, http://www.execunet.com/m_releases_content.cfm?id=3096.

6. Ulf Lundberg, Marianne Granqvist, Tommy Hansson, Marianne Magnusson, and Leif Wallin, "Psychological and Physiological Stress Responses During Repetitive Work at an Assembly Line," *Work and Stress* 3, no. 2 (April 1989): 143–153.

7. Seth Mullins, "Some of the Most Stressful Jobs Ever Invented: Perils of the Restaurant Business," *Associated Content*, December 15, 2006, http://www.associated-content.com/article/100303/some_of_the_most_stressful_jobs_ever.html?cat=31.

8. Greg Noll, in *Riding Giants* (directed by Stacy Peralta), Forever Films, 2004.

9. Ibid.

10. In fact they already do. See Alex Edmans, "Does the Stock Market Fully Value Intangibles? Employee Satisfaction and Equity Prices," Social Science Research Network, Working Paper Series, August 12, 2009, http://finance.wharton.upenn.edu/~aedmans/Rowe%20Summary.pdf.

11. Matt Richtel and Jenna Wortha, "Weary of Looking for Work, Some Create Their Own," *New York Times*, March 13, 2009, http://www.nytimes.com/2009/03/14/technology/start-ups/14startup.html?partner=rss&emc=rss.

12. Steampunk, as practiced by its enthusiasts, is a retroactive application of science fiction to the steam age, marrying an Edwardian industrial aesthetic with a do-it-yourself mentality. A steampunk, for example, might refashion a computer with old typewriter pieces to look like something out of Jules Verne.

13. A steampunk innovator made exactly this kind of homemade respirator. See Jake von Slatt, "Gas Mask Sawdust Respirator," *Steampunk Workshop*, http://steampunkworkshop.com/respirator.shtml.

14. Luke Plunkett, "Americans Spent 2008 Playing World of Warcraft, PlayStation 2 Games," *Kotaku*, January 1, 2009, http://kotaku.com/5121962/americans-spent-2008-playing-world-of-warcraft-playstation-2-games#c.

15. Douglas Thomas, "Scalable Learning: From Simple to Complex in World of Warcraft," *On the Horizon* 17, no. 1 (2009): 35–46

16. Ibid.

17. See, for instance, Wesley Yin-Poole, "French WoW Player Reaches Level 70 in 28 Hours," Videogamer.com, January 17, 2007, http://www.videogamer.com/news/french_wow_player_reaches_level_70_in_28_hours.html.

18. SAP has more than 121,000 installed systems today.

19. Conversation with authors, October 2008.

20. Greg Noll, *Riding Giants*.

21. Matt Higgins, "Rough Waves, Tougher Beaches," *New York Times*, January 22, 2009, http://www.nytimes.com/2009/01/23/sports/othersports/23surfing.html?_r=1.

Chapter 5

1. Ellen Levy, interview with authors, September 20, 2009.

2. Ibid.

3. Ibid.

4. For more about how monetizing intangible assets drives corporate wealth creation, see Lowell Bryan and Claudia Joyce, *Mobilizing Minds* (New York: McGraw-Hill, 2007).

5. See John Hagel III, John Seely Brown, and Lang Davison, *The 2009 Shift Index: Measuring the Forces of Long-Term Change* (San Jose, Calif.: Deloitte Development, June 2009).

6. Andrew Keen, *The Cult of the Amateur: How Today's Internet Is Killing Our Culture* (New York: Broadway Business, 2007).

7. Ian Millhiser, "Clarence Thomas's America," *Huffington Post*, April 14, 2009, http://www.huffingtonpost.com/ian-millhiser/clarence-thomas-america_b_186425.html.

8. Clay Shirky, "Newspapers and Thinking the Unthinkable," blog posting, March 13, 2009, http://www.shirky.com/weblog/2009/03/newspapers-and-thinking-the-un-thinkable/.

9. Matthew B. Crawford, *Shop Class as Soulcraft: An Inquiry into the Value of Work* (New York: Penguin, 2009).

10. Grant McCracken, *Chief Culture Officer: How to Create a Living, Breathing Corporation* (New York: Basic Books, 2009).

Chapter 6

1. Details about Shai Agassi's early days at SAP and his later work at Better Place are drawn in part from Daniel Roth, "Driven: Shai Agassi's Audacious Plan to Put Electric Cars on the Road," *Wired*, August 18, 2008.

2. Trailing his hand in the wave was the spontaneous innovation made by Laird Hamilton while surfing a "death-defying" wave in Teahupoo, Tahiti, in August 2000. See Wikipedia entry for Laird Hamilton, http://en.wikipedia.org/wiki/Laird_Hamilton.

3. See Shai Agassi, "I LOVE Open Source—Really!" SAP Network Blogs, November 11, 2005, https://www.sdn.sap.com/irj/scn/weblogs?blog=/pub/wlg/1700.

4. See John Hagel III, John Seely Brown, and Lang Davison, *The 2009 Shift Index: Measuring the Forces of Long-Term Change* (San Jose, Calif.: Deloitte Development, June 2009).

5. See Daniel Pink, *Free Agent Nation* (New York: Warner Books, 2001).

6. Tara Lemmey, interview with the authors, July 10, 2009.

7. Note that what we're advocating here flips "strategic HR" on its head. Strategic HR is about ensuring that HR policies are aligned with strategy. What we suggest is making sure the firm's strategies are aligned with its need to develop talent more rapidly.

8. In an e-mail to the authors on September 28, 2004, Bill Joy indicated that he had made this statement many times in speeches throughout the 1980s.

9. That's precisely what Shai Agassi did when he developed the SAP Developer Network. Realizing that adoption of NetWeaver would occur more quickly if he har-

nessed the power of talented individuals outside of SAP, he reached across the boundaries of the company (after first convincing SAP's internal groups to create one rather than many communities) to knit together a broad network of developers, consultants, users, pundits, and experts. Few of them were on the SAP payroll, but nearly all were passionate about software. At minimal cost to SAP—relative to push models—SAP harnessed the collective power of hundreds of thousands of talented individuals to help achieve the company's strategic goals.

10. For more about this crucial question, see John Hagel III and Marc Singer, "Unbundling the Corporation," *Harvard Business Review*, March 1, 1999, which asserts that most companies are an unnatural bundle of three very different types of businesses: They are customer-relationship businesses, infrastructure-management businesses, and product-development and innovation businesses.

11. See Thomas H. Davenport, *Thinking for a Living: How to Get Better Performance and Results from Knowledge Workers* (Cambridge: Harvard Business School Press, 2005).

12. Thomas B. Winans and John Seely Brown, "Cloud Computing: A Collection of Working Papers," July 31, 2009, Deloitte Development.

Chapter 7

1. Zoe Baird and James Barksdale et al., "Creating a Trusted Network for Homeland Security," Markle Foundation, December 2, 2003, http://www.markle.org/downloadable_assets/nstf_report2_overview.pdf.

2. See Saxby Chambliss, "Counterterrorism Intelligence Capabilities and Performance Prior to 9-11," Subcommittee on Terrorism and Homeland Security, A Report to the Speaker of the House of Representatives and the Minority Leader, July 2002, http://www.fas.org/irp/congress/2002_rpt/hpsci_ths0702.html.

3. John Franke, "SAP CEO Heir-Apparent Resigns," March 28, 2007, TechTarget.com, http://searchsap.techtarget.com/news/article/0,289142,sid21_gci1249379,00.html#.

4. This and other details are drawn from Daniel Roth, "Driven: Shai Agassi's Audacious Plan to Put Electric Cars on the Road," *Wired*, August 18, 2008, http://www.wired.com/cars/futuretransport/magazine/16-09/ff_agassi?currentPage=all.

5. An article in *The New Yorker* indicated that Tesla Motors CEO Elon Musk may be no fan of Better Place. "I think Shai is going to spend a lot of money and not have a lot to show for it," Musk said of Agassi. Nonetheless, to hedge his bets, Musk was making Tesla's Model S with an exchangeable battery. Tad Friend, "Plugged In," *The New Yorker*, August 24, 2009.

6. See Roth, "Driven."

7. Ibid.

8. Ibid.

9. Clayton M. Christensen and Michael E. Raynor, *The Innovator's Solution: Creating and Sustaining Successful Growth* (Cambridge: Harvard Business Press, 2003).

Further Reading

Though neither comprehensive nor exhaustive, the following list of books and articles represents a reasonably diverse set of essential readings covering a wide range of the themes central to this book. We include it here for evocative purposes as well: to suggest places and domains where you might be able to take the ideas presented in this book further.

Arthur, Brian. *Increasing Returns and Path Dependence in the Economy.* Ann Arbor: University of Michigan Press, 1994.

Beinhocker, Eric. *The Origin of Wealth.* Boston: Harvard Business School Press, 2006.

Benkler, Yochai. *The Wealth of Networks.* New Haven, Conn.: Yale University Press, 2006.

Boisot, Max H., Ian C. MacMillan, and Kyeong Seok Han. *Explorations in Information Space.* New York: Oxford University Press, 2007.

Brandenburger, Adam, and Barry Nalebuff. *Co-opetition.* New York: Doubleday, 1996.

Burt, Ronald. *Brokerage and Closure.* New York: Oxford University Press, 2005.

Chesbrough, Henry. *Open Innovation.* Boston: Harvard Business School Press, 2003.

Clippinger, John. *A Crowd of One: The Future of Individual Identity.* New York: PublicAffairs, 2007.

Corneliussen, Hilde G., and Jill Rettberg, eds. *Digital Culture, Play, and Identity: A World of Warcraft Reader.* Cambridge: MIT Press, 2008.

Florida, Richard. *The Rise of the Creative Class.* New York: Basic Books, 2002.

Friedman, Thomas. *The World Is Flat.* New York: Farrar, Straus and Giroux, 2005.

Hagel, John III, and John Seely Brown. *Edge Perspectives.* www.edgeperspectives.com.

Hall, Peter. *Cities in Civilization.* New York: Pantheon Books, 1998.

Hock, Dee. *Birth of the Chaordic Age.* San Francisco: Berrett-Koehler, 1999.

Iansiti, Marco, and Roy Levien. *The Keystone Advantage.* Boston: Harvard Business School Press, 2004.

Jacobs, Jane. *The Economy of Cities.* New York: Vintage Books, 1970.

Kauffman, Stuart. *Reinventing the Sacred.* New York: Basic Books, 2008.

Langlois, Richard, and Paul Robertson. *Firms, Markets and Economic Change.* New York: Routledge, 1995.

Loasby, Brian. *Knowledge, Institutions and Evolution in Economics.* New York: Routledge, 2002.

Malone, Thomas W. *The Future of Work.* Boston: Harvard Business School Press, 2004.

McKelvey, Bill, and Pierpaolo Andriani. "Extremes and Scale-Free Dynamics in Organization Science." *Strategic Organization* 3, no. 2 (2005): 219–228.

Page, Scott E. *The Difference.* Princeton, N.J.: Princeton University Press, 2007.

Perez, Carlota. *Technological Revolutions and Financial Capital.* Northampton, Mass.: Edward Elgar, 2002.

Polanyi, Michael. *Personal Knowledge.* Chicago: University of Chicago Press, 1958.

Robinson, Ken. *The Element.* New York: Viking Penguin, 2009.

Shirky, Clay. *Here Comes Everybody.* New York: Penguin, 2008.

Taleb, Nassim Nicholas. *The Black Swan.* New York: Random House, 2007.

Tuomi, Ilkka. *Networks of Innovation.* New York: Oxford University Press, 2002.

Warshaw, Matt. *The Encyclopedia of Surfing.* New York: Harcourt, 2005.

Weber, Steven. *The Success of Open Source.* Boston: Harvard University Press, 2004.

Williamson, Oliver E. *The Mechanisms of Governance.* New York: Oxford University Press, 1996.

Index